**NO POSTAGE
NECESSARY
IF MAILED
IN THE
UNITED STATES**

BUSINESS REPLY CARD

FIRST CLASS   PERMIT NO. 33107   PHILADELPHIA, PA

POSTAGE WILL BE PAID BY ADDRESSEE

HANLEY & BELFUS, INC.
Medical Publishers
P.O. Box 1377
Philadelphia, PA 19105-999(

D1345753

I₁₁₁lll₁l₁₁₁₁lll₁₁₁l₁l₁l₁l₁l₁l₁l₁llₗₗlₗₗll

**NO POSTAGE
NECESSARY
IF MAILED
IN THE
UNITED STATES**

BUSINESS REPLY CARD

FIRST CLASS   PERMIT NO. 33107   PHILADELPHIA, PA

POSTAGE WILL BE PAID BY ADDRESSEE

HANLEY & BELFUS, INC.
Medical Publishers
P.O. Box 1377
Philadelphia, PA 19105-9990

I₁₁₁lll₁l₁₁₁₁lll₁₁₁l₁l₁l₁l₁l₁l₁l₁llₗₗlₗₗll

STATE OF THE ART REVIEWS (STARs)

SUBJECT	FREQUENCY	PRICE (U.S.)	PRICE (Foreign)	PRICE (Single)
☐ ADOLESCENT MEDICINE	Triannual	$57.00	$67.00	$28.00
☐ CARDIAC SURGERY	Triannual	$88.00	$98.00	$38.00
☐ OCCUPATIONAL MEDICINE	Quarterly	$72.00	$82.00	$34.00
☐ PATHOLOGY	Biannual	$60.00	$70.00	$40.00
☐ PHYSICAL MED & REHAB (PM&R)	Triannual	$68.00	$80.00	$32.00
☐ SPINE	Triannual	$78.00	$88.00	$35.00

☐ 1990 subscription   ☐ 1991 subscription   ☐ Single issue
   Check subject title above.   Title _____

Name _____   I enclose payment: ☐ Check ☐ Visa ☐ MasterCard

Company/Hospital _____   Credit Card # _____

Street Address _____   Expiration Date _____

City/State/Zip _____   Signature _____

Send order to:
HANLEY & BELFUS, INC.
210 South 13th Street / Philadelphia, PA 19107 / 215-546-7293 / 800-962-1892

STATE OF THE ART REVIEWS (STARs)

SUBJECT	FREQUENCY	PRICE (U.S.)	PRICE (Foreign)	PRICE (Single)
☐ ADOLESCENT MEDICINE	Triannual	$57.00	$67.00	$28.00
☐ CARDIAC SURGERY	Triannual	$88.00	$98.00	$38.00
☐ OCCUPATIONAL MEDICINE	Quarterly	$72.00	$82.00	$34.00
☐ PATHOLOGY	Biannual	$60.00	$70.00	$40.00
☐ PHYSICAL MED & REHAB (PM&R)	Triannual	$68.00	$80.00	$32.00
☐ SPINE	Triannual	$78.00	$88.00	$35.00

☐ 1990 subscription   ☐ 1991 subscription   ☐ Single issue
   Check subject title above.   Title _____

Name _____   I enclose payment: ☐ Check ☐ Visa ☐ MasterCard

Company/Hospital _____   Credit Card # _____

Street Address _____   Expiration Date _____

City/State/Zip _____   Signature _____

Send order to:
HANLEY & BELFUS, INC.
210 South 13th Street / Philadelphia, PA 19107 / 215-546-7293 / 800-962-1892

1.09
SUR

Adolescent Medicine

Sports and the Adolescent

Paul G. Dyment, M.D.
Editor

Volume 2/Number 1
HANLEY & BELFUS, INC.

February 1991
Philadelphia

STATE OF THE ART REVIEWS

Publisher: HANLEY & BELFUS, INC.
             210 South 13th Street
             Philadelphia, PA 19107
             (215) 546-7293

ADOLESCENT MEDICINE: State of the Art Reviews is indexed in the *Combined Cumulative Index to Pediatrics*, ISI/ISTP&B online database, Index to Scientific Book Contents, and Current Contents (Clinical Medicine and Social & Behavioral Sciences).

ADOLESCENT MEDICINE: State of the Art Reviews   ISSN 1041-3499
February 1991   Volume 2, Number 1   ISBN 1-56053-039-1

© 1991 by Hanley & Belfus, Inc. under the International Copyright Union. All rights reserved. No part of this book may be reproduced, reused, republished, or transmitted in any form or by any means without written permission of the publisher.

ADOLESCENT MEDICINE: State of the Art Reviews is published triannually (three times per year) by Hanley & Belfus, Inc., 210 South 13th Street, Philadelphia, Pennsylvania 19107.

POSTMASTER: Send address changes to ADOLESCENT MEDICINE: State of the Art Reviews, Hanley & Belfus, Inc., 210 South 13th Street, Philadelphia, PA 19107.

This issue is Volume 2, Number 1

The Editor of this publication is Linda C. Belfus.

ADOLESCENT MEDICINE:
STATE OF THE ART REVIEWS

Developed in cooperation with the
Section on Adolescent Health of the American Academy of Pediatrics

EDITORS-IN-CHIEF

Victor C. Strasburger, M.D.
Chief, Division of Adolescent Medicine
Associate Professor of Pediatrics
University of New Mexico
  School of Medicine
Albuquerque, New Mexico

Donald E. Greydanus, M.D.
Professor of Pediatrics
Michigan State University and
Pediatrics Program Director
Kalamazoo Center for Medical Studies
Kalamazoo, Michigan

ASSOCIATE EDITORS

Robert T. Brown, M.D.
Columbus, Ohio

George D. Comerci, M.D.
Tucson, Arizona

Susan M. Coupey, M.D.
Bronx, New York

John W. Kulig, M.D., M.P.H.
Boston, Massachusetts

Manuel Schydlower, M.D.
El Paso, Texas

EDITORIAL ADVISORY BOARD

Boston, MA
  Johanna Dwyer, D.S.C.
  David Elkind, Ph.D.
  S. Jean Emans, M.D.

New Haven, CT
  Lorraine V. Klerman, Dr.P.H.

New York, NY
  Michael I. Cohen, M.D.

Rochester, NY
  Christopher Hodgman, M.D.

Philadelphia, PA
  Gail Slap, M.D.

Baltimore, MD
  Marianne E. Felice, M.D.

Rockville, MD
  Robert B. Shearin, M.D.

Washington, DC
  Renee R. Jenkins, M.D.

Parris Island, SC
  Robert Senior, M.D.

Augusta, GA
  Robert H. DuRant, Ph.D.

Jackson, MS
  William A. Long, Jr., M.D.

Oklahoma City, OK
  Marilyn G. Lanphier, B.S.N., M.P.H.

New Orleans, LA
  Hyman C. Tolmas, M.D.

Cleveland, OH
  Trina Anglin, M.D., Ph.D.

Bluffton, IN
  Donald A. Dian, M.D.

Chicago, IL
  Arthur B. Elster, M.D.
  M. Susan Jay, M.D.

Madison, WI
  John N. Stephenson, M.D.

Minneapolis, MN
  Robert Wm. Blum, M.D., Ph.D.

Boulder, CO
  Richard Jessor, Ph.D.

Albuquerque, NM
  Robert L. Hendren, D.O.

Phoenix, AZ
  Mary Ellen Rimsza, M.D.

San Francisco, CA
  Mary-Ann Shafer, M.D.

Los Angeles, CA
  Lawrence S. Neinstein, M.D.

Orange, CA
  Adele D. Hofmann, M.D.

Seattle, WA
  James A. Farrow, M.D.

INTERNATIONAL

Australia
  David L. Bennett, M.D.

Toronto, Ontario, Canada
  Eudice Goldberg, M.D.

Vancouver, B.C., Canada
  Roger S. Tonkin, M.D.

Tel Aviv, Israel
  Emanuel Chigier, M.D.

Published Issues 1990–91

The At-Risk Adolescent
Edited by Victor C. Strasburger, M.D.
Albuquerque, New Mexico
and Donald E. Greydanus, M.D.
Kalamazoo, Michigan

Adolescent Dermatology
Edited by Steven C. Shapiro, M.D.
Staten Island, New York
Victor C. Strasburger, M.D.
Albuquerque, New Mexico
Donald E. Greydanus, M.D.
Kalamazoo, Michigan

AIDS and Other Sexually Transmitted Diseases
Edited by Manuel Schydlower, M.D.
El Paso, Texas
and Mary-Ann Shafer, M.D.
San Francisco, California

Sports and the Adolescent
Edited by Paul G. Dyment, M.D.
Portland, Maine

Future Issues 1991–92

Parenting the Adolescent: Practitioner Concerns
Edited by George D. Comerci, M.D.
Tucson, Arizona
and William A. Daniel, Jr., M.D.
Montgomery, Alabama

Acute and Chronic Medical Disorders
Edited by John W. Kulig, M.D., M.P.H.
Boston, Massachusetts

Adolescent Sexuality: Preventing Unhealthy Consequences
Edited by Susan M. Coupey, M.D.
Bronx, New York
and Lorraine V. Klerman, Dr.P.H.
New Haven, Connecticut

Psychosocial Problems in Adolescents
Edited by Robert T. Brown, M.D.
and Barbara A. Cromer, M.D.
Cleveland, Ohio

Subscriptions and single issues available from the publisher—Hanley & Belfus, Inc., Medical Publishers, 210 South 13th Street, Philadelphia, PA 19107
(215) 546-7293

Contents

This chapter discusses the preparticipation examination and outlines its components. Sports participation history and physical forms recently published by the Sports Medicine Committee of the American Academy of Pediatrics are provided. The author stresses the importance of performing a musculoskeletal assessment as part of the sports physical, and describes the "two-minute orthopedic examination."

This chapter presents the American Academy of Pediatrics guidelines for participation in competitive sports, and discusses several conditions that may require exclusion. These conditions include absence of paired organs, hernia, Down syndrome, hypertension, cardiac and respiratory diseases, diabetes mellitus, dermatologic infections, and neurologic disorders.

In the past 20 years, a large number of female children and adolescents have begun participating in sports and physical activities previously not open to them. Female athletes may present with disorders of menstruation, such as delayed menarche, amenorrhea, oligomenorrhea, dysmenorrhea, and anovulation with irregular cycles. This chapter addresses these clinical situations and methods of treatment.

Some degree of stress is inherent in all competitive situations. But some athletes experience excessive chronic stress that can contribute to a variety of psychological as well as physical maladies. This chapter emphasizes that an understanding of the antecedents, dynamics, and consequences of athletic stress can pave the way for preventive, diagnostic, and remedial measures. The role of physicians in helping coaches, parents, and adolescent athletes to keep competition within a healthy perspective is addressed, and a relaxation training program is described.

Over the past decade numerous reports have cited the health benefits associated with physical activity and regular exercise. This chapter reviews the current status of adolescent physical fitness, describes the benefits of physical fitness, and suggests methods the physician can use to improve the physical activity and fitness of adolescents.

Anabolic steroids have been used by athletes for more than three decades in an attempt to improve athletic performance in sports requiring great strength and size. Within the last decade, use of these drugs has spread, involving not only elite athletes, but recreational athletes as well. In the last several years it has become apparent that adolescents are using anabolic steroids. The author describes the physiological effects and side effects of steroids, and reasons for their use by adolescents. The role of the physician in screening for and preventing steroid use is also addressed.

Sudden death during activity in children and adolescents is a rare event, considering the larger number of hours spent by this population in recreational and organized physical activities. The shock following such an occurrence frequently results in the family and physician's questioning whether the death could have been avoided. Common misconceptions are (1) that the physical fitness of a child correlates with the condition of the heart, and (2) that cardiac disorders responsible for sudden death give ample symptoms or clues to forecast these tragedies. This article discusses the more common disorders that cause sudden death during exercise, and addresses what, if any, practical measures can be taken to prevent it.

This chapter discusses the epidemiology of injuries in organized sports in adolescents from junior high school through college age. Epidemiology includes the study of the distribution, causes, and prevention of disease. Epidemiologic data on sports injuries can help pediatricians to counsel families about the risks of specific sports, to know what injuries to expect in a given activity, to help athletic programs plan for medical care, and to advise athletes and coaches on injury prevention.

This chapter is intended to help primary care physicians and other providers of health care to adolescents to become more knowledgeable about the management of soft tissue injuries. Discussion includes the pathophysiology of injury, the assessment of the degree of injury, and the rationale for the RICE (rest, ice, compression, and elevation) method of acute treatment. Principles of rehabilitation are also discussed along with objective criteria that can be used to make return-to-play decisions following a soft tissue injury.

This chapter describes the incidence, diagnosis, and management of cerebral concussions. A scheme for grading the severity of a concussion is presented and guidelines are given for when to allow the athlete to return to competition. Other types of head injuries described include epidural and subdural hematoma, subarachnoid hemorrhage, and malignant brain edema syndrome.

Joseph S. Torg and Thomas A. Gennarelli

Although all athletic injuries require careful attention, the evaluation and management of injuries to the head and neck should proceed with particular consideration. The actual or potential involvement of the nervous system creates a high-risk situation in which the margin for error is low. This chapter presents guidelines for classification, evaluation, and emergency management of catastrophic injuries that occur to the head and neck as a result of participation in competitive and recreational activitites.

Arthur M. Pappas

The purpose of this chapter is to provide the physician with guidelines for the diagnosis and treatment of overuse syndromes. The author describes the normal anatomy of the shoulder and elbow, the physical examination of the patient with overuse syndrome, and various possible etiologies. The value of a conditioning program for the prevention of overuse syndromes is also discussed.

Jack T. Andrish

Common overuse syndromes of the back and lower extremities are discussed in terms of relevant history, physical examination, and treatment options. These syndromes are most often associated with a significant change or increase in normal training habits or with repetitive stresses to structures that are abnormally loaded. Strategies for treatment and prevention of recurrence are emphasized, along with the philosophy of "let the kids play the game at their own pace."

Contributors

Jack T. Andrish, M.D.
Department of Orthopedics, Cleveland Clinic Foundation, Cleveland, Ohio

Robert C. Cantu, M.D., F.A.C.S., F.A.C.S.M.
Chief, Neurosurgery Service; Chairman, Department of Surgery; and Director, Service of Sports Medicine, Emerson Hospital, Concord, Massachusetts

Paul G. Dyment, M.D.
Chief of Pediatrics, Maine Medical Center, Portland, Maine; Professor of Pediatrics, University of Vermont College of Medicine, Burlington, Vermont

Thomas A. Gennarelli, M.D.
Professor of Neurosurgery, University of Pennsylvania School of Medicine, Philadelphia, Pennsylvania

Gita P. Gidwani, M.D.
Staff Physician, Department of Gynecology, Cleveland Clinic Foundation, Cleveland, Ohio

Jorge E. Gomez, M.S., M.D.
Nathan Smith Fellow in Adolescent and Sports Medicine, and Clinical Instructor, Department of Pediatrics, University of Wisconsin Medical School, Madison, Wisconsin

Mimi D. Johnson, M.D.
Clinical Instructor, Division of Adolescent Medicine, Department of Pediatrics, University of Washington School of Medicine; Team Physician, Department of Athletics, University of Washington, Seattle, Washington

Gregory L. Landry, M.D.
Associate Professor of Pediatrics, University of Wisconsin Medical School, Madison; Head Medical Team Physician, University of Wisconsin, Madison, Wisconsin

Richard C. McFaul, M.D.
Director, Pediatric and Adolescent Cardiology, Maine Medical Center, Portland, Maine; and University of Vermont College of Medicine, Burlington, Vermont

Michael A. Nelson, M.D.
Clinical Associate Professor of Pediatrics, University of New Mexico School of Medicine, Albuquerque, New Mexico

Arthur M. Pappas, M.D.
Professor and Chairman, Department of Orthopedics and Physical Rehabilitation, University of Massachusetts Medical Center, Worcester, Massachusetts

R. Austin Raunikar, M.D.
Pediatric Cardiology Fellow, Medical College of Georgia, Augusta, Georgia

William L. Risser, M.D.
Professor of Pediatrics, University of Texas Medical School–Houston, Houston, Texas

Ronald E. Smith, Ph.D.
Professor of Psychology, University of Washington, Seattle, Washington

Frank L. Smoll, Ph.D.
Professor of Psychology, University of Washington, Seattle, Washington

William B. Strong, M.D.
Leon Henri Charbonnier Professor of Pediatrics, and Chief, Section of Pediatric Cardiology, Medical College of Georgia, Augusta; Director, Georgia Institute for the Prevention of Human Disease and Accidents, Augusta, Georgia

Joseph S. Torg, M.D.
Professor of Orthopaedic Surgery, and Director, Sports Medicine Center, University of Pennsylvania School of Medicine, Philadelphia, Pennsylvania

Preface

Many adolescents participate in high school or college athletics. Most, but not all, benefit more than they lose from their encounters with sports. Participation in athletics is, unfortunately, almost always associated with some degree of risk of injury, the amount depending on the sport. Football is by far the most dangerous one as measured by the frequency of injuries, with over 600,000 high school players injured each year in the United States.[1] Each high school football team will average one player hospitalized with an injury each season, and another one will undergo knee surgery then or at a later time. Wrestling, ice hockey, and girl's gymnastics are the sports with the next highest injury rates. To these physical risks must be added the psychologically destructive effects of the overly demanding parent or the poorly trained coach who teaches by humiliation or actual abuse, both of whom can instill negative feelings of self-worth in adolescents regardless of their athletic abilities.

If these are the risks, what are the gains for the adolescent who participates in sports? Athletes experience the exhilaration of winning and the despair of defeat; having undergone these experiences, they will be better able to face the successes and failures that will be their lot as adults. If they take part in a team sport, they can learn the importance of cooperation as an integral part of competition—the ice hockey player who learns to pass the puck to a teammate who is in a better position to make a goal rather than to attempt the shot himself. Learning and mastering skills increase the young person's feelings of self-worth. Instilling in adolescents the desire for a physically fit body may lead to an adult life-style that includes regular physical activity, with its well-known benefits of longevity, weight control, and positive self-image. Last, but not least, there is something to be said for the sheer joy of playing a game or competing against others.

In balancing the risks of athletic participation against the potential gains, for most young people the risks are worth it. The sole exception is if they compete in boxing, a sport "condemned" by both the American Academy of Pediatrics and the American Medical Association.

The field of sports medicine has long been considered the domain of orthopedic surgeons, and for years it focused on the management of athletic trauma. As the field has expanded to encompass the epidemiology and prevention of athletic injuries, the preparticipation assessment, the special problems of female athletes, and the psychological consequences of sports (both good and bad), increasing numbers of primary care physicians are becoming knowledgeable about sports medicine. An enthusiastic and suitably trained primary care physician can care for most of the injuries sustained by athletes. All of these subjects are covered in this volume of **Adolescent Medicine: State of the Art Reviews**. This book has been written for primary care physicians who have a particular interest in adolescents and who are looking for information that will help them care for the young athletes in their practices.

I would like to express my gratitude to the contributors for their valuable time and expertise, which made this text possible.

Reference

1. Powell J: 636,000 injuries annually in high school football. Athletic Training 22:19–22, 1987.

Paul G. Dyment, M.D.
GUEST EDITOR

The Sports Physical

PAUL G. DYMENT, M.D.

Chief of Pediatrics
Maine Medical Center
Professor of Pediatrics
University of Vermont
Portland, Maine

For most primary care physicians, performing a sports physical examination will be their principal contact with sports medicine. Nearly 7 million high-schoolers participate in team sports, and most of them undergo regular preparticipation examinations. Unfortunately, most physicians for good reasons place little or no faith in these examinations as being very effective in preventing athletic injuries. Only about 1% of these almost universally healthy athletic teenagers will have an abnormality detected as a result of the examination, *at least as it is usually performed,* which is without a comprehensive musculoskeletal assessment. And even these "abnormalities," i.e., a benign heart murmur, a trace of albuminuria, or an elevated blood pressure determination, usually turn out to be of no consequence as far as participation is concerned. This has caused several authors to question the cost-effectiveness of this examination.[8,9,18] Knowing this, and knowing how keen athletes are to "pass" the examination, it is not surprising that *both* the physician and the athlete are only too ready to make the examination a brief cursory affair.

One solution to the problem of examining the large number of athletes in a school is the mass "locker-room" physical examination. One or two physicians are induced to volunteer their time as good citizens for one evening, and each athlete receives a brief physical examination. This format is to be deplored for several reasons. (1) The lack of privacy and time precludes any kind of health counseling. (2) The yield of abnormalities from a strictly medical

ADOLESCENT MEDICINE: State of the Art Reviews—Vol. 2, No. 1, February 1991
Philadelphia, Hanley & Belfus, Inc.

1

examination is low. (3) Even though the consent form from the school may indicate that this examination is just a screening examination and "not a substitute for a complete physical examination," the parents deem it otherwise. One study revealed that for 78% of these athletes, the school examinations were their *only* health assessments.[4] This meant that these athletes did not have the opportunity to undergo a comprehensive health maintenance examination with appropriate anticipatory guidance from their personal physician. For these reasons, schools should be encouraged to have participation examinations performed in physicians' offices whenever possible.

Most sports injuries are reinjuries, and therefore the preparticipation sport examination should include a detailed assessment of the musculoskeletal system. The physician should look for signs of muscle or ligament weakness or pain signifying an incompletely healed injury from a previous season which may recur unless rehabilitative exercises are performed. The musculoskeletal assessment is the most productive part of the sports physical, and the "two-minute orthopedic examination" should be incorporated into all of these examinations. A Cleveland Clinic study using a similar technique demonstrated that in 10% of their high school football players undergoing an examination, musculoskeletal abnormalities, generally from previous injuries, were detected.[11]

A physician who is performing an annual health maintenance examination of an adolescent at any time during the year should ask if the youth plans to play a sport during the coming year. If this is a possibility, then a musculoskeletal assessment should be performed *as part of a complete physical examination,* and the patient urged to forward subsequent sport physical forms to the physician's office for completion.

When physicians are asked to perform sports physicals in their offices, they should convert that visit to a health maintenance examination, which will require additional time. Practitioners should allot 30 minutes for annual health maintenance examinations of adolescents. Physicians' appointment secretaries should inform parents that 30 minutes is the physician's standard of practice for this kind of visit, and, of course, the charges should reflect this additional time.

Adolescents should receive a comprehensive examination every year so that there will be enough of a relationship between the physician and the teenager that appropriate anticipatory guidance will be more likely to be accepted by the young person. A physician will not be effective if he or she is considered to be just one more adult telling the adolescent what not to do.

THE MEDICAL HISTORY

The Sports Medicine Committee of the American Academy of Pediatrics (AAP) has recently (1990) published sports preparticipation history and physical forms, and school districts should be encouraged to adopt them (Figs. 1 and 2). There are two components to the medical history. One is an *interim history,* which should be completed prior to *each sport season.* Otherwise there is no mechanism for assessing whether an athlete who successfully passed his preparticipation examination before the football season, but who

SPORTS PARTICIPATION HEALTH RECORD

This evaluation is only to determine readiness for sports participation. It should not be used as a substitute for regular health maintenance examinations.

NAME _____ AGE _____(YRS) GRADE _____ DATE _____

ADDRESS _____ PHONE _____

SPORTS _____

The Health History (Part A) and Physical Examination (Part C) sections must both be completed, at least every 24 months, before sports participation. The Interim Health History section (Part B) needs to be completed at least annually.

PART A — HEALTH HISTORY:
To be completed by athlete and parent

	YES	NO
1. Have you ever had an illness that:		
a. required you to stay in the hospital?	____	____
b. lasted longer than a week?	____	____
c. caused you to miss 3 days of practice or a competition?	____	____
d. is related to allergies? (ie, hay fever, hives, asthma, insect stings)	____	____
e. required an operation?	____	____
f. is chronic? (ie, asthma, diabetes, etc)	____	____
2. Have you ever had an injury that:		
a. required you to go to an emergency room or see a doctor?	____	____
b. required you to stay in the hospital?	____	____
c. required x-rays?	____	____
d. caused you to miss 3 days of practice or a competition?	____	____
e. required an operation?	____	____
3. Do you take any medication or pills?	____	____
4. Have any members of your family under age 50 had a heart attack, heart problem, or died unexpectedly?	____	____
5. Have you ever:		
a. been dizzy or passed out during or after exercise?	____	____
b. been unconscious or had a concussion?	____	____
6. Are you unable to run 1/2 mile (2 times around the track) without stopping?	____	____
7. Do you:		
a. wear glasses or contacts?	____	____
b. wear dental bridges, plates, or braces?	____	____
8. Have you ever had a heart murmur, high blood pressure, or a heart abnormality?	____	____
9. Do you have any allergies to any medicine?	____	____
10. Are you missing a kidney?	____	____

11. When was your last tetanus booster? _____

12. For Women
  a. At what age did you experience your first menstrual period? _____
  b. In the last year, what is the longest time you have gone between periods? _____

EXPLAIN ANY "YES" ANSWERS _____
_____
_____
_____

I hereby state that, to the best of my knowledge, my answers to the above questions are correct.

Date _____

Signature of athlete _____

Signature of parent _____

PART B — INTERIM HEALTH HISTORY:
This form should be used during the interval between preparticipation evaluations. Positive responses should prompt a medical evaluation.

1. Over the next 12 months, I wish to participate in the following sports:
  a. _____
  b. _____
  c. _____
  d. _____

2. Have you missed more than 3 consecutive days of participation in usual activities because of an injury this past year?
  Yes _____ No _____
  If yes, please indicate:
  a. Site of injury _____
  b. Type of injury _____

3. Have you missed more than 5 consecutive days of participation in usual activities because of an illness, or have you had a medical illness diagnosed that has not been resolved in this past year?
  Yes _____ No _____
  If yes, please indicate:
  a. Type of illness _____

4. Have you had a seizure, concussion or been unconscious for any reason in the last year?
  Yes _____ No _____

5. Have you had surgery or been hospitalized in this past year?
  Yes _____ No _____
  If yes, please indicate:
  a. Reason for hospitalization _____
  b. Type of surgery _____

6. List all medications you are presently taking and what condition the medication is for.
  a. _____
  b. _____
  c. _____

7. Are you worried about any problem or condition at this time?
  Yes _____ No _____
  If yes, please explain: _____
  _____
  _____
  _____

I hereby state that, to the best of my knowledge, my answers to the above questions are correct.

Date _____

Signature of athlete _____

Signature of parent _____

FIGURE 1. Health history and interim health history form. (Reproduced with permission. Copyright © 1990 by The American Academy of Pediatrics, Elk Grove Village, Illinois.)

Part C – PHYSICAL EXAMINATION RECORD

NAME _____ DATE _____ AGE _____ BIRTHDATE _____

Height _____   Vision: R _____/_____, corrected _____, uncorrected _____

Weight _____   L _____/_____, corrected _____, uncorrected _____

Pulse _____   Blood Pressure _____ Percent Body Fat (optional) _____

	Normal	Abnormal Findings	Initials
1. Eyes			
2. Ears, Nose, Throat			
3. Mouth & Teeth			
4. Neck			
5. Cardiovascular			
6. Chest and Lungs			
7. Abdomen			
8. Skin			
9. Genitalia - Hernia (male)			
10. Musculoskeletal: ROM, strength, etc.			
a. neck			
b. spine			
c. shoulders			
d. arms/hands			
e. hips			
f. thighs			
g. knees			
h. ankles			
i. feet			
11. Neuromuscular			
12. Physical Maturity (Tanner Stage)	1. 2. 3. 4. 5.		

Comments re: Abnormal Findings: _____
_____
_____
_____

PARTICIPATION RECOMMENDATIONS:

1. No participation in: _____
_____

2. Limited participation in: _____
_____

3. Requires: _____
_____

4. Full participation in: _____

Physician Signature _____

Telephone Number _____ Address _____

American Academy of Pediatrics

©Copyright 1990
HE0086

FIGURE 2. Physical examination form. (Reproduced with permission. Copyright © 1990 by The American Academy of Pediatrics, Elk Grove Village, Illinois.)

sprained his ankle playing football, should be allowed to compete for the basketball team. The school nurse or team physician should review the interim history of all the team members before the season and request a full physical examination if a questionnaire is significantly abnormal. Note that the medical history addresses not only recent injuries, including concussions, but also family history of early heart disease and a menstrual assessment in young women.

LABORATORY TESTS

Neither a routine *hemoglobin/hematocrit* nor *urinalysis* is recommended by the AAP as a necessary part of a preparticipation examination, although either may well be indicated at certain intervals during a health maintenance examination. Although there is a definite but small incidence of iron deficiency anemia in adolescents, there is conflicting evidence as to whether the far more frequent situation of iron deficiency without anemia can impair athletic performance. It is reasonable, albeit expensive, to measure the serum ferritin or iron at least in national-level competitors, and treat those who are abnormal with ferrous sulphate. Many elite athletes whose gender or athletic events (such as marathon running) make them quite likely to develop iron deficiency take ferrous sulfate prophylactically as a part of their "training."

Sickle cell screening for all athletes in at-risk populations is controversial, as there seems to be no particular risk to athletes with sickle cell trait unless they exercise at a high altitude.[3] Such screening should therefore be considered in certain geographical locations, but it is not an essential component in most of the country.

THE PHYSICAL EXAMINATION

If the examination is being done as part of a health maintenance examination, then, in addition to the usual examination and anticipatory guidance, a musculoskeletal assessment should be performed—"the two-minute orthopedic examination" (Table 1, Figs. 3–14). The sports physical may be done in the school locker room, but in both instances the AAP forms (Figs. 1 and 2) should be used. The musculoskeletal assessment is spelled out in some detail on that form. The reader is encouraged to reproduce Table 1 and have a copy in each examining room so it can be consulted while actually performing the examination.

What does the physician do when a musculoskeletal abnormality—generally muscle or ligament weakness remaining from an incompletely reha-bilitated ankle sprain, or pain from an overuse syndrome such as the patellofemoral syndrome or "swimmer's shoulder—is detected? Most primary care physicians are unfamiliar with the rehabilitative exercises necessary to treat these conditions, so a referral to a certified athletic trainer or a physio-therapist experienced in sports injuries may be necessary. In almost all cases, however, the athlete should be allowed to play that season, as the treatments are aimed at reducing the possibility of a reinjury. Because it takes 3–6 weeks

TABLE 1. The Two-minute Orthopedic Examination

Figure*	Instructions	Observations
3	Stand facing examiner	Acromioclavicular joints, general habitus
4	Look at ceiling, floor, over both shoulders; touch ears to shoulders	Cervical spine motion
5	Shrug shoulders (examiner resists)	Trapezius strength
6	Abduct shoulders 90° (examiner resists at 90°)	Deltoid strength
7	Full external rotation of arms	Shoulder motion
8	Flex and extend elbows	Elbow motion
9	Arms at sides, elbows 90° flexed; pronate and supinate wrists	Elbow and wrist motion
10	Spread fingers; make fist	Hand or finger motion and deformities
	Tighten (contract) quadriceps; relax quadriceps	Symmetry and knee effusion; ankle effusion
11	"Duck walk" four steps (away from examiner with buttocks on heels)	Hip, knee and ankle motion
12	Back to examiner	Shoulder symmetry, scoliosis
13	Knees straight, touch toes	Scoliosis, hip motion, hamstring, tightness
14	Raise up on toes, raise heels	Calf symmetry, leg strength

* Refers to Figure numbers in the present article.
Reproduced with permission from Sports Medicine: Health Care of the Young Athlete, 2nd ed., 1991, published by The American Academy of Pediatrics, Elk Grove Village, Illinois.

for these exercises to become effective, the preparticipation examination should be performed at least 6 weeks before the beginning of the playing season.

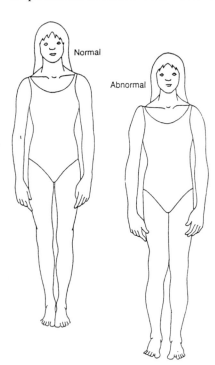

Stand straight with arms at sides
Symmetry of upper and lower extremities and trunk.

Common abnormalities:
1. Enlarged acromioclavicular joint
2. Enlarged sternoclavicular joint
3. Asymmetrical waist (leg length difference or scoliosis)
4. Swollen knee
5. Swollen ankle

FIGURE 3

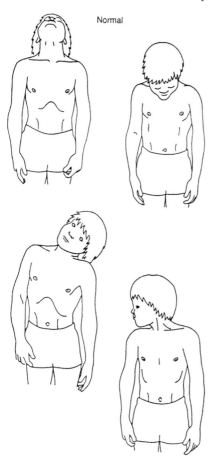

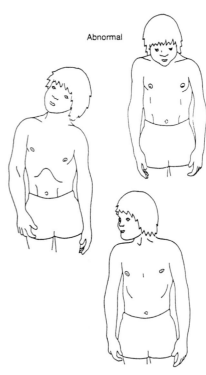

Look at ceiling; look at floor; touch right (left) ear to shoulder; look over right (left) shoulder.

Should be able to touch chin to chest, ears to shoulders and look equally over shoulders.

Common abnormalities (may indicate previous neck injury): 2. Loss of lateral bending.
1. Loss of flexion   3. Loss of rotation

FIGURE 4

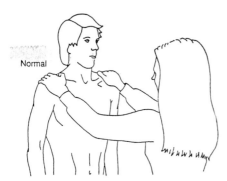

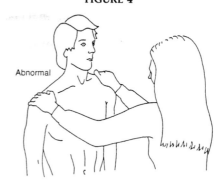

Shrug shoulders while examiner holds them down.

Trapezius muscles appear equal; left and right sides equal strength.

Common abnormalities (may indicate neck or shoulder problem):
1. Loss of strength   2. Loss of muscle bulk

FIGURE 5

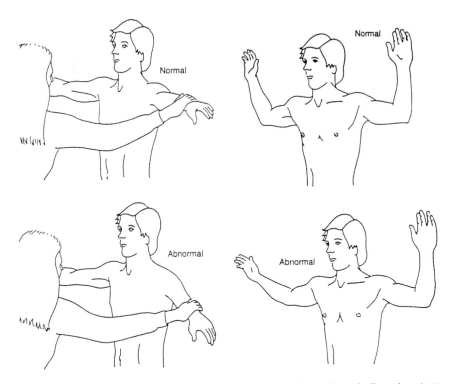

Hold arms out from sides horizontally and lift while examiner holds them down.

Strength should be equal and deltoid muscles should be equal in size.

Common abnormalities:
1. Loss of strength
2. Wasting of deltoid muscle

FIGURE 6

Hold arms out from sides with elbows bent (90°); raise hands back vertically as far as they will go.

Hands go back equally and at least to upright vertical position.

Common abnormalities (may indicate shoulder problem or old dislocation):
1. Loss of external rotation

FIGURE 7

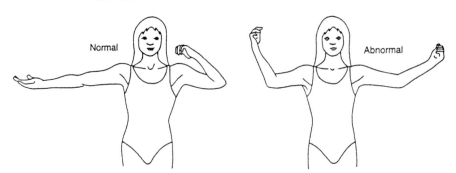

Hold arms out from sides, palms up; straighten elbows completely; bend completely.

Motion equal left and right.

Common abnormalities (may indicate old elbow injury, old dislsocation, fracture, etc.):
1. Loss of extension   2. Loss of flexion

FIGURE 8

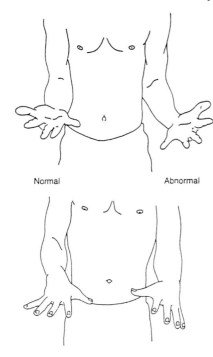

Normal   Abnormal

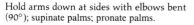

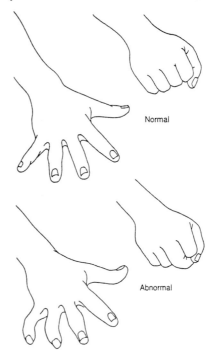

Normal

Abnormal

Hold arms down at sides with elbows bent (90°); supinate palms; pronate palms.

Palms should go from facing ceiling to facing floor.

Common abnormalities (may indicate old forearm, wrist, or elbow injury):
1. Lack of full supination
2. Lack of full pronation

FIGURE 9

Make a fist; open hand and spread fingers.

Fist should be tight and fingers straight when spread.

Common abnormalities (may indicate old finger fractures or sprains):
1. Protruding knuckle from fist
2. Swollen and/or crooked finger

FIGURE 10

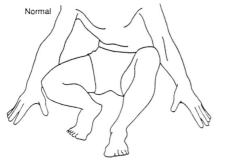

Normal

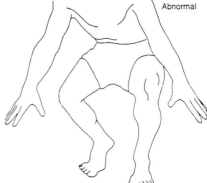

Abnormal

Squat on heels; duck walk 4 steps and stand up.

Maneuver is painless; heel to buttock distance equal left and right; knee flexion equal during walk; rises straight up.

Common abnormalities:
1. Inability to full flex one knee 2. Inability to stand up without twisting or bending to one side

FIGURE 11

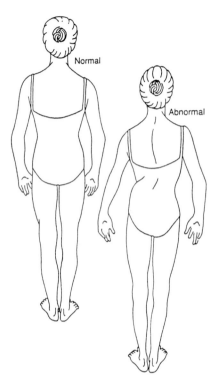

With back to examiner stand up straight.

Symmetry of shoulders, waist, thighs, and calves.

Common abnormalities:
1. High shoulder (scoliosis) or low shoulder (muscle loss)
2. Prominent rib cage (scoliosis)
3. High hip or asymmetrical waist (leg length difference or scoliosis)
4. Small calf or thigh (weakness from old injury)

FIGURE 12

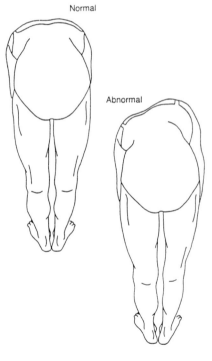

Bend forward slowly as to touch toes.

Bends forward straightly and smoothly.

Common abnormalities:
1. Twists to side (low back pain)
2. Back asymmetrical (scoliosis)

FIGURE 13

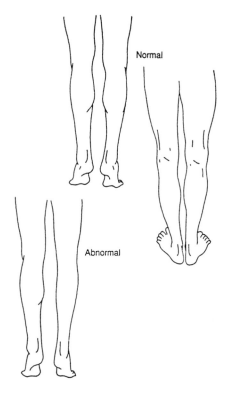

Stand on heels; stand on toes.

Equal elevation right and left; symmetry of calf muscles.

Common abnormalities:
1. Wasting of calf muscles (Achilles injury or old ankle injury)

FIGURE 14

UNEXPECTED DEATH DURING ATHLETICS

Sudden death in athletics is discussed in further detail in the chapter "Death on the Playing Field." In instances of sudden death, cardiac abnormalities are generally found on postmortem examination, but they are either detected or suspected prior to death in only about 25% of such cases.[5] Unfortunately, most of the rest of the causes of these deaths could not have been detected by even a meticulous medical history and thorough physical examination. The most common cardiovascular causes of sudden death in young athletes are hypertrophic cardiomyopathy (formerly called idiopathic hypertrophic sub-aortic stenosis, or IHSS), congenital coronary artery anomalies, atherosclerotic coronary artery disease, and aortic rupture associated with Marfan syndrome.

Some clues in the history that should trigger a more extensive cardiologic evaluation include family history of early nontraumatic sudden death, premature coronary artery disease in the family up to second degree relatives, and episodes of palpitations or actual syncope during exercises. During the physical examination of a tall athlete, the physician should look for the stigmata of Marfan syndrome. Any apparent arrhythmia warrants referral of the patient to a cardiologist. If a murmur and mid-systolic click typical of mitral valve prolapse are found, that diagnosis should be pursued, as there have been a few reported cases of sudden death during exercise in athletes with this condition.

If cardiac abnormalities are detected, national guidelines are available (the 16th Bethesda Conference on Cardiovascular Abnormalities in the Athlete: Recommendations Regarding Eligibility for Competition, 1984)[7] to assist the primary physician or cardiologist in questions of participation.

DISQUALIFICATION FROM SPORTS

In 1988 the American Academy of Pediatrics proposed a list of athletic events from which athletes with certain medical conditions should be excluded.[1,2] This system is the best working document available for the practitioner, and it is reproduced in Tables 1 and 2 on pages 14–16 in the chapter "Medical Exclusion from Sport." Athletic events are divided into groups depending upon their degree of strenuousness and probability for collision. Sports such as downhill skiing, which are generally noncontact but have definite risks of collision (i.e., with a tree), are included in the "limited contact/ impact" group of sports. The recommendations for participation, depending on the kind of sport and the athlete's medical condition, are provided. The usual caveat exists, that such tables should be used only as a guideline; they are no substitute for a physician's clinical judgment.

ACKNOWLEDGMENT

Figures 3–14 reproduced with permission of Ross Laboratories, Columbus, Ohio.

References

1. Committee on Sports Medicine, American Academy of Pediatrics: Recommendations for participation in competitive sports. Pediatrics 81:737–739, 1988.
2. Dyment PG: New guidelines for sports participation. Phys Sportsmed 16:45–46, 1988.
3. Eichner ER: Sickle cell trait, exercise, and altitude. Phys Sportsmed 14:144–151, 1986.
4. Goldberg B, Saraniti A, Witman P, et al: Preparticipation sports assessments—an objective evaluation. Pediatrics 66:736–745, 1980.
5. Maron BJ, Epstein SE, Roberts WC: Causes of sudden death in competitive athletes. J Am Coll Cardiol 7:1186–1232, 1985.
6. McClain LG: The tall athlete and Marfan syndrome. J Adolesc Health Care 10:564–566, 1989.
7. Mitchell JH, Maron BJ, Epstein SE: The 16th Bethesda Conference on Cardiovascular Abnormalities in the Athlete: Recommendations regarding eligibility for competition. J Am Coll Cardiol 6:1186–1232, 1985.
8. Risser WL, Hoffman HA, Bellah GG, et al: A cost-benefit analysis of preparticipation sports examinations of adolescent athletes. J School Health 55:270–273, 1985.
9. Rowland TW: Preparticipation sports examination of the child and adolescent athlete: Changing views of an old ritual. Pediatrician 13:3–9, 1986.
10. Samples P: Preparticipation exams: Are they worth the time and trouble? Phys Sportsmed 14:180–187, 1986.
11. Thompson TR, Andrish JT, Bergfeld JA: A prospective study of preparticipation sports examinations of 2,670 young athletes: Method and results. Cleve Clin Q 49:225–233, 1982.

Medical Exclusion from Sport

MICHAEL A. NELSON, M.D.

Associate Clinical Professor of
  Pediatrics
University of New Mexico School
  of Medicine
Albuquerque, New Mexico

Reprint requests to:
Michael A. Nelson, M.D.
4801 McMahon Blvd., N.W.
Albuquerque, NM 87114

More adolescents with chronic disease or disability are safely participating in sports than at any time in history. This, in part, is due to recent scientific and technologic innovations: sophisticated exercise stress testing is available for athletes with cardiovascular or pulmonary disease, blood glucose monitoring for diabetics, and protective devices including eyewear, face guards and flak jackets facilitate a safer sport environment for adolescents with a lack of paired organs. Nonetheless, the physician will routinely need to determine eligibility for patients with illness or disability based on the likelihood of morbidity or mortality resulting from participation in sports.

The disqualifying conditions for sports participation published in 1976 by the American Medical Association (AMA)[2] do not reflect recent advances in disease management and protective equipment. In 1988 the American Academy of Pediatrics (AAP) published new guidelines for Participation in Competitive Sports (Tables 1 and 2).[8] A 1990 report of the Board of Trustees of the AMA states "The guidelines developed by the American Academy of Pediatrics are thorough and provide physicians the most current source on what conditions disqualify athletes from what sports."[3] These new guidelines recognize the need for individualization regarding sports participation for athletes with variable degrees of illness and severity of disability.

The AAP developed new categories of sports events based on strenuousness and

ADOLESCENT MEDICINE: State of the Art Reviews—Vol. 2, No. 1, February 1991
  Philadelphia, Hanley & Belfus, Inc.

13

TABLE 1. Classification of Athletic Events According to Probability for Contact and Degree of Strenuousness

| Contact/Collision | Limited Contact/Impact | Noncontact | | |
		Strenuous	Moderately Strenuous	Nonstrenuous
Boxing	Baseball	Aerobic dancing	Badminton	Archery
Field hockey	Basketball	Crew	Curling	Golf
Football	Bicycling	Fencing	Table tennis	Riflery
Ice hockey	Diving	Field		
Lacrosse	Field	Discus		
Martial arts	High jump	Javelin		
Rodeo	Pole vault	Shot put		
Soccer	Gymnastics	Running		
Wrestling	Horseback riding	Swimming		
	Skating	Tennis		
	Ice	Track		
	Roller	Weight lifting		
	Skiing			
	Cross-country			
	Downhill			
	Water			
	Softball			
	Squash, handball			
	Volleyball			

Reprinted with permission from *Pediatrics*, May 1988; 81:5. Copyright © 1988 American Academy of Pediatrics.

probability of collision. Some sports such as football inherently involve contact or collision. Other sports such as skiing are not inherently contact sports but involve the potential for serious collisions and resultant injury. A category reflecting inadvertent risk of collision not inherent to a particular sport is uncommon in many sport classification schemes. However, consideration of the risk of inadvertent trauma is an important factor in determining eligibility for participation in certain sports.

PHYSICIAN RESPONSIBILITY

When determining eligibility for participation, it is critical to maintain a good relationship with the athletes and their families. Every attempt should be made to make decisions regarding participation jointly with the athlete, family and perhaps the coach. However, the physician's primary responsibility is to safeguard the health of the athlete. Practitioners who work as team physicians should have final authority for decisions regarding participation.

In spite of the authority granted to a physician to determine disqualification, other factors may influence the decision-making process. If the desires of athletes and their families conflict with physician recommendations, an adversarial relationship may develop. Numerous options are available to athletes who wish to circumvent the decision-making process. It is usually not difficult for adolescents to find another physician who will provide a participation recommendation that will coincide with their desires. In some school systems a

TABLE 2. Recommendations for Participation in Competitive Sports

	Contact/ Collision	Limited Contact/ Impact	Noncontact		
			Strenuous	Moderately Strenuous	Nonstrenuous
Atlantoaxial instability	No	No	Yes*	Yes	Yes
* Swimming: no butterfly, breast stroke, or diving starts.					
Acute illness	*	*	*	*	*
* Needs individual assessment, e.g., contagiousness to others, risk of worsening illness.					
Cardiovascular					
Carditis	No	No	No	No	No
Hypertension					
Mild	Yes	Yes	Yes	Yes	Yes
Moderate	*	*	*	*	*
Severe	*	*	*	*	*
Congenital heart disease	†	†	†	†	†
* Needs individual assessment.					
† Patients with mild forms can be allowed a full range of physical activities; patients with moderate or severe forms, or who are postoperative, should be evaluated by a cardiologist before athletic participation.					
Eyes					
Absence or loss of					
function of one eye	*	*	*	*	*
Detached retina	†	†	†	†	†
* Availability of American Society for Testing and Materials (ASTM)-approved eye guards may allow competitor to participate in most sports, but this must be judged on an individual basis.					
† Consult ophthalmologist.					
Inguinal hernia	Yes	Yes	Yes	Yes	Yes
Kidney: Absence of one	No	Yes	Yes	Yes	Yes
Liver: Enlarged	No	No	Yes	Yes	Yes
Musculoskeletal disorders	*	*	*	*	*
* Needs individual assessment.					
Neurologic					
History of serious head or spine trauma, repeated concussions, or					
craniotomy	*	*	Yes	Yes	Yes
Convulsive disorder					
Well controlled	Yes	Yes	Yes	Yes	Yes
Poorly controlled	No	No	Yes†	Yes	Yes‡
* Needs individual assessment.					
† No swimming or weight lifting.					
‡ No archery or riflery.					

(Continued on next page)

TABLE 2. *(Continued.)*

	Contact/ Collision	Limited Contact/ Impact	Noncontact		
			Strenuous	*Moderately Strenuous*	*Nonstrenuous*
Ovary: Absence of one	Yes	Yes	Yes	Yes	Yes
Respiratory					
Pulmonary insufficiency	*	*	*	*	Yes
Asthma	Yes	Yes	Yes	Yes	Yes
* May be allowed to compete if oxygenation remains satisfactory during a graded stress test.					
Sickle cell trait	Yes	Yes	Yes	Yes	Yes
Skin: Boils, herpes, impetigo, scabies	*	*	Yes	Yes	Yes
* No gymnastics with mats, martial arts, wrestling, or contact sports until not contagious.					
Spleen: Enlarged	No	No	No	Yes	Yes
Testicle: Absence or undescended	Yes*	Yes*	Yes	Yes	Yes
* Certain sports may require protective cup.					

Reprinted with permission from *Pediatrics*, May 1988; 81:5. Copyright © 1988 American Academy of Pediatrics.

waiver system is used whereby after physician counseling of the athlete, family, and coach regarding the risk of participation and recommending against such participation, the athlete and family may sign a waiver accepting responsibility for the risks involved. Because "informed consent" or waiver forms are frequently challenged in the courts, physicians who choose to participate in a waiver process should be meticulous in documenting an adequate provision of pertinent information and subsequent understanding of the material by all involved. If all else fails for the adolescent determined to participate, application to the courts to overturn the disqualification for sport participation is possible.

Regardless of which course of action athletes and their families may take, the physician's primary responsibility is to make recommendations or decisions based on his or her best medical opinion. The physician should never subordinate regard for safety to the desires of athlete, coach, or family. The following sections are intended to provide the practitioner with expanded guidelines that may be used in conjunction with the AAP Recommendations for participation in competitive sports.

ANATOMIC CONDITIONS

Absence of Paired Organs

Serious eye injuries resulting in blindness or loss of vision are relatively common in racquet and contact/collision sports. However, technologic advances in the development of protective eyewear should allow participation of all but a few athletes with loss of vision in one eye.[11] These devices should have lenses made of polycarbonate material. Open eye protection devices are not adequate for any sport involving a significant risk of eye injury. Eye protection devices acceptable for use include those that meet the American Society for Testing Materials standard F803 for racquet sports. For the athlete with corrected vision in one eye of 20/200 or less, participation in boxing should not be allowed because no protective devices can be worn. For other contact/collision sports, 20/200 or worse corrected vision in one eye mandates use of certified protective eyewear. Consideration should be given to requiring protective eyewear for any athlete with significantly decreased corrected vision in one eye. A history of a detached retina should prompt consultation with an ophthalmologist regarding participation in contact/collision, limited contact/impact, or strenuous noncontact sports. Strenuous exertion as well as head trauma may have catastrophic consequences.

Participation in contact/collision sports by an athlete with a single kidney poses an unacceptably high risk. The actual incidence of renal trauma in these sports is unknown. New, lightweight protective devices (flak jackets) are touted to protect against internal injury; however, until such time that these devices are shown to provide adequate protection, the dire consequences of significant trauma to a single kidney should preclude participation in contact sports for these adolescents.[10]

The development of "hard cups" (scrotal protectors) has minimized the risk of significant testicular trauma and allows participation in all sports for adolescents with a single testicle.[10] There are no reported cases of ovarian damage from sports participation and absence of an ovary should not preclude participation in any sport.

The absence of an arm or leg would place the adolescent at risk for significant disability if the opposite, intact extremity were to be traumatized. However, some athletes have been able to demonstrate adequate proficiency that lessens the risk. One has only to look at Jim Abbott, a one-armed pitcher for the California Angels, who is able to field baseballs with the skill of someone with both arms, to realize that some players may still be able to participate in certain sports. For contact/collision sports that involve significant risk of injury to the remaining extremity, participation should not be allowed. However, for some sports (i.e., baseball) in which skill is required to avoid other types of injuries, if proficiency can be demonstrated, participation should be allowed.

Hernia

There is no evidence to indicate that participation in sports increases the risk of incarceration of an indirect inguinal hernia. Because smaller hernias are more likely to incarcerate than larger hernias, if sports participation resulted in enlargement of a hernia the risk of incarceration would not be increased.[18] The athlete should be counseled about the symptoms of incarceration but allowed to finish the competitive season. Repair can safely be accomplished after the completion of the sport season.

Down Syndrome

Current guidelines for participation in sports that involve possible trauma to the head and neck for adolescents with Down syndrome include a single radiographic screening for atlantoaxial instability. Specific guidelines are published in the AAP statement "Atlantoaxial Instability in Down Syndrome."[7] However, controversy exists regarding the appropriateness of radiographic screening because most, if not all, cases of subluxation resulting in paralysis or death have been preceded by a period of neurologic symptomatology.[9] The AAP is currently reassessing its recommendation for this screening procedure. On the basis of current guidelines, individuals with Down syndrome should be screened, and those with neurologic symptoms or an atlantoaxial separation of greater than 4 mm should not participate in sports in which there is significant risk of head and neck trauma.

CHRONIC MEDICAL CONDITIONS

Hypertension

Adult hypertension is associated with increased risk of coronary heart disease, stroke, and renal and retinal disease. Evidence exists that adult hypertension has its origins in childhood, but the classification for severity of hypertension in adolescents is based on clinical experience and consensus rather than risk data. The AAP guidelines for participation use the adult classification schema of mild, moderate and severe hypertension developed by the Sixteenth Bethesda Conference.[13] The National Heart, Lung and Blood Institute Task Force has also developed a classification system for children and adolescents which defines significant hypertension as those values persistently between the 95th and 99th percentiles for age, and severe hypertension as persistent values at or above the 99th percentile for age.[22] A comparison of these two classification systems is provided in Figure 1. Although there is considerable overlap of categories between the two systems, significant hypertension can reasonably be considered the equivalent of mild hypertension. Severe hypertension encompasses the moderate and severe categories derived from adult standards.

The diagnosis of hypertension should never be made without serial measurements, using proper technique, on at least three separate occasions. Specific guidelines for measurement of blood pressure and appropriate diagnostic evaluation are described elsewhere.[22] Decisions regarding sports participation for adolescents with essential hypertension should be reassessed on a regular basis since up to 50% of those with blood pressure greater than the 95th percentile may become normotensive without treatment within 2 years.[13]

Regardless of the severity of essential hypertension, individuals with target organ involvement (i.e., renal parenchymal disease, polycystic kidneys, etc.) should not participate in contact/collision sports. The risk of renal trauma from participation in limited contact/impact sports is unknown, but

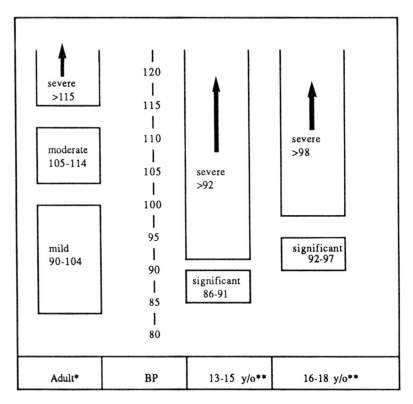

FIGURE 1. Categories of hypertension (diastolic, mm Hg). (Adapted from *Task Force IV: Systemic arterial hypertension,[13] and **Second Task Force on Blood Pressure in Children.[22])

probably not greater than injury risk during participation in unsupervised recreational activities. Participation in these sports should be based on the desires of and acceptance of potential risks by the athlete and family.

Dramatic elevations of blood pressure are known to occur during static exercise in normotensive individuals. Adolescents with hypertension have been shown to have significantly higher elevations of blood pressure than normotensive controls during static (isometric) exercise.[23] The significance of blood pressure elevations during static exercise remains to be elucidated. Regardless of the level of resting blood pressure, cerebrovascular accidents have occurred during maximal weight lifting. However, there is no direct evidence linking hypertension with sudden death or cerebrovascular accidents (CVAs) during sports activities. Additionally, studies indicating how exercise stress testing may be used to predict risks of participation in sports are lacking.[28] While stress testing may eventually have a role in evaluating athletes for sports participation, at this time it is not recommended as part of the determination regarding readiness for sports participation.

Children with mild (significant) hypertension should be allowed to participate in all sports. Participation in strenuous sports may be beneficial in that lowering of blood pressure has been demonstrated in adolescents participating in running and strength training programs.

A diagnosis of moderate or severe hypertension should prompt a recommendation to avoid sports with high static demands. No evidence indicates any immediate risk from participation in strenuous sports for adolescents with moderate or severe hypertension. However, because of a paucity of data, caution should be exercised in recommending participation for these patients.[11]

Cardiac Diseases

Studies of individuals with sudden cardiac death in sports reveal that many experienced previous symptoms (see the article in this issue on Death on the Playing Field). Adolescents with a history of exertional syncope, palpitations, or chest pain may participate in all sports only after cardiovascular evaluation, which may include chest x-ray, electrocardiogram (EKG), echocardiogram, and exercise stress testing. Individuals at risk include those with myocarditis, hypertrophic cardiomyopathy, severe aortic stenosis, and anomalous left coronary artery, among others.[27] These adolescents should be excluded from all but nonstrenuous sports. Long-term studies of individuals with coronary artery disease associated with Kawasaki disease are not yet available. However, whether in the acute phase of the disease, or after resolution of coronary artery aneurysms, a pediatric cardiologist should be consulted to determine eligibility for competition.

Children with an arrhythmia may require evaluation by a cardiologist. Resting premature ventricular or atrial contractions are common. If premature contractions disappear with exercise (enough to raise the heart rate to 120–140) and are unifocal and not associated with structural heart disease, participation in all sports should be allowed.

In both the preoperative and postoperative repair state a wide range of severity is associated with individual congenital heart lesions. After surgical repair, individuals with even mild forms of structural heart disease often have residual decreases in exercise tolerance. Many adolescents with structural heart disease will require exercise stress testing prior to participation in sports. Specific guidelines have been published elsewhere.[12,21] For those with more severe forms of heart disease, a cardiac specialist should be consulted about advisability of sports participation.

Respiratory Diseases

Asthma is the most common chronic disease in childhood and adolescence. Approximately 10% of the normal population and 80–90% of asthmatics will experience exercise-induced asthma (EIA).[16] With proper management, only those with the most severe form need exclusion from any sport.

Although no improvements in pulmonary function have been demonstrated through sports or exercise participation, other significant benefits include decreases in non-exercise-induced asthma, use of medication, hospitalization, and school absenteeism.[26] The goal of the physician should be to design a treatment program that will allow participation.

Symptoms of EIA include shortness of breath, dyspnea, chest pain, headache, abdominal pain, and a feeling of being out of shape. Except for very severe asthmatics, exercise stress testing or methacholine challenge is not necessary to establish the diagnosis. Once an index of suspicion is established, a clinical trial of treatment is sufficient.[17]

Exercise-induced asthma can be reduced by the use of repetitive short warmup drills, surgical face masks, or exercise in warm, humidified environments. More commonly, medication is used to prevent EIA. Among the most convenient and effective treatments are beta-2-agonists or cromolyn inhaled shortly before the onset of exercise. More extensive recommendations are published elsewhere.[17]

Exercise stress testing may be necessary for adolescents with severe forms of pulmonary insufficiency such as severe asthma, cystic fibrosis, or other diseases that result in severe reductions in pulmonary function (i.e., FEV_1 less than 50% of predicted). Many of these individuals will experience oxygen desaturation with exercise. Less strenuous sports may be more appropriate for them.[17]

Diabetes Mellitus

Adolescents with type I or II diabetes mellitus can safely participate in all sports if they demonstrate good diabetic control, have family support, and are willing to increase monitoring and alter lifestyle. Complications include hypoglycemia if there is excess insulin present or inadequate carbohydrate available during sports participation. Hypoglycemia may occur during participation or several hours later, particularly during sleep. Paradoxically, those with blood sugars > 350 mg/dl just prior to participation may actually develop ketoacidosis. Those with ketosis prior to competition are particularly prone to this complication.[4]

Because individual responses to exercise vary, at the beginning of the sport season the athlete should monitor blood sugars before, at frequent intervals during, and for several hours after practice or competition. Ideally, preparticipation blood sugar levels should be between 100 and 250 mg/dl. Once a pattern is established, less frequent monitoring is required. The athlete may need to modify eating habits, insulin doses, and site of injection in order to participate successfully in sports. Detailed recommendations have been published elsewhere.[15]

Hematologic Diseases

Studies in military recruits have demonstrated an increased incidence of sudden death in black military recruits with sickle cell trait.[16] No similar studies have been done in athletes and there have been no reports of increased death among black athletes. Studies in military recruits should not be applied in determining eligibility for sport participation for adolescents with sickle cell trait. With proper attention to exercise and heat acclimatization, as well as hydration, adolescents with sickle cell trait should be able to participate in all sports.

Adolescents with sickle cell disease have exhibited abnormal cardiac responses to exercise dependent on the degree of anemia present. Those with hemoglobin levels below 8 gm% have shown temporary ischemic EKG changes during exercise.[1] Whether those with milder degrees of anemia are at risk is unclear. However, all patients with sickle cell anemia should be screened by a cardiologist. If participation is allowed, attention to good hydration and avoidance of heat stress are critical to avoid potential complications of vaso-occlusive phenomena or hemolysis.

Adolescents with hemophilia should avoid contact/collision sports. A decision regarding participation in limited contact/impact sports should be guided by the severity of the individual's disease, which tends to stay at the same level throughout a life span. There is a direct correlation between disease severity and both quantity and quality of clotting factors.[19] However, there are individuals with low levels of factor VIII who have never had significant bleeding with anything other than surgery or life-threatening trauma. Recommendation for participation in limited contact/collision sports requires individual assessment.

Neurologic Disorders

Concussions occur during collision sports such as football at an alarming rate, with many very mild (no loss of consciousness, or post-traumatic amnesia) concussions going unrecognized by other players and coaching staff. The cumulative effect of these so-called "dings" is unknown and their significance for deciding future participation has not been determined. However, one should seriously question continued participation in contact/collision sports for players who have experienced multiple episodes.

Different categorizations for severity of concussion make recommendations for participation or return to play difficult. Specific recommendations are available in the article on minor head trauma in this issue, and elsewhere,[5] but some basic guidelines should be followed. Following a concussion, adolescents who wish to participate in contact/collision or limited contact/ impact sports should be totally asymptomatic both at rest and during strenuous exercise. Some authorities recommend fixed time periods of sport exclusion after resolution of symptoms, depending on the degree of severity of the concussion.[5] Three recognized concussions, regardless of severity, during the previous year should result in exclusion of the athlete for that season. Consideration for participation in subsequent seasons may be given after individual assessment.

The AAP has recommended excluding children with epilepsy from sports in which significant injury or death could occur as a result of a seizure.[6] Some of these activities include underwater swimming, high diving, rope climbing, or use of certain gymnastic apparatus such as parallel bars, rings, or high bars. Swimming should be performed with appropriate supervision using the "buddy system." Participation in sports other than those listed above is acceptable for athletes who demonstrate good seizure control. Participation in contact/collision or limited contact/impact sports should depend on the

TABLE 3.   Qualification Factors for Seizure Disorders

Seizure:	Seizure-free duration
Type	Medical compliance
Severity	Sport-specific injury risk
Frequency	Patient age
Etiology	

medical management, degree of control, and type of supervision available during sports activity.

Some factors to consider regarding eligibility for participation with epilepsy are listed in Table 3. An adolescent who has experienced a recent seizure secondary to electrolyte abnormalities associated with gastroenteritis need not be excluded from any sport. Alternatively, the occurrence of generalized major motor seizures on a monthly basis should disqualify an adolescent from contact/collision sports.

Because there is great variation in individual circumstances, precise definition of "good control" are not available. Participation decisions should weigh the potential benefit of participation against the risk of serious harm should a seizure occur. Responsibility for the decision should be shared among the physician, adolescent and parents.

ACUTE MEDICAL CONDITIONS

Dermatologic Infections

Adolescents with acute herpes simplex or zoster should be excluded from sports that involve close physical contact with opposing players. Numerous outbreaks, with secondary attack rates between 20 and 50%, of herpes gladiatorum have been reported in wrestling.[13a] Any adolescent with active lesions should be excluded from wrestling until the risk of contagion is decreased. Herpes simplex virus can be recovered from lesions for an average of 5 days, but, in general, it is safe to return the athlete to participation when the crusts have come off the lesion, leaving a pink epithelialized base.[24] If the lesion can be covered adequately, participation may be allowed in sports requiring less physical contact.

Pyoderma resulting from streptococcal or staphylococcal infection may present as impetigo, furuncles, carbuncles, folliculitis, and cellulitis.[24] These athletes should not participate in contact/collision sports or those involving shared equipment (i.e., gymnastic mats) until the infection is controlled. Shared equipment should be isolated or cleansed with disinfectant solutions. In general, if there is clinical improvement, risk of contagion is adequately reduced after 48 hours of appropriate antimicrobial treatment.

Infectious Mononucleosis

Infectious mononucleosis is a self-limited disease with an average duration of symptoms of 20–30 days. Splenomegaly occurs in approximately

50% of patients. However, ultrasound studies reveal that significant spleno-megaly is often not detectable clinically and may persist for several weeks after clinical symptoms have resolved.[25] The complication of greatest concern is splenic rupture, which may occur in 0.1–0.2% of cases. There are no clinical guidelines to predict which patients may be at risk for splenic rupture. However, most ruptures have occurred during the first 3 weeks of illness in spleens that are enlarged two to three times normal.[20] Splenomegaly detected by ultrasound after resolution of clinical symptoms beyond 4 weeks from onset of illness has not been demonstrated to be associated with risk of rupture.

Recommendations for return to sports have varied from the point of resolution of clinical symptoms to 6 months after illness. In light of recent ultrasound studies, neither of these recommendations seems appropriate. Absence of splenomegaly demonstrable by ultrasound and resolution of clinical symptoms are certainly safe criteria to use for return to participation. The risk of splenic rupture for the asymptomatic athlete beyond 4 weeks of illness with ultrasonically demonstrable splenomegaly awaits further study. Based on clinical data, if persistent splenomegaly is mild (less than twice normal size), the risk of rupture after 4 weeks seems extremely low. If the athlete and family are willing to accept the theoretical risk of splenic rupture at that point in the course of the disease, participation may be permissible.

CONCLUSION

The opportunities for adolescents with chronic disease or disability to participate safely in sports is increasing in a direct relationship with advances in medicine and science. Exclusion from sports should be based on current recommendations and AAP guidelines that reflect improvements in medical care and sport technology. Knowledge of the limited number of conditions that require exclusion and recognition of recent advances in disease treatment and injury prevention will allow the physician to qualify the vast majority of adolescents for safe sports participation.

References

1. Alpert BS, Dover V, Strong WB, et al: Longitudinal exercise hemodynamics in children with sickle cell anemia. Am J Dis Child 138:1021–1024, 1984.
2. American Medical Association: Medical Evaluation of the Athlete: A Guide, rev. ed. Chicago, American Medical Association, 1976.
3. American Medical Association, Report of the Board of Trustees (I-90): Athletic Preparticipation Examination for Adolescents. Chicago, American Medical Association, 1990.
4. Berger M, Berchtold HJ, Cuppers H, et al: Metabolic and hormonal effects of muscular exercise in juvenile type diabetics. Diabetologia 13:355–365, 1977.
5. Cantu RC: Guidelines for return to contact sports after a cerebral concussion. Phys Sportsmed 14(10):75–79, 1986.
6. Committee on Children with Handicaps and Committee on Sports Medicine, American Academy of Pediatrics: Sports and the child with epilepsy. Pediatrics 72:884–885, 1983.
7. Committee on Sports Medicine, American Academy of Pediatrics: Atlantoaxial instability in Down syndrome. Pediatrics 81:857–865, 1988.
8. Committee on Sports Medicine, American Academy of Pediatrics: Recommendations for participation in competitive sports. Pediatrics 81:737–739, 1988.

9. Davidson RG: Atlantoaxial instability in individuals with Down syndrome: A fresh look at the evidence. Pediatrics 81:857–865, 1988.
10. Dorsen PJ: Should athletes with one eye, kidney, or testicle play contact sports? Phys Sportsmed 14:130–138, 1986.
11. Easterbrook M: Eye protection in racquet sports. Clin Sports Med 7:253–266, 1988.
12. Freed MD: Recreational and sports recommendations for the child with heart disease. Pediatr Clin North Am 31:1307–1320, 1984.
13. Frolich ED, et al (eds): Task Force IV: Systemic arterial hypertension. J Am Coll Cardiol 6:1218–1221, 1985.
13a. Goodman JL, Holland EJ, Andres CW, et al: Herpes gladiatorum at a high school wrestling camp—Minnesota. MMWR 39:5, 1990.
14. Hagberg JM, Ehsani AA, Goldring D, et al: Effect of weight training on blood pressure and hemodynamics in hypertensive adolescents. J Pediatr 104:147–151, 1984.
15. Horton ES: Exercise and diabetes in youth. In Gisolfi CV, Lamb DR (eds): Perspectives in Exercise Science and Sports Medicine: Youth Exercise and Sport. Carmel, IN, Benchmark Press, 1989, pp 539–574.
16. Kark JA, Posey DM, Schumacher HR, et al: Sickle cell trait as a risk factor for sudden death in physical training. N Engl J Med 317:781–787, 1987.
17. Lemanske RF, Henke KG: Exercise-induced asthma. In Gisolfi CV, Lamb DR (eds): Perspectives in Exercise Science and Sports Medicine: Youth Exercise and Sport. Carmel, IN, Benchmark Press, 1989, pp 465–511.
18. McArthy P: Hernias in athletes: What you need to know. Phys Sportsmed 18(5):115–122, 1990.
19. Berman RE, Vaughn VC (eds): Coagulation disorders. In Nelson Textbook of Pediatrics, 13th ed. Philadelphia, W.B. Saunders, 1987, pp 1067–1069.
20. McKeag DB, Kinderknecht J: A basketball player with infectious mononucleosis. In Smith NJ (ed): Common Problems in Pediatric Sports Medicine. Chicago, Year Book Medical Publishers, 1989.
21. McNamara DG, Bricker JT, Galioto FM, et al: Cardiovascular abnormalities regarding eligibility for competition: Task Force I: Congenital heart disease. J Am Coll Cardiol 6:1200–1208, 1985.
22. National Heart, Lung and Blood Institute: Report of the Second Task Force on Blood Pressure Control in Children. Pediatrics 79:1–25, 1987.
23. Nudel DB, Gootman N, Brunson SC, et al: Exercise performance of hypertensive adolescents. Pediatrics 65:1073–1078, 1980.
24. Olerud JE: Common skin problems encountered in young athletes. In Smith NJ (ed): Common Problems in Pediatric Sports Medicine. Chicago, Year Book Medical Publishers, 1989.
25. Primos WA, Landry GL, Scanian KH: The course of splenomegaly in infectious mononucleosis (abstract). Am J Dis Child 144:438–439, 1990.
26. Szentagothai K, Gyene I, Szocska M, et al: Physical exercise program for children with bronchial asthma. Pediatr Pulmonol 3:166–172, 1987.
27. Tunstall-Pedde D: Exercise and sudden death. Br J Sports Med 12:215–219, 1979.
28. Wong HO, Kasser IS, Bruce LA: Impaired maximal exercise performance with hypertensive cardiovascular diseases. Circulation 39:633–638, 1969.

The Athlete and Menstruation

GITA P. GIDWANI, M.D.

Head, Section of Pediatric
  and Adolescent Gynecology
The Cleveland Clinic Foundation
Cleveland, Ohio

Reprint requests to:
Gita P. Gidwani, M.D.
The Cleveland Clinic Foundation
One Clinic Center
9500 Euclid Avenue
Cleveland, OH 44195

Why has there been such interest in the special problems of the female athlete in the past 10–15 years? In 1971, the National Organization of Women filed suit against the Little League of New Jersey, seeking to allow girls to play baseball competitively. Title IX of the Federal Education Assistance Act in 1972 legitimized the concept of equal support for male and female sports at the school level. In the past 20 years, a large number of female children and adolescents have begun participating in sports and physical activities previously not open to them. Female athletes may present with disorders of menstruation, such as delayed menarche, amenorrhea, oligomenorrhea, dysmenorrhea, and anovulation with irregular cycles. Occasionally, the anxious parent of the athlete needs reassurance and guidance from the physician. Coaches and school leaders may have questions about normal and abnormal signs and symptoms in young female athletes. This chapter addresses these clinical situations in a practical manner.

PUBERTY AND MENSTRUATION

The onset of menstruation (menarche) is a positive landmark in a young girl's growth and development. However, significant changes in the hypothalamic-pituitary-ovarian axis are initiated long before the first menstrual period. Puberty in the female begins with the first sign of secondary sexual development and growth spurt and continues until ovulatory cycles occur. Figures 1 and 2 illustrate the

ADOLESCENT MEDICINE: State of the Art Reviews—Vol. 2, No. 1, February 1991
  Philadelphia, Hanley & Belfus, Inc.

27

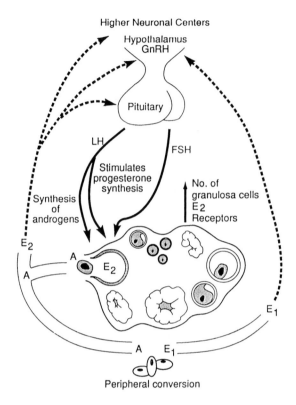

Higher Neuronal Centers

GnRH   Gonadotropin Releasing Hormone
LH   Luteinizing Hormone
FSH   Follicle Stimulating Hormone
E_2 Estradiol
A   Androstenedione
E_1 Estrone

FIGURE 1.   Hypothalamic pituitary ovarian cycle.

relationship of the hypothalamus to the production of gonadotropin-releasing hormone (GnRH). GnRH is transmitted to the pituitary gland, which in turn produces follicle-stimulating hormone (FSH) and luteinizing hormone (LH). The pituitary hormones stimulate maturation of ovarian follicles and production of estrogen and progesterone (sex steroids). These hormones then initiate change in the end-organ, namely the endometrium of the uterus, and produce the first menstrual period. The sex steroids exert a feedback effect on gonadotropin secretion. The positive feedback at the level of the hypothalamus modulates the frequency and amplitude of GnRH release, and its pulses govern the production of LH and FSH. The negative feedback of sex steroids allows estrogen in very small amounts to suppress gonadotropin secretion, whereas positive feedback allows menstrual midcycle surge of estrogen to trigger increased pulses of FSH and LH, producing ovulation. Central nervous

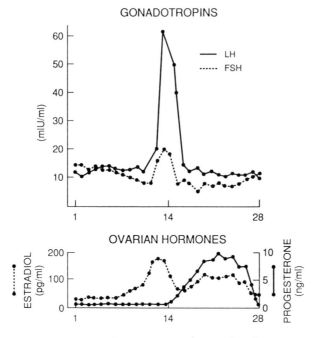

FIGURE 2. Hormones in menstrual cycle.

system endorphins appear to have an inhibitory effect and catecholamines a stimulatory effect on GnRH secretion. This interplay of hormones may be disrupted during the female reproductive years and cause the menstrual cycle to regress to the pubertal and prepubertal level. Some changes in female athletes and in patients with anorexia nervosa seem to be explained by this regression.

The hypothalamic-pituitary-ovarian cycle is intact at the time of birth. However, there is a reduction in the amplitude and frequency of GnRH pulses and decreased pituitary responsiveness to GnRH. This inactivity appears to occur in response to a central nervous signal. The earliest hormonal changes associated with future pubertal maturation are the secretion of adrenal androgens, dehydroepiandrosterone sulfate (DHEA-S) and androstenedione. DHEA-S and its relationship to the other pituitary hormones are depicted in Figure 3.

LH stimulates the theca interna cells of the ovary to synthesize precursors and FSH increases the enzyme aromatase, which is responsible for the conversion of androgen precursors to estrogen. Estrogen seems to peak 10–12 hours after gonadotropin secretion and causes follicular growth.

The initiation of puberty seems to be triggered by the central nervous system, but the stimulus for the initiation is still unknown. Many factors influence the onset and process of puberty, including nutrition, age, body weight, and body composition.

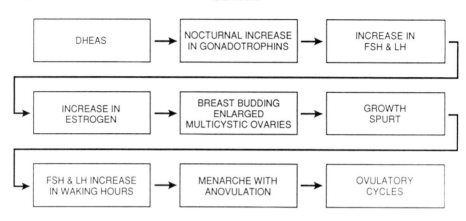

FIGURE 3.   Hormonal events in puberty.

Rising estrogen levels are responsible for changes in the body, such as breast budding, increase in vaginal discharge, and lengthening of the uterus. The Tanner stages of pubertal development are very useful in determining whether an adolescent is developing normally or slowly (Table 1). The Tanner stages of breast and pubic hair development and measurements of height and weight must be recorded by the clinician in the office evaluation of every athlete. Table 2 provides common working numbers that a clinician must keep in mind when evaluating a female adolescent.

MENARCHE AND MENSTRUATION IN THE ATHLETE

A female athlete may present with the following problems: (1) delay in onset of thelarche and menarche, (2) amenorrhea, which is defined as cessation

TABLE 1.   Stages of Pubertal Development

	Age (years)*	
Stage and Description	Mean	Range (95% limits)
Breast Growth		
B-1 Preadolescent		
B-2 Breast budding and areolar enlargement	11.2	8.9–13.3
B-3 Breast tissue enlarged beyond areola in visible mound	12.2	10.0–14.3
B-4 Areola and papilla projecting beyond contour of breast	13.1	10.8–15.3
B-5 Mature breast with areola recessed to contour of breast	15.3	11.9–18.8
Pubic hair growth		
PH-1 Absence of hair		
PH-2 Sparse hair, usually along labia majora	11.7	9.3–14.1
PH-3 Coarse, curled hair sparsely over mons veneris	12.4	10.2–14.6
PH-4 Abundant hair limited to mons veneris	13.0	10.8–15.1
PH-5 Adult hair spread to medial aspects of thighs	14.4	12.2–16.7

Adapted from Marshall WA, Tanner JM: Variations in the pattern of pubertal changes in girls. Arch Dis Child 44:291–303, 1969.

* Ages for English and European girls. For American and Canadian girls, each stage occurs approximately 6 months earlier.

TABLE 2.   Facts and Dates in Female Puberty

Pubertal Event	Date
1. Peak height velocity (PHV)	Occurs before Tanner stages B3 and PH2
2. Menarche (Mean)	13.46 ± .46 years (Tanner) 12.6 ± 1.2 years (Zacharias) Stages B4 and PH4 (Tanner)
3. Interval between B2 and menarche	2.3 ± 0.1 years (Tanner) (range 0.5–5.75 years)
4. Interval between menarche and regular periods Interval between menarche and painful ovulatory cycle	14 months (Zacharias) 24 months (Zacharias)
5. Frisch's "fatness" level: weight to attain menarche Initiate periods Maintain ovulatory cycles	46–47 kg 17% fatness level of body weight 22% fatness level of body weight

of menses for 6 or more cycles after they have been established, (3) anovulatory cycles or short luteal phase cycles that may appear as regular cycles or irregular cycles but by definition may not be accompanied by dysmenorrhea, and (4) regular cycles.

Exercise-related menstrual changes have been studied by numerous investigators but the exact mechanism is still unclear. Most clinicians believe that the effect is at the level of the hypothalamus, and a variety of patterns of GnRH and gonadotropins from prepubertal to early pubertal to late pubertal can be seen in these athletes. Because athletes can suffer from medical conditions, the diagnosis of menstrual aberrations caused by athletics must be made cautiously and only after a careful work-up.

The following section addresses the differential diagnosis and work-up of delayed puberty and menstrual problems in young athletes. We believe that any female athlete is a "female with amenorrhea" rather than an "athlete with amenorrhea," and therefore all physiologic and pathologic conditions, e.g., pregnancy, pituitary tumors, thyroid dysfunction, mullerian agenesis, polycystic ovarian disease, or premature ovarian failure, must be ruled out. As outlined by the Committee on Sports Medicine of the American Academy of Pediatrics, any medical evaluation of a female athlete should include a focus on menstrual history. Athletes, parents, and coaches must be counseled to monitor closely growth velocity, weight changes, and menstrual function during the active sport seasons.

DELAYED THELARCHE AND MENARCHE

Pubertal development appears to be delayed in thin athletes, especially ballet dancers and runners (Fig. 4). Frisch et al.[10] found that athletes who began their training premenarcheally experienced a delay in menarche and had a higher incidence of amenorrhea than athletes who began their training postmenarcheally (Fig. 5). For each year of training before menarche, menarche is delayed 5 months (Fig. 6). Malina et al.[15] proposed that this delay may be attributed to preselection of girls with thin body type and familial late

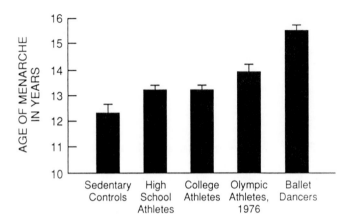

FIGURE 4. Exercise and age of menarche. Pubertal development appears to be delayed in thin athletes.

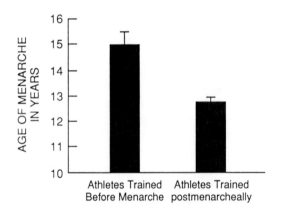

FIGURE 5. Athletes who began their training premenarcheally experienced a delay in menarche.

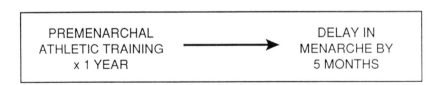

FIGURE 6. For each year of training before menarche, menarche is delayed by 5 months.

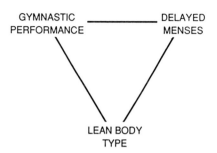

FIGURE 7.   In order to maintain superior performance, gymnasts and ballet dancers may be compelled to stay thin, thus delaying menarche.

development. These young women also excel in athletics and some of the delay in menarche may be related to athletic activity. Relatively low body fat gives the prepubertal female a greater strength-weight ratio, which is useful in gymnastics and ballet dancing. In order to maintain superior performance, such individuals may feel compelled to stay thin, thus delaying menarche (Fig. 7). Warren et al.[23] have pointed out that scoliosis and stress fractures in young ballet dancers are related to delayed menarche and secondary amenorrhea.[7]

Work-up of a Patient with Delayed Menarche

Some common causes of delayed pubertal development are listed in Table 3. When should initiation of pubertal changes in an athlete be considered abnormal? The following recommendations are offered:

(1) If no pubertal changes occur by the chronologic age of 13 years ("two standard deviations outside the normal variation"), examination must be done to rule out thyroid abnormalities, prolactin-secreting adenomas, ovarian dysgenesis, and chromosomal abnormality.

TABLE 3.   Some Common Causes of Delayed Menarche

Hypothalamic
Space-occupying lesions (e.g., craniopharyngioma, glioma)
Functional disturbances of hypothalamic-pituitary axis (e.g., anorexia nervosa, emotional stress, athletics, eating disorders, drugs)

Pituitary
Hypopituitarism—idiopathic
Prolactin-secreting adenomas

Ovarian
Gonadal dysgenesis—chromosomal abnormalities
Tumors
Polycystic ovaries
Resistant ovary syndrome

Uterine or vaginal
Absence of uterus (e.g., mullerian agenesis)
Complete or partial absence of vagina
Imperforate hymen resulting in hematocolpos

Other
Congenital adrenal hyperplasia
Hypothyroidism or hyperthyroidism
Debilitating chronic disease (e.g., congenital heart disease, Crohn's disease, collagen disorders, renal failure)

(2) If there is no period by the age of 16 with some pubertal growth, then a definite search must be made for anatomic causes of amenorrhea and mullerian agenesis.

(3) The Committee on Sports Medicine of the American Academy of Pediatrics has recommended that a work-up be instituted if menarche is delayed by 1 year beyond the age of onset of menses of other female family members.

(4) If the patient, her parents, or coach are anxious about late menarche or delayed puberty, a limited individualized work-up must be offered. Failure to diagnose an abnormality may later haunt the physician and the patient. The patient's family should be counseled about nutrition and weight after adequate data have been gathered and goals determined. It is important that the physician discuss the entire gamut of delayed menarche in an athlete, and the practice of patting the patient on the back and saying that "you are a late bloomer" must be discouraged. The patient may be worried about cancer or fertility and therefore it is important that these issues be addressed in a forthright and honest fashion. The development of pubic hair, breasts, and axillary hair must be noted and staged according to the Tanner classification. A thin female may be noted to have "no development" but may have a normal adrenarche. Warren[24] observed a pubertal developmental dichotomy in athletes in whom ovarian but not adrenal events of puberty were delayed. In contrast, in constitutional delay of puberty, adrenarche, thelarche, and menarche are all delayed. Similarly, scant axillary hair and pubic hair with adequate breast development and amenorrhea are seen in a patient with complete testicular feminization syndrome (Fig. 8). Ambiguous genitalia must be ruled out and a pelvic examination obviously will show whether the uterus and vagina are present and whether there is an abnormality of the hymen. The degree of estrogenization of vaginal mucous membrane will further help to determine whether the patient is hypoestrogenic or has enough estrogen so she can be challenged with medroxyprogesterone acetate. In a number of young hypoestrogenic patients, the absence or presence of the uterus is difficult to define on pelvic or rectal examination and even on ultrasound; therefore this examination may have to be repeated after the patient has been given estrogen orally.

Laboratory evaluation includes skull x-rays, bone age films, thyroid tests, complete blood count, sedimentation rate, serum FSH, and prolactin. Table 4 shows the differential diagnosis after a physical examination and history, growth charts, and laboratory evaluation have been completed.

Well-developed secondary sex characteristics may be seen in the adolescent with delayed menarche. Table 5 describes the complete work-up. Figure 9 depicts an athlete with mullerian agenesis or Rokitansky-Kuster-Hauser syndrome. Reindollar et al.[21] reported this syndrome in 15% of their patients who presented with pubertal abnormality (Table 6). The patient with an obstructed hematocolpos or incomplete mullerian agenesis, namely a transverse vaginal septum, is more dramatic in presentation at menarche because of the obstructed quantum of blood and does not present with the silent amenorrhea that is seen in total mullerian agenesis.

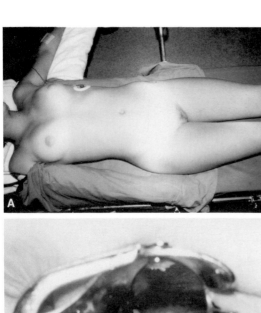

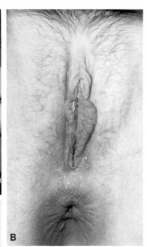

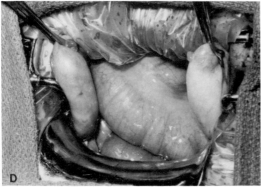

FIGURE 8. A 14.5-year-old white female athlete was referred following routine school examination for left inguinal hernia and primary amenorrhea. Weight, 52 kg; height, 162.5 cm. Normal breasts and external genitalia (A). Sparse pubic hair (B). Uterus and cervix absent (C). Vagina: 4 cm long, well-estrogenized. Karyotype: 46XY. Serum testosterone: 540 ng% (male range 37–100 ng%). Diagnosis: testicular feminization syndrome. Plan: (1) laparotomy with gonadectomy (D) and (2) estrogen replacement.

TABLE 4.   Evaluation of Delayed Pubertal Development

History
    Amount and intensity of exercise
    Nutrition
    Social activities
Physical examination
Growth charts
Thyroid function tests
CBC and sedimentation rate
Bone age
Measure FSH and LH
    I. If low or normal FSH and LH:
        Dx: Hypogonadotropic hypogonadism
             (see Table 8)
    II. If high FSH and LH:
        Dx: Hypergonadotropic hypogonadism
             Do karyotype
        DD: Gonadal dysfunction
             Autoimmune premature ovarian failure (46XX)
             Other causes of ovarian failure such as radiation, chemotherapy (46XX)

The patient in whom abnormal genitalia have been ruled out, and who has well-developed secondary sex characteristics, normal internal and external genital organs, and has had no periods but shows enough estrogen, could be challenged with progesterone, which will initiate menstrual flow in patients with inappropriate positive feedback. In a small unpublished study, we have found that prolactin-secreting adenomas in adolescent females were usually diagnosed late if the youngster was active in athletics. Therefore we recommend that a serum prolactin be done even if the patient responds to progesterone

TABLE 5.   Delayed Menarche with Well-developed Secondary Sex Characteristics

I.   Uterus and vagina present: rule out pregnancy
     A. Oral progesterone, 10 mg for 5 days
        1. Withdrawal bleeding
           a. Check serum prolactin and continue induction of withdrawal
              bleeding every 3 months with progesterone
     B. If sexually active, prescribe oral contraception

II. Uterus and/or vagina absent
     A. Rokitansky-Kuster-Hauser syndrome
     B. Testicular feminization syndrome
     C. Vaginal agenesis
     D. Transverse vaginal septum
     E. Uterine agenesis

III. Uterus and vagina present but no withdrawal bleeding with progesterone
     A. Rule out pregnancy
     B. Check FSH and LH
     C. Proceed as in Tables 4 and 8

IV. Ambiguous genitalia external or signs of androgen excess
     A. Differential diagnosis
        1. Adult-onset congenital adrenal hyperplasia
        2. Pseudohermaphroditism
        3. Hyperthecosis or polycystic ovarian syndrome
        4. Ovarian or adrenal tumors

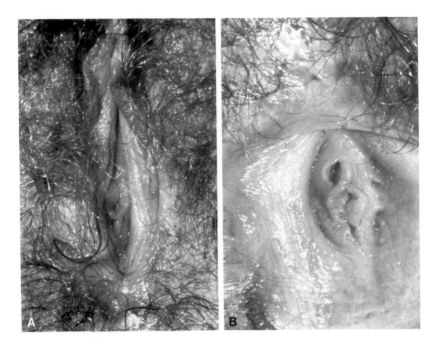

FIGURE 9. A 16-year-old white female athlete with primary amenorrhea. Normal 46XX and normal breast development. Normal external genitalia *(A)*. Labia retracted *(B)*. Diagnosis: Rokitansky-Kuster-Hauser syndrome. Plan: vaginoplasty.

by having a period. If the serum prolactin is normal and the patient is not sexually active and responds to progesterone, the progesterone challenge may be administered every 2–3 months. The athlete should be monitored every 6 months for weight, amount of athletic activity, and diet history. She can be allowed to continue her athletic activity and reassured that all is well. If she has adequate estrogen, she will not be prone to stress fractures and osteopenia; she can be reassured that fertility will not be impaired and that the use of medication, namely progestins, will prevent hyperplasia of the endometrium. We have always been impressed by the anxiety of some of these youngsters

TABLE 6.   Etiologic Breakdown of 252 Patients Presenting
with Prepubertal Abnormalities

	No. of Patients	Percentage
Hypergonadotropic hypogonadism	109	43
Hypogonadotropic hypogonadism	77	31
Eugonadism	66	26
* (Rokitansky-Kuster-Hauser)	(37)	(15)
Total	252	100

From Reindollar RH, Byrd TR, McDonough PG: Delayed sexual development: A study of 252 patients. Am J Obstet Gynecol 140:371, 1981, with permission.
* 37 of 66 patients in eugonad group had Rokitansky-Kuster-Hauser syndrome.

that they may "not be normal." The patient may be kept under surveillance until she develops normal ovulatory cycles. If the patient has persistent amenorrhea (no spontaneous periods for over 2 years with response to progesterone), then a further detailed work-up will be necessary.

Work-up of a patient with delayed menarche and ambiguous genitalia (or signs of androgen excess such as hirsutism, acne, or alopecia). The work-up should rule out congenital adrenal hyperplasia, male or female pseudohermaphroditism, and ovarian or adrenal tumors. Figure 10 describes a patient who had been told that her periods were delayed because of her athletic activity but had not been given an adequate examination of her external genitalia, which were obviously abnormal. She presented to a community hospital with acute torsion of a dysgerminoma. She was later referred to us for further work-up, which included a laparotomy with excision of the other gonad and surgical revision of the enlarged clitoris.

Work-up of an athlete with delayed menarche with no secondary sex characteristics or poorly developed secondary sex characteristics. The next and most common problem in female athletes is no or poorly developed secondary sex characteristics, no ambiguous genitalia, and poor estrogenization with no other signs of androgen excess. Measurement of gonadotropins must be included in the work-up. If the level of gonadotropins is high, the patient should be carefully examined for stigmata of gonadal dysgenesis, and chromosomal studies must be done. FSH levels above the level of 50 mIU/ml repeated on two different occasions will confirm the diagnosis of ovarian failure. As shown in Figure 11, this patient happened to have a Y fragment on the chromosomes that was not seen on the chromosomal pattern but was suspected. This Y fragment could be diagnosed only on a DNA study; on subsequent exploration and removal of the ovaries, an early gonadoblastoma was discovered. Patients with premature ovarian failure may present similarly. These patients are 46XX, and after ovarian failure has been diagnosed, an antibody work-up and an evaluation of the thyroid and other endocrine glands must be done to rule out autoimmune failure of other endocrine glands.

A more difficult group includes **hypoestrogenic females with low gonadotropins**, in which most patients with anorexia nervosa and other causes of hypothalamic amenorrhea will fall. The work-up depends on the presenting symptoms and differential diagnosis (Tables 7 and 8). These patients should be closely monitored for incipient anorexia nervosa. It is important to remember that adolescents with anorexia may have joined the track team and may exercise compulsively to lose additional weight. Eating disorders (dieting, binging, and purging) are prevalent among ballet dancers.

SECONDARY AMENORRHEA IN ATHLETES

The incidence is as variable as the definitions. The Committee on Sports Medicine of the American Academy of Pediatrics has defined secondary amenorrhea as occurring in the mature girl "menarcheal for 3 years who has missed menses for 6 or more cycles." The International Olympic Committee

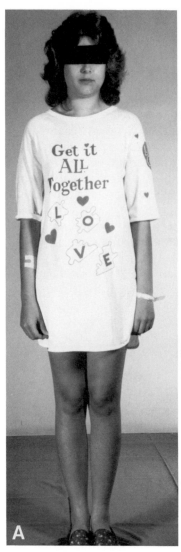

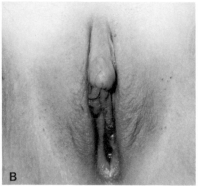

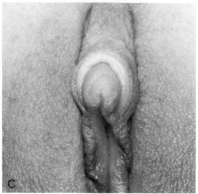

FIGURE 10. A 15-year-old white female: height 64 cm, weight 119 pounds *(A)*. Breasts: Tanner stage 3. Clitoris enlarged *(B and C)*. History: oophorectomy for twisted ovary and appendectomy 4 months previously. Karyotype: 46 XY. Diagnosis: True hermaphroditism. Plan: Clitoral reduction, vaginoscopy, laparotomy with excision of dysgenetic gonad, excision of periaortic lymph nodes, biopsy of omentum.

(The patient is now 6 years postoperative, has regular periods, is married, and has had no recurrence of dysgerminoma. She is an athlete and is considering in vitro fertilization later in life.)

has defined athletic amenorrhea as one period or fewer per year. Wilson et al.,[25] in a study of boarding school athletes who exercised 1½ hours daily including interschool competition, showed that these athletes did not have an increase in menstrual dysfunction compared with nonathletic controls in a similar boarding school. However, it is quite clear from the literature and practice that a clinician will see an increased incidence of oligomenorrhea and amenorrhea in the following clinical situations:[3]

(1) Ballet dancers, runners, and gymnasts are more prone to amenorrhea or oligomenorrhea than swimmers, cyclists, and racketball players.

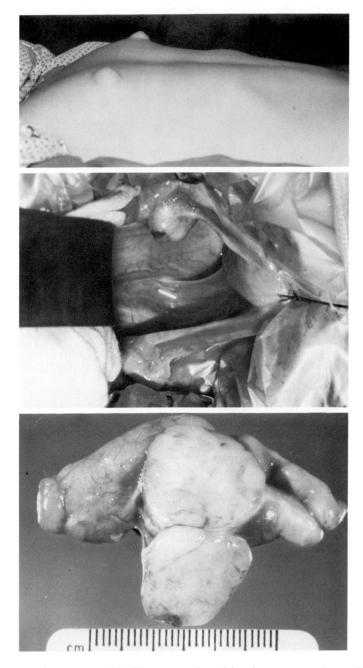

FIGURE 11.   This 13-year-old athlete was referred for short stature. Serum FSH: 90 mIu/cc. Breasts: Tanner stage 2. Karyotype: 46X with a fragment suggestive of Y (later confirmed Y by DNA study). At laparotomy, a gonadoblastoma was found.

TABLE 7. Differential Diagnosis of Hypogonadotrophic Hypogonadism

1. Hypothalamic causes
   stress
   weight loss
   obesity
   athletics
   constitutional
   drugs
2. Central nervous system tumors
3. Hypothyroidism, hypopituitarism
4. Chronic systemic disease (e.g., Crohn's)
5. Kallmann's syndrome

(2) Thin body build or low weight:height ratio with a decreased percentage of body fat is associated with secondary amenorrhea. Frisch[9] has proposed that low body fat causes secondary amenorrhea; however, other investigators have failed to find low body fat as the only factor causing secondary amenorrhea.

(3) Excessive weekly mileage in runners may be a causative factor. Feicht et al.[8] found that the incidence of amenorrhea was 20% in women running 20 miles per week and 43% for those running 60 miles per week.

(4) Diet is considered suboptimal in many athletes with amenorrhea (Table 9).

(5) Stress may increase the incidence of amenorrhea. Gadpaille and colleagues[12] have found an association between athletes, eating disorders, and family history of major affective disorders. Stress alone may cause amenorrhea. Adolescents often experience secondary amenorrhea when they go away to college or camp. Ballet dancers resume normal growth patterns and menstruation when they are not in training sessions.

At present, the most tempting hypothesis is that neurotransmitters are involved in hypothalamic-pituitary alteration of gonadotropins in the exercising athlete.

The study of hypoestrogenic amenorrhea in athletes, whether primary or secondary, has focused on the possible role of lowered bone mass. We demonstrated in 1984 that adolescents with amenorrhea and anorexia nervosa have significant decrease in cortical bone thickness independent of nutritional status.[2] In 1984, Drinkwater[6] showed decreased bone mineral content in

TABLE 8. Work-up of Amenorrhea Related to Hypogonadotrophic Hypogonadism

1. Neurologic assessment including sense of smell
2. Check serum prolactin, thyroid function tests
3. Bone age
4. Consider
   - Skull x-ray films, CT scan of head or MRI to rule out tumors
   - Malabsorption work-up: liver function tests, GI series, etc., if chronic disease is suspected
   - GnRH stimulation test
   - Other measurements of DHEA-S, androgen levels

TABLE 9. Studies of Influence of Diet and Exercise on Menstrual Function:
Comparisons of Amenorrheic and Eumenorrheic Runners

Drinkwater et al., 1984[6]	Caloric intake deficiency
Marcus et al., 1985[16]	Caloric intake deficiency
Deuster et al., 1986[4]	Fat and zinc deficiency
Nelson et al., 1986[18]	Caloric intake deficiency
Schweiger et al., 1988	Caloric intake deficiency
Pirke et al., 1986[19]	Vegetarian diet

amenorrheic athletes. Ayers[1] concluded that premenopausal bone mineral density (BMD) was associated with the following variables: (1) amenorrhea, (2) competitive physical endurance and training, and (3) anthropomorphic thinness. Warren et al.[23] found that the incidence of stress fractures rose with increasing age of menarche, and that the incidence of amenorrhea was twice as high among dancers with stress fractures as in those without. Dancers with delayed menarche may also be more likely to have scoliosis. All this has resulted in considerable controversy about the effect of hypoestrogenic amenorrhea on the skeleton of the adolescent athlete.

The Committee on Sports Medicine of the American Academy of Pediatrics recommends that: (1) amenorrheic athletes within 3 years of menarche should be counseled to decrease the intensity of exercise and improve nutritional intake, especially protein. The use of hormonal therapy for these younger girls is not advised. (2) The mature amenorrheic athlete, generally greater than 3 years postmenarche or age 16 years, who is found to be hypoestrogenic may benefit from estrogen supplementation. Optimal therapy has yet to be determined but supplementation with low-dose contraceptives (less than 50 μg of estrogen) is reasonable.

We recommend counseling thin menstruating adolescents to adhere to diets with adequate calcium and protein. Coaches are helpful in pointing out that "stress fractures are a nuisance" in the competitive season, and they may be avoided by an adequate diet. Patients with hypoestrogenic amenorrhea should be counseled about intake of calcium (at least 1500 mg daily). This amenorrhea is usually associated with a serum estradiol of less than 30 pg/ml and with no withdrawal bleeding following administration of progesterone. Estrogen decreases bone resorption, increases absorption of calcium, and increases renal tubular resorption of calcium. A baseline skeletal assessment by bone densitometry will be useful to detect decreased BMD and can be used to monitor progressive loss of cortical bone. If bone age is retarded by 2 years or bone mass is less than 25% of normal, we recommend doses of estrogen equivalent to 0.625 mg of conjugated estrogen (this dose is for prevention of postmenopausal osteoporosis) for 25 days followed by progesterone 5 mg for 14 days monthly. Reassuringly, Drinkwater in 1986[6] showed the BMD increased in a 14-month follow-up of amenorrheic runners (with a mean duration of amenorrhea of 14 months). No differences were found in risk of bone fractures in college athletes versus nonathletes in older women in a study by Wyshak et al.[26] Emans et al.[7] state that their estrogen regimen was started at 16 years of age in such patients, and this prevented further bone loss but did not bring mass to the level of age-matched controls. More recently, estrogen patches have been used in postmenopausal and adolescent patients. Even though we have not had any personal experience, it seems to be a nice alternative for young patients who do not like to take pills. Naturally, even the estrogen patches must be accompanied by the use of progesterone, 5 mg for 14 days monthly.

If an athlete is sexually active and hypoestrogenic, a simple solution may be the use of an oral contraceptive to substitute estrogen for prevention of osteoporosis, and also for the treatment of dyspareunia, which is common in these young people secondary to vaginal atrophy.

IRREGULAR MENSTRUAL CYCLES IN ATHLETES

Prior et al.[20] showed that on the measurement of basal body temperatures in 14 women who had apparently normal menstrual cycles, one-third of the athletic women had anovulation, one-third had luteal phase inadequacy, and one-third had normal phase function. Irregular bleeding can usually be controlled with oral contraceptives or progestins. It may be prudent to measure serum prolactin as a baseline in such patients, especially if oral contraceptives are to be used over a long period of time. Some athletes with chronic anovulation have marked hyperandrogenism and increasingly high LH levels with large multicystic ovaries. These patients may present with occasional acne and fine lanugo hair, or with acute abdominal pain caused by rupture of an ovarian cyst, or a small bleed in an ovarian cyst. The treatment consists of ruling out any major tumor of the ovary or adrenal gland and administering an oral contraceptive to "dissolve the cyst" for a period of 3–6 months. An athlete with anovulation must be monitored. Progesterones and/or oral contraceptives may be used to prevent endometrial hyperplasia and to prevent bouts of metromenorrhagia that follow periods of amenorrhea.

DYSMENORRHEA

Dysmenorrhea in any teenager can be severe enough to interfere with school activities. In a study by Klein and Litt,[13] 14% of 12–17 year old females missed school because of menstrual cramps. An athlete naturally finds dysmenorrhea to be disabling and an attempt must be made to treat her aggressively with antiprostaglandins. Manipulation of the menstrual cycle is discussed below. In cases of dysmenorrhea that do not respond to antiprostaglandins, an aggressive work-up to rule out congenital anomalies of the mullerian system, endometriosis, or other pelvic disease is required.

PREMENSTRUAL TENSION SYNDROME

This syndrome, especially when accompanied by fluid retention, is also bothersome in an athlete. We have found the use of a diet free of caffeine and sugar to be useful in control of these symptoms. Occasionally, a mild diuretic such as spironolactone, in doses of 25 mg twice daily, may be administered to relieve symptoms of "water logging." Oral contraceptives may be useful in the control of dysmenorrhea and premenstrual symptoms and can be used effectively in sexually active athletes. A nonsexually active athlete may wish to use an oral contraceptive in order to relieve troublesome symptoms for an occasional special event.

MANIPULATION OF MENSTRUAL CYCLES

Occasionally coaches discover that athletes are using androgenic steroids. This practice must be avoided because most steroids have serious side effects and may cause amenorrhea or a rise in serum testosterone. Olympic physicians have suspected that drugs used to treat precocious puberty, such as danazol or GnRH agonists, may be used to retard the onset of pubertal changes in international gymnasts. Occasionally, a female athlete may wish to postpone her period for a competitive event. A menstrual cycle can be delayed easily by 5–7 days with oral contraceptives and by continuing the pill beyond the 21 days for an extra 5–8 days. Progesterone can also be used in 20–30-mg doses daily from the 20th day of cycle for about 15 days. Progesterone can cause bloating and breakthrough bleeding and athletes should be cautioned accordingly.

CONTRACEPTION

Most athletes can be managed either by barrier contraceptive methods or oral contraception. We do not recommend the intrauterine device (IUD) in nulligravida, although it is a very good method in a multigravida who has a single partner.

Oral contraceptives have a very low failure rate, correct irregular periods, and may help to relieve symptoms of dysmenorrhea and premenstrual bleeding; they also provide estrogen for the hypoestrogenic athlete.

Diaphragm, sponge, condoms, and various chemical barriers can be used in teenagers who have normal estrogen function.

Menstruation in an athlete may be normal or abnormal. Coaches, parents, and athletes should be educated about the myths and misconceptions surrounding this subject. Preparticipation evaluations of menstruation and nutrition must be emphasized and such surveillance continued during the athletic career of the youngster. The effect of prolonged hypoestrogenemia on bones ("stress fractures") is fairly well known. Every attempt should be made to stress that all menstrual dysfunction in athletes is reversible if there is no underlying structural or hormonal abnormality.

References

1. Ayers JWT: Hypothalamic osteopenia—body weight and skeletal mass in the premenopausal woman. Clin Obstet Gynecol 28:670–680, 1985.
2. Ayers JWT, Gidwani GP, Schmidt, Gross: Osteopenia in hypoestrogenic young women with anorexia nervosa. Fertil Steril 41:224–229, 1984.
3. Baker ER: Menstrual dysfunction and hormonal status in athletic women: A review. Fertil Steril 36:691–697, 1981.
4. Deuster PA, Kylem SB, Moser PB, et al: Nutritional intakes and status of highly trained amenorrheic and eumenorrheic women runners. Fertil Steril 46:636–643, 1986.
5. Drinkwater BL, Nelson K, Ott S, et al: Bone mineral density after resumption of menses in amenorrheic athletes. JAMA 256:380, 1986.
6. Drinkwater BL, Nilson K, Chestnut CH III, et al: Bone mineral content of amenorrheic and eumenorrheic athletes. N Engl J Med 311:277–281, 1984.
7. Emans SJ, et al: Personal communication.
8. Feicht FB, Johnson TS, Martin BJ: Secondary amenorrhea in athletes. Lancet 2:1145, 1978.
9. Frisch RE, McArthur JW: Menstrual cycles: Fatness as a determinant of minimum weight necessary for their maintenance and onset. Science 185:949, 1974.
10. Frisch RE, Wishak G, Vincent L: Delayed menarche and amenorrhea in ballet dancers. N Engl J Med 303:17–19, 1980.
11. Frisch RE, Gotz Welberg AV, McArthur JW, et al: Delayed menarche and amenorrhea of college athletes in relation to age of onset of training. JAMA 246:1559–1563, 1981.
12. Gadpaille WJ, Sanborn CF, Wagner WW: Athletic amenorrhea, major affective disorders and eating disorders. Am J Psychiatry 144:939, 1987.
13. Klein JR, Litt IF: Epidemiology of adolescent dysmenorrhea. Pediatrics 68:661, 1981.
14. Malina RM, Bouchard C, Shoup RF, et al: Age at menarche, family size and birth order in athletes at the Olympic Games of 1976. Med Sci Sports Exerc 11:354–358, 1979.
15. Malina RM: Menarche in athletes—a synthesis and hypothesis. Ann Human Biol 10:1–24, 1983.
16. Marcus R, Cann C, Mading P, et al: Menstrual function and bone mass in elite women distance runners. Ann Intern Med 102:158–163, 1985.
17. Marshall WA, Tanner JM: Variations in the pattern of pubertal changes in girls. Arch Dis Child 44:291–303, 1969.
18. Nelson ME, Fisher EC, Castsos PD, et al: Diet and bone status in amenorrheic runners. Am J Clin Nutr 43:910–916, 1986.
19. Pirke KM, Scheweiger U, Laessle W: Dieting influences the menstrual cycle—vegetarian versus nonvegetarian diet. Fertil Steril 46:1083, 1986.
20. Prior JC: Menstrual cycle changes with training: Anovulation and short luteal phase. Can J Appl Sports Sci 7:173–177, 1982.
21. Reindollar RH, Byrd TR, McDonough PG: Delayed sexual development: A study of 252 patients. Am J Obstet Gynecol 140:371, 1981.
22. Schweiger VF, Herman R, Laessle W, et al: Caloric intake, stress and menstrual function in athletes. Fertil Steril 49:447–450, 1988.
23. Warren MP, Brooks-Gunn J, Hamilton LH, et al: Scoliosis and fractures in young ballet dancers. N Engl J Med 314:1348–1353, 1986.
24. Warren MP: Effect of exercise in pubertal progression and reproductive function in girls. J Clin Endocrinol Metab 51:1150–1157, 1980.
25. Wilson C, Emans SJ, Mansfield J, et al: The relationship of calculated percent body fat, sports participation, age and place of residence on menstrual patterns in healthy adolescent girls at an independent New England high school. J Adolesc Health Care 5:248–253, 1984.
26. Wyshak G, Frisch RE, Albright TE, et al: Bone fractures among former college athletes compared with nonathletes in the menopausal and postmenopausal years. Obstet Gynecol 69:121, 1987.
27. Zacharias L, Wurtman R: Age at menarche: Genetic and environmental influences. N Engl J Med 280:868, 1969.

Additional Reading

Recommendations of Sports Medicine Committee, American Academy of Pediatrics. Pediatrics 2:394–396, 1989.

Stress and the Adolescent Athlete

FRANK L. SMOLL, PH.D.
RONALD E. SMITH, PH.D.

Professors of Psychology
University of Washington
Seattle, Washington

Reprint requests to:
Dr. Frank L. Smoll
Department of Psychology NI-25
University of Washington
Seattle, WA 98195

Athletic competition places numerous demands on the participants' physical and psychological resources. Consequently, it is not surprising that three fundamental requirements of sports have considerable importance for psychosocial development. First, sports involve the demonstration of athletic prowess, which is a highly prized attribute among children and youth. Second, there is an opportunity for comparison of athletic ability with that of peers, which provides athletes with information about their physical competence. Third, youth sport participants are extensively evaluated by highly significant people, including coaches, parents, and peers.[12,16] These features of the athletic environment not only attract youngsters to sports, but they also serve as potential sources of stress. The physical and mental tests that are opportunities and challenges to some can be psychological threats to others. Some adolescent athletics have a positive drive to succeed, and they regard pressure situations as challenges and rise to the occasion. Others, unfortunately, are motivated primarily by a fear of failing. When faced with the trials of competition, they are likely to be paralyzed by their fear and to "choke."

In spite of its potential harm, some degree of stress can have beneficial effects. In fact, one of the virtues of youth sports is that they provide a training ground for acquiring certain adaptive attitudes and coping skills.

ADOLESCENT MEDICINE: State of the Art Reviews—Vol. 2, No. 1, February 1991
Philadelphia, Hanley & Belfus, Inc.

47

"Competitive stress may be likened to a virus. A heavy dose all at once can make a child ill. A small dose carefully regulated permits the psyche to build antibodies and to successfully resist subsequent stress."[8] Thus, exposure to moderately stressful sport experiences might actually help adolescent athletes to deal effectively with stress in other areas of their lives.

Pediatricians and family physicians with a particular interest in adolescent medicine have become increasingly concerned with the effects of sport participation. There is increased recognition that contact with athletes, coaches, and parents and the consultant roles they occupy in many organizations place physicians in a position to influence positively both the physical and psychological welfare of adolescent athletes. It is our opinion that the youth sport setting can foster psychological growth, and physicians can play an important role in helping to facilitate this process.

THE NATURE OF ATHLETIC STRESS

Although numerous models and definitions of psychological stress have been proposed, some recurrent themes appear and a basic attempt at integration can be made. The term *stress* is typically used in two different but related ways. The first usage refers to situations that tax the physical and/or psychological capabilities of the individual.[6] The focus here is on the balance between the demands of the situation and the personal and environmental resources available to the person. Situations are likely to be labeled stressful (or "stressors") when their demands test or exceed the resources of the person. The second use of the term *stress* refers to the individual's cognitive, affective, and behavioral responses to situational demands and includes aversive emotional states, such as anxiety, depression, and anger. Clearly, these two uses of the term are not synonymous, as people may vary considerably in how "stressful" they find the same situation.

A conceptual model showing the dynamics of stress is presented in Figure 1.[20] The model encompasses relations among situational factors, cognitive appraisal of various aspects of the transaction between the person and the situation, physiological responses, and behavioral responses. Each of these components is, in turn, influenced by personality and motivational variables.

The first component of the model, the **situation**, involves interactions between demands and personal and environmental resources. Demands can be external, as when an athlete confronts a strong opponent in an important contest, or they can have an internal origin in the form of desired goals, personal performance standards relating to values or commitments, or unconscious motives and conflicts. Resources include personal characteristics of the athlete that contribute to coping with the demands, as well as people in the social environment who provide help and support. Stress results from a significant imbalance between demands and resources. When demands are not met, costs in the form of anxiety, guilt, anger, and self-derogation may occur.

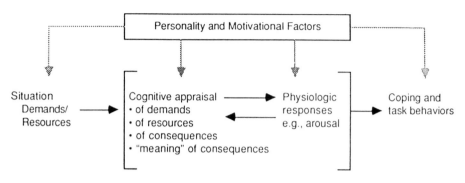

FIGURE 1. A conceptual model of stress showing hypothesized relations among situational, cognitive, physiological, and behavioral components. Motivational and personality variables are assumed to affect and interact with each of the components. (From Smith RE: A component analysis of athletic stress. In Weiss MR, Gould D (eds): Sport for Children and Youths. Champaign, IL, Human Kinetics, 1986, p 108. Copyright 1986 by Human Kinetics Publishers. Reprinted by permission.)

Stress is usually thought to occur in situations in which demands exceed resources ("overload"). However, stress can also result when resources greatly exceed demands or when the person is not challenged to use his or her resources. Feelings of boredom, stagnation, and staleness are common responses to this state of affairs, and a condition of "underload" can take a toll on an adolescent athlete. Thus, both overtaxing and undertaxing situations have been hypothesized to cause athletes to burn out.[21]

Of all the components of the stress model, **cognitive appraisal** may be the most important. Although athletes often view their emotions as direct reactions to situations, in most instances situations exert their effects through the intervening influence of thought. Through their own thought processes, people create the psychological reality to which they respond. Cognitive appraisal processes play a central role in understanding stress because the nature and intensity of emotional responses are a function of at least four different elements: appraisal of the situational demands; appraisal of the resources available to deal with them; appraisal of the nature and likelihood of potential consequences if the demands are not met; and the personal meaning of those consequences, which derive from the person's belief system, self-concept, and conditions of self-worth.

It is important to note that excessive or inappropriate stress responses can result from errors in any of the cognitive appraisal elements. For example, an athlete with low self-confidence may misappraise the balance between demands and resources so that failure seems imminent. Likewise, appraisal errors may occur in relation to the subjective likelihood of the potential consequences, as when an athlete anticipates that the worst is *certain* to happen. Finally, personal belief systems and internalized standards influence the ultimate meaning of the situation for the athlete. For example, an athlete who believes that his or her self-worth depends on success will attach a different meaning to sport outcomes than will an athlete who can divorce self-worth from success or failure. Many adolescent athletes appear to be victimized by irrational beliefs concerning the meaning and importance of success and approval of others, and such beliefs predispose them to inappropriate stress reactions.

The third component of the model, **physiological responses**, is reciprocally linked to cognitive appraisal. When appraisal indicates the existence of threat or danger, physiological arousal occurs as part of the mobilization of resources to deal with the situation. Arousal, in turn, provides feedback concerning intensity of the emotion being experienced, thereby contributing to the ongoing process of appraisal and reappraisal. An athlete who becomes aware of an increasing level of arousal may thus appraise the situation as more threatening than if arousal remained low. It follows that the reciprocal nature of the appraisal-arousal relation can easily elevate levels of stress in an anxious individual, whereas some degree of cognitive or somatic coping ability may serve to control or reduce anxiety.

The fourth component of the model consists of output **behaviors** that constitute the person's attempt to cope with the situation. The model emphasizes that task-oriented, social, and other classes of coping behaviors are mediated by cognitive appraisal processes and by the nature and intensity of physiological responses that may occur. Furthermore, the adequacy or success of these behaviors affects the balance between demands and rescources as well as the ongoing appraisal process.

This component analysis of stress indicates that a variety of elements interact with one another in complex ways. A change in any one of the components can influence all of the others, and all of the components can be strongly affected by **personality and motivational factors**. Individual differences in personality and motivational variables influence the kinds of situations to which people expose themselves, how they appraise themselves and the situations, how they react physiologically, and how they customarily respond at the behavioral level.

The mediational model of stress helps to provide a foundation for the topics to follow. First, we describe the consequences of stress for adolescent athletes. Next, we discuss implications for diagnosing competitive anxiety. Finally, we consider a variety of intervention strategies designed to reduce stress.

HOW COMPETITIVE ANXIETY AFFECTS ADOLESCENT ATHLETES

As noted earlier, sport is an important achievement arena where ability is publicly tested, scrutinized, and evaluated. Because of this, youngsters must learn to cope with the demands and pressures of competition if they are to enjoy and succeed in sports. Fortunately, some athletes develop effective ways of coping with potential sources of stress. Others are prone to suffer adverse psychological, behavioral, and health-related effects. Consideration is now given to the negative consequences of excessive stress (Fig. 2).[22]

FIGURE 2. Negative effects of excessive stress in youth sports.

Fear and anxiety are unpleasant emotions that most people try to avoid. There is evidence that this is precisely what many stress-ridden athletes do. Avoiding sports is one of the ways some youngsters cope with an activity they find threatening rather than pleasant. Evidence also suggests that competitive stress contributes significantly to attrition in youth sports. For example, a study of over 1,000 age-group swimmers indicated that too much pressure, conflict with coaches, and insufficient success were among the reasons that swimmers reported for why their teammates dropped out of competition.[11] In addition to influencing decisions about entering and/or continuing to participate, competitive stress can detract from athletes' enjoyment of sports. This is particularly true for those who perceive more parental pressure and feel that their parents and coaches are less satisfied with their overall sport performance.

In recent years, the notion of burnout has received increasing attention in sports. Elite athletes and coaches have dropped out of sports at the peak of their careers, maintaining that they are too "burned out" to continue. Likewise, youth sport authorities have become increasingly concerned about the large numbers of youth who are dropping out of sports during the adolescent years. While research suggests that in many cases children drop out because they become more interested in other things, there is also concern that intense competitive pressures and too many sport demands may cause some youngsters to burn out and abandon sports.[21] Sport burnout is a legitimate concern, because burned out athletes often show depression, loss of drive and energy, and a lowered sense of self-esteem that carries over into other areas of their lives.

Stress affects not only how athletes feel but also how they perform. All of us have seen athletes fall apart or "choke" under high levels of stress. When under great stress, even gifted athletes can perform poorly. A key to understanding how stress affects performance is the relation between emotional arousal and performance (Fig. 3).

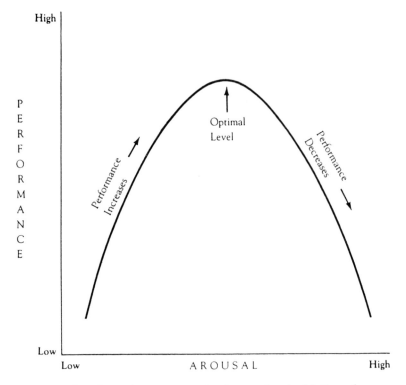

High

P
E
R
F
O
R
M
A
N
C
E

Optimal
Level

Performance
Increases

Performance
Decreases

Low

Low   A R O U S A L   High

FIGURE 3. The relation between emotional arousal and athletic performance.

The manner in which emotional arousal affects performance takes the form of the familiar inverted U, which is predicted by the Yerkes-Dodson law advanced in 1908. When arousal is absent or extremely low, athletes frequently describe themselves as flat and do not perform as well as they are able. As arousal increases, so does performance, but only up to a certain point. Beyond that optimal arousal point, arousal begins to interfere with behavior, and a drop-off in performance occurs. Research has also shown that the more complicated or difficult the task, the less arousal it takes to interfere with performance. Thus, it takes less arousal to interfere with a figure skater or a golfer's performance than with a sprinter's or a weight lifter's.

High-stress athletes who cannot control their emotions are likely to experience higher-than-optimal levels of arousal and to perform poorly. The failure experiences that result only serve to reinforce these athletes' fears and undermine their confidence. Thus, a vicious circle involving anxiety, impaired performance, and increased anxiety can result. Many adolescent athletes never succeed in achieving their potential in sports because of their inability to control their anxiety.

Several other effects of stress should be noted. There is mounting medical evidence that high levels of chronic stress can impair health. The physical nature of the stress response taxes the resources of the body and appears to increase susceptibility to illness and disease. For example, the unfortunate effects of severe competitive pressures are all too frequently seen in adolescent athletes who develop stress-related dermatologic and gastrointestinal problems. In addition, disruption of youngsters' eating and sleeping patterns is directly related to competitive stress. This is surely a high and unnecessary price to pay for the pursuit of athletic excellence!

Stress affects physical well-being in yet another way: Research indicates that, for both college and high school athletes, stressful life changes are related to an increased likelihood of injury. Specifically, studies of college football players have shown injury rates of 68–73% in athletes who had recently experienced many major life changes, compared with 30–39% in athletes who had not experienced such events.[1] For high-school football players, Coddington and Troxell[2] found no association between overall life stress and injury rates. However, athletes who suffered the actual loss of a parent were five times more likely to be injured than were teammates who had experienced no loss of a close personal relationship. In addition, May, Veach, Southard, and Herring[10] reported life changes to be related to injuries in a diverse group of male and female athletes, including gymnasts, figure skaters, basketball players, and biathletes.

Although there is a reasonable basis for considering life stress as a potential risk factor in athletic injuries, stressors do not affect people in a uniform fashion. In fact, some people are highly susceptible, whereas others are quite resilient. Results from a recent prospective study involving 451 high school male and female athletes suggest that the stress-injury relation may be enhanced dramatically by a combination of poor psychological coping skills and low social support.[24] Major negative life changes in themselves were essentially unrelated ($r = .09$) to a measure of subsequent injury (time loss from participation). However, among athletes in the lower quartiles in *both* classes of psychological assets, a correlation of .55 was found between the number of major negative life events experienced in the 6 months prior to the start of the season and subsequent injury. No other low-high combination of social support and coping skills yielded a statistically significant stress-injury correlation. Thus, coping skills and social support operated as moderator variables in an interactive manner: low levels of both variables were required for injury vulnerability in the face of high life stress.

In addition to being at greater risk for injury, sports medicine specialists have observed that athletes who find participation to be stressful and unpleasant often appear to take longer to recover from injuries.[9,14] Depression, anxiety, and anger are frequently experienced by injured athletes, but the effects of such reactions on recovery are unclear. Speculation exists that athletes who are high in fear of failure might find an injury a socially acceptable means of avoiding exposure to the sources of stress, resulting in a longer required recovery period. In other words, some athletes may find an injury to be a temporary and legitimate haven from the stresses of competition.

In light of the above, it seems appropriate to ask whether youth sports are *too* stressful. Research results indicate that for most youngsters, sport participation is not exceedingly stressful, especially in comparison with other activities involving performance evaluation.[18] Indeed, the amount of stress in youth sports does not appear to be as widespread or as intense as critics have claimed. We therefore agree with others (e.g., Martens,[7] Seefeldt and Gould[17]) who have suggested that the problem of competitive stress has been over-emphasized. But it is equally clear that the sport setting is capable of producing high levels of stress for a minority of youngsters. Instead of finding athletic competition enjoyable and challenging, some participants undoubtedly experience anxiety and discomfort, and, as emphasized earlier, excessive stress can have harmful psychological, behavioral, and health-related effects. Consequently, high priority should be given to minimizing sources of undue stress in youth sports.

DIAGNOSTIC PROCEDURES

Although sport participation is not an overly taxing psychological experience for the majority of athletes, stress can be a moderate to serious problem for some adolescents involved in highly competitive situations. The harmful effects of excessive stress, particularly at advanced stages, are rather obvious. On the other hand, the etiological factors involved may be less evident.

For the purpose of illustration, let us assume that your patient is a male high-school athlete who frequently exhibits an inability to perform well in critical situations. This is one of the most common and perplexing of all stress-related problems. In helping him to identify and to deal effectively with competitive anxiety, the conceptual model of stress provides a useful framework for guiding diagnostic efforts. More specifically, you will want to assess situational, cognitive, physiological, behavioral, and personality/motivational factors that might contribute to his substandard performance.

The first step is to obtain information concerning the demands being faced by the athlete and the resources that he has to cope with them. The athlete's coach should be able to give you accurate information about this. A written or verbal report should therefore be obtained, including an assessment of the athlete's physical attributes, his performance in games versus practices, and his ability to perform in pressure situations. Because of the importance of coaching roles and the manner in which their behaviors affect young athletes, it would also be desirable to obtain information about the coach's philosophy of sport as well as his leadership/teaching style. Some of the necessary data may be available from your own observations of the athlete and his coach.

An interview with the athlete in which confidentiality is assured and support is rendered could be helpful to you and to the athlete in understanding what is happening to him. The first issue, of course, is whether or not the athlete views the situation as problematic. If he does not, it will be difficult to provide assistance. Assuming that he does, a physical examination to rule out the possibility of a physical cause for his poor performance can be followed by an attempt to identify psychosocial causes and decide on a course of action.

A good starting point would be to explore the role that the particular sport plays in the young man's life. How important is it to him in comparison with other activities? How committed is he to it? How much does he enjoy it? Does he want to continue to participate? How important is his sport participation to significant others in his life, such as his parents? What are the rewards and costs of sport participation for him? To what does he attribute his performance failures in specific situations? Answers to such questions may provide important information, and they also have implications regarding the degree of commitment he is likely to demonstrate to possible intervention programs.

In examining the demands/resources balance, the coach's report could clarify the role of certain situational and behavioral factors. For example, analysis of the athlete's skill and ability may reveal that his difficulties cannot be attributed to a lack of physical competence. This might be further substantiated by the fact that he tends to perform well in practices and in most game situations. Thus, a purely physical interpretation of the problem would seem inappropriate, leading one to explore the potential role of stress in his performance.

At the situational level, coaches are often important sources of stress. In addition to the inherent tension of competitive events, the nature of the coach-athlete relationship could be a debilitating factor. In their efforts to promote optimal performance, coaches may unwittingly create excessive situational demands. The coach may be interested in his athlete's performance, but the manner in which this is communicated might well be interpreted as pressure rather than encouragement. If there is evidence that the coach pushes his athletes to excel and constantly attempts to gain a "competitive edge," this might place undue importance on the outcome of games. Under such conditions, it is not surprising that an otherwise proficient athlete founders at critical times.

Several other situational sources of stress deserve mention. Stress from different areas of the adolescent's life could carry over into the sport setting. This might include stress from academics, part-time employment, and interpersonal situations involving family or peers. Problems in any of these areas may reduce the athlete's ability to cope in an intensely competitive environment.

Key factors in the athlete's stress response may exist at the cognitive level. It is possible that untoward pressure placed on the athlete has reinforced his already existing beliefs and self-statements. The young man may consequently exaggerate the importance of his performance in relation to his self-worth, his esteem in the eyes of his peers and family, and his value as a member of the team. In addition, because he has repeatedly displayed poor performance at crucial times, despite his ability, this may have led the athlete to believe that he is, in fact, incapable of meeting challenges. With every failure, his appraisal of his own ability to cope might decrease, and an increasing number of situations might become threatening to him.

It is important to explore with the athlete his personal standards for self-worth. Athletes who suffer from performance anxiety usually have high fears of failure or social disapproval that underlie their anxiety. Typically, these have been acquired in relationships with parents or with other important people who have made approval or love contingent on success and have reacted in a punitive manner or withdrawn support in response to failure. It may be possible to assess the extent to which this is the case in his past and current relationships with significant others.

At the physiological level, we would expect that the athlete's performance is adversely affected by high levels of arousal during competition. Athletes are usually able to describe their physiological responses, and your patient should be asked about his emotional arousal level during intense game situations compared with those experienced in practices. It is also well to ask if the athlete has identified any association between his level of arousal and specific thought patterns. Athletes sometimes have surprising levels of insight into how their thoughts and feelings are related, and such information can be very useful from diagnostic and treatment perspectives. If the athlete is unaware of such relations, he should be asked to focus on the contents of his thoughts, images, and memories during subsequent practices and games.

INTERVENTION STRATEGIES

The conceptual model of stress not only provides a frame of reference for diagnostic purposes, but also suggests a number of points at which intervention strategies might be applied. In a general sense, any of the model's components may be a target for intervention. It is important to recognize, however, that the model is a reciprocally interactive and recursive one, so that measures taken to modify any one of the components will almost certainly affect other components as well.

The broadest level at which intervention might be directed is that of personality and motivation. In cases in which athletes' stress responses are a reflection of deep-seated personality problems that threaten personal adjustment, formal counseling or psychotherapy may be appropriate. If assessment of your patient's difficulties suggests the presence of severe personal maladjustment, then referral to a clinical sport psychologist is warranted. In most cases, however, other less expensive and time-consuming approaches are sufficient to alleviate athletic stress problems. Moreover, focused intervention strategies can have a generalized effect on more global aspects of personality.

At the situational level, changes in certain features of the athletic environment can dramatically alter its capacity to generate stress. These may involve the reduction of demands, the increasing of resources, or both. Environmental demands can be reduced by making changes in the organization and administration of a sport program, particularly for athletes at younger ages. For example, some progressive programs use homogeneous grouping procedures to match competitors on such variables as size, physical maturity, and ability. Likewise, programs may be organized to differ in degree of competitive intensity, allowing participants to select the level at which they wish to play. Another approach involves modification of the sport itself.[13] For example, the height of the basketball hoop can be lowered, or a smaller ball can be used. This decreases performance demands and increases the chances for success and enjoyment. Although such changes are desirable improvements, they may not be entirely appropriate for adolescent-level athletics. In any event, adoption of worthy policies and practices can be facilitated by a physician's input on a sports advisory council or management board.

With respect to environmental resources, the availability of social support is perhaps the most important asset that one might have. Substantial evidence indicates that social support acts as a buffer against stressors, and that low social support or a loss of support constitutes a significant stressor in its own right.[5,15] Recognizing that coaches are important potential sources of social support for athletes, it follows that intervention programs that increase the amount and/or quality of their support can help tip the balance of the demands/resources scale in a positive direction. One such program, known as Coach Effectiveness Training (CET), provides instruction for coaches in creating a more supportive and enjoyable psychological environment for athletes.

The core of CET consists of a series of behavioral guidelines that are based primarily on (1) social influence techniques that involve principles of positive control rather than aversive control, and (2) a conception of success or "winning" as consisting of giving maximum effort.[27] A primary goal of the guidelines is to increase the level of social support within the team and to increase the desire of athletes to learn and to give maximum effort while reducing fear of failure. The importance of reinforcement, encouragement, and sound technical instruction is emphasized, while aversive control procedures based on punishment and criticism are discouraged. If coaches only require their athletes to give maximum effort, and if they reinforce effort rather than focusing solely on outcome, athletes can learn to set similar standards for themselves. Athletes have complete control over effort and only partial control over outcome, and it is well established that lack of perceived control is a major contributing factor to stress responses.[4] As far as winning is concerned, CET emphasizes that if athletes are well-trained, give maximum effort, and have positive achievement motivation rather than performance-disrupting fear of failure, winning will take care of itself within the limits of their ability. Evaluation of CET in an experimental field study indicated that coaches can be trained to relate more effectively to young athletes, to create a more supportive athletic environment, and to enhance athletes' feelings of self-worth, all of which might ultimately serve as buffers against competitive stress.[23]

In addition to educating coaches, there is sometimes a need for intervention with athletes' parents. A companion program has therefore been developed to provide parents with parallel guidelines for promoting the development of a positive desire to achieve rather than fear of failure, but the effects of this program have not been evaluated experimentally.[26] Many of the concepts and guidelines contained in CET would undoubtedly assist parents in fostering their youngster's personal growth through sports.[25] For example, the philosophy of winning is as relevant for parents as it is for coaches. Indeed, the notion may be more important for parents to grasp because they can apply it to many areas of the adolescent's life in addition to athletics. The basic principles contained in the positive approach to coaching also apply to parents. By encouraging adolescents to do as well as they are currently able, by reinforcing effort as well as outcome, and by avoiding the use of criticism and punishment, coaches and parents can promote the development of positive motivation to achieve and help prevent fear of failure. Physicians are in a favorable position to facilitate this process by performing an important educational/guidance function. Specifically, you can counsel coaches and parents about their youth sport roles and responsibilities and provide them with guidelines for relating effectively to adolescent athletes. Detailed guidelines for both coaches and parents are available in two recent publications and can serve as a basis for counseling, talks, and workshops for parents and coaches.[25,27]

Returning to the conceptual model of stress, environmental changes can also be produced by changes occurring within the behavioral component. Behavior is affected by the environment, but the opposite is also true; that is, the environment is influenced and sometimes transformed by behavioral changes. Thus, acquisition of effective problem-solving behaviors can increase personal resources and reduce demands. For example, training that increases sport skills can make athletic demands easier to cope with, and increased social skills can help athletes develop a more positive social environment and increase the quality of social support received from coaches and teammates.

Stress can also be reduced by modifying the cognitive appraisal of athletes. This is in many ways the key component in the model, because most interventions directed at other model components ultimately are mediated by and/or exert their effects on the appraisal processes. Even if the situation cannot be changed (as is often the case), athletes can be trained to discover, challenge, and change the appraisal elements that are, in actuality, generating their stress responses. In athletes, these internal self-statements generally relate to fear of failure and/or disapproval (e.g., "How horrible it would be if I messed up." "I couldn't stand it if I let down my coach and teammates."). Worrying and dwelling upon the seemingly catastrophic consequences of failure dominate the thought patterns of many high-stress athletes. Such cognitions interfere with productive planning and attention to the task at hand, thus resulting in lowered performance. Training in cognitive coping skills may be required in instances where dysfunctional thoughts play a major role in the adolescent athlete's stress response. This kind of training is best referred to a certified sport psychologist who is knowledgeable about the specific techniques.

The final point at which intervention can be directed is at the level of physiological arousal. Muscular relaxation is one of the most useful coping skills that athletes can have for preventing or lowering excessive physiological arousal, and this important skill can be easily taught. The rationale for relaxation training is that deep muscle relaxation is incompatible with arousal, and, to the extent that athletes can voluntarily control their level of relaxation, they can also control stress responses. It is important to note, however, that the goal is *not* to eliminate arousal completely, as some degree of arousal enhances performance. Rather, the goal of the training is to give athletes greater control over emotional responses, thereby enabling them to prevent or reduce high or aversive levels of arousal that interfere with performance and enjoyment. Because of their generally superior ability to control motor responses, athletes tend to learn relaxation skills rather quickly. The learning of relaxation skills also helps athletes to become more sensitive to their bodily arousal, so that they can use their coping skills before their level of arousal becomes excessive and difficult to control.

A relaxation training program that can be used by physicians is presented in the Appendix. We have been using the techniques for many years as part of a comprehensive approach to stress management. Our experience has shown that children as young as 8 or 9 years of age, adolescents, and adults can easily learn voluntary relaxation skills to provide them with a means of counteracting physiological arousal.

From the perspective of the stress model, the "mentally tough" athlete is one who is able to keep arousal within an optimal range and who is able to direct attentional and other cognitive processes to performing instrumental behaviors under adverse environmental conditions. In working with athletes (and other groups) we have therefore focused on the development and rehearsal of specific coping skills at both the cognitive and physiological levels that serve to prevent and/or reduce stress responses. Stress Management Training (SMT)[19] consists of a number of clinical treatment techniques combined into an educational program for self-control of emotion. Originally developed for use in individual and group psychotherapy with clinical populations, the program components have been adapted and combined to form a training package that has been applied to a variety of nonclinical populations, including child, adolescent, college, and professional athletes. In essence, SMT provides for the learning of an **integrated coping response** having a physiologic-somatic component (relaxation training) and a cognitive component (cognitive and self-instructional training). SMT also includes a skill-rehearsal phase that involves practicing the coping skills to reduce arousal elicited by imagining stressful athletic events. Although it has been presented as a 1- or 2-day workshop, the group SMT program typically consists of six 1-hour sessions conducted over a 3-week period. The spaced sessions give participants more opportunity to practice and integrate their coping skills.

CONCLUDING COMMENTS

Some degree of stress is inherent in all competitive situations. Like striving for victory, it is an integral part of sports. But some athletes experience excessive chronic stress that can contribute to a variety of psychological as well as physical maladies. This chapter has emphasized that an understanding of the antecedents, dynamics, and consequences of athletic stress can pave the way for preventive, diagnostic, and remedial measures. Physicians can play an important role in helping coaches, parents, and adolescent athletes to keep competition within a healthy perspective. Through your professional efforts, you can help to alleviate needless stress within sports and thus provide adolescent athletes with enjoyment and personal growth.

ACKNOWLEDGMENT

Preparation of this chapter was facilitated by Grant 86-1066-86 from the William T. Grant Foundation.

References

1. Bramwell ST, Masuda M, Wagner NN, Holmes TH: Psychosocial factors in athletic injuries: Development and application of the Social and Athletic Readjustment Rating Scale (SARRS). J Human Stress 1:6–20, 1975.
2. Coddington RD, Troxell JR: The effect of emotional factors on football injury rates—A pilot study. J Human Stress 6:3–5, 1980.
3. Cryan PD, Alles WF: The relationship between stress and college football injuries. J Sports Med 23:52–58, 1983.
4. Folkman S: Personal control and stress and coping processes: A theoretical analysis. J Pers Soc Psychol 46:839–852, 1984.
5. Heller K, Swindle RW: Social networks, perceived social support, and coping with stress. In Felner RD, Jason LA, Moritsugu JN, Farber SS (eds): Preventive Psychology: Theory, Research, and Practice. Elmsford, NY, Pergamon, 1983.
6. Lazarus RS, Folkman S: Stress, Appraisal, and Coping. New York, Springer, 1984.
7. Martens R: Joy and Sadness in Children's Sports. Champaign, IL, Human Kinetics, 1978.
8. Martens R: An examination of some frequent concerns in youth sports from a psychological perspective. In Smith NJ (ed): Sports Medicine for Children and Youth. Columbus, OH, Ross Laboratories, 1979.
9. May JR, Sieb GE: Athletic injuries: Psychosocial factors in the onset, sequelae, rehabilitation, and prevention. In May JR, Asken MJ (eds): Sport Psychology: The Psychological Health of the Athlete. New York, PMA Publishing, 1987.
10. May JR, Veach TL, Southard SW, Herring M: The effects of life change on injuries, illness, and performance in elite athletes. In Butts NK, Gushikin TT, Zarins B (eds): The Elite Athlete. Jamaica, NY, Spectrum, 1985.
11. McPherson B, Marteniuk R, Tihanyi J, Clark W: The social system of age group swimmers: The perception of swimmers, parents and coaches. Can J Appl Sport Sci 4:142–145, 1980.
12. Passer MW: Determinants and consequences of children's competitive stress. In Smoll FL, Magill RA, Ash MJ (eds): Children in Sport, 3rd ed. Champaign, IL, Human Kinetics, 1988.
13. Potter M: Game modifications for youth sport: A practitioner's view. In Weiss MR, Gould D (eds): Sport for Children and Youths. Champaign, IL, Human Kinetics, 1986.
14. Rotella RJ, Heyman SR: Stress, injury, and the psychological rehabilitation of athletes. In Williams JM (ed): Applied Sport Psychology: Personal Growth to Peak Performance. Palo Alto, CA, Mayfield, 1986.
15. Sarason IG, Sarsason BR (eds): Social Support: Theory, Research and Applications. Boston, Nijhoff, 1985.
16. Scanlan TK: Social evaluation and the competition process: A developmental perspective. In Smoll FL, Magill RA, Ash MJ (eds): Children in Sport, 3rd ed. Champaign, IL, Human Kinetics, 1986.
17. Seefeldt V, Gould D: Physical and psychological effects of athletic competition on children and youth. Report No SP 015398. Washington, D.C., ERIC Clearinghouse on Teacher Education, 1980.
18. Simon JA, Martens R: Children's anxiety in sport and nonsport evaluative activities. J Sport Psychol 1:160–169, 1979.

19. Smith RE: A cognitive-affective approach to stress management training for athletes. In Nadeau CH, Halliwell WR, Newell KM, Roberts GC (eds): Psychology of Motor Behavior and Sport–1979. Champaign, IL, Human Kinetics, 1980.
20. Smith RE: A component analysis of athletic stress. In Weiss MR, Gould D (eds): Sport for Children and Youths. Champaign, IL, Human Kinetics, 1986.
21. Smith RE: Toward a cognitive-affective model of athletic burnout. J Sport Psychol 8:36–50, 1986.
22. Smith RE, Smoll FL: Sport performance anxiety. In Leitenberg H (ed): Handbook of Social and Evaluation Anxiety. New York, Plenum, 1990.
23. Smith RE, Smoll FL, Curtis B: Coach Effectiveness Training: A cognitive-behavioral approach to enhancing relationship skills in youth sport coaches. J Sport Psychol 1:59–75, 1979.
24. Smith RE, Smoll FL, Ptacek JT: Conjunctive moderator variables in vulnerability and resiliency research: Life stress, social support and coping skills, and adolescent sport injuries. J Pers Soc Psychol 58:360–370, 1990.
25. Smith RE, Smoll FL, Smith NJ: Parents' Complete Guide to Youth Sports. Reston, VA, American Alliance for Health, Physical Education, Recreation, and Dance, 1989.
26. Smoll FL: Parent sport orientation: A workshop for athletes' parents. Your Public Schools 23:11, 1984.
27. Smoll FL, Smith RE: Sport Psychology for Youth Coaches. Washington, DC, National Federation of Catholic Youth Ministries, 1987.

APPENDIX

Training in Muscle Relaxation

Relaxation training provides a useful stress management coping skill. The following procedure can be used to train most people to a satisfactory skill level in approximately 1 week. The practitioner should explain the rationale for relaxation training and then take the patient through the procedure on at least the first occasion. The patient then receives a copy of the instructions to follow in practice. We recommend practice at least twice daily.

Our procedure starts by concentrating on the hands and arms; moves to the legs, chest, shoulder, stomach, back, neck and jaw muscles; and finishes up with the facial and scalp muscles. After going through the exercises a few times, the patient will be able to memorize the sequence and will no longer need the printed relaxation instructions.

Tensing and relaxing of the muscles are important not only in the learning of the relaxation response, but also in increasing the patient's awareness of states of bodily tension. As practice proceeds, the patient can decrease the tension level to the halfway point and incorporate larger and larger groups of muscles (i.e., the entire lower body) at the same time. This also reduces practice time appreciably. The goal is to reach the point where the breathing component and the self-command to relax are sufficient to produce a state of relaxation within a few breaths.

1. Get as comfortable as possible. Loosen tight clothing. Legs should not be crossed. Take a deep breath, let it out slowly, and become as relaxed as possible.

2. While sitting comfortably, bend your arms at the elbow. Now make a hard fist with both hands, and bend your wrists downward while also tensing the muscles of your upper arms. This will produce a state of tension in your hands, forearms, and upper arms. Hold this tension for 5 seconds and study it carefully, then slowly let the tension out halfway while concentrating on the sensations in your arms and fingers as tension decreases. Hold the tension at the halfway point for 5 seconds, and then slowly let the tension out the rest of the way and rest your arms comfortably in your lap. Concentrate carefully on the contrast between the tension just experienced and the relaxation that deepens as you voluntarily relax the muscles for an additional 10 to 15 seconds. As you breathe normally, concentrate on those muscles and give yourself the mental command to relax each time you

exhale. Do this for 7 to 10 breaths. The following is a sample of how you can phrase the instructions when presenting this exercise:

> We're going to start out with the arms and hands. What I'd like you to do while keeping your eyes closed is to bend your arms and make a fist like this. [*Demonstrate*] Now make a hard fist and tense those muscles in your arms hard. Notice the tension and the pulling throughout your arm as those muscles stretch and bunch up like rubber bands. Focus on those feelings of tension in your arms and hands.
>
> [*After 5 seconds*] Now slowly begin to let that tension out halfway, and concentrate very carefully on the feeling in your arms and hands as you do that. Now hold the tension at the halfway point and notice how your arms and hands are less tense than before, but that there is still tension present.
>
> [*After 5 seconds*] Now slowly let the tension out all the way and let your arms and hands become completely relaxed, just letting go and becoming more and more relaxed, feeling all the tension draining away as the muscles let go and become completely relaxed. And now, each time you breathe out, let your mind tell your body to relax, and concentrate on relaxing the muscles even more. That's good . . . just let go.

3. Tense the calf and thigh muscles by straightening out your legs while at the same time pointing your toes downward. Hold the tension for 5 seconds, then slowly let it out halfway. Hold the halfway point for an additional 5 seconds, and then slowly let the tension out all the way and concentrate on relaxing the muscles as completely as possible. Again, pay careful attention to the feelings of tension and relaxation as they develop. Finish by giving the muscles the mental command, "Relax," each time you exhale (7 to 10 times), and concentrate on relaxing them as deeply as possible.

4. Cross the palms of your hands in front of your chest and press them together to tense the chest and shoulder muscles. At the same time, tense your stomach muscles. As before, hold the tension for 5 seconds, then slowly let the tension out halfway and focus on the decreasing level of tension as you do so. Hold again for 5 seconds at the halfway point and then slowly let the tension out completely. Again, do the breathing procedure with the mental command to deepen the relaxation in your stomach, chest, and shoulder muscles.

5. Arch your back and push your shoulders back as far as possible so as to tense your upper and lower back muscles. (Be careful not to tense these muscles too hard.) Repeat the standard procedure of slowly releasing the tension halfway, then all the way. Finish by doing the breathing exercise and mental command as you relax your back muscles deeply.

6. Tense your neck and jaw muscles by thrusting your jaw outward and drawing the corners of your mouth back. Release the tension slowly to the halfway point, hold for 5 seconds, and then slowly release the tension in these muscles all the way. Let your head droop into a comfortable position and your jaw slacken as you concentrate on relaxing these muscles totally with your breathing exercise and mental command. (You can also tense your neck muscles in other ways, such as by bending your neck forward, backward, or to one side. Experiment to find the way that is best for you, but remember to tense your jaw at the same time.)

7. Wrinkle your forehead and scalp to tense those muscles. Hold the tension for 5 seconds, then release it halfway for an additional 5 seconds. Finally, relax the tension all the way. Focus on relaxing your facial and scalp muscles completely, and use your breathing and associated mental command to deepen relaxation.

8. While sitting in a totally relaxed position, take a series of short inhalations, about one per second, until your chest is filled and tense. Hold this for about 5 seconds, then exhale slowly while thinking silently to yourself, "Relax." Most people can deepen their relaxation by doing this. Repeat this exercise three times.

9. Finish off your relaxation practice by concentrating on breathing with your abdomen (rather than with your chest). Simply let your abdominal area fill with air as you inhale, and deepen your relaxation as you exhale. Abdominal breathing is far more relaxing than chest breathing.

10. When you are under stress, monitor your body to identify your tension points so that you can devote special attention to learning to relax those areas. Also, repeat Exercise 8 whenever you have the opportunity to help you condition your bodily relaxation to the mental command to relax. This command, combined with exhalation, can then be used to help control emotional arousal in stressful situations.

As you guide your patients through the exercises, you can practice them yourself. You will find relaxation very useful in your own life. It not only serves as a weapon against tension and stress, but it produces an enjoyable state in its own right.

The Status of Adolescent Physical Fitness

R. AUSTIN RAUNIKAR, M.D.
WILLIAM B. STRONG, M.D.

R. Austin Raunikar, M.D.
Fellow, Pediatric Cardiology
Medical College of Georgia
Augusta, Georgia

William B. Strong, M.D.
Leon Henri Charbonnier
    Professor of Pediatrics
Chief, Section of Pediatric
    Cardiology
Director, Georgia Institute for the
    Prevention of Human Disease
    and Accidents
Medical College of Georgia
Augusta, Georgia

Reprint requests to:
William B. Strong, M.D.
Chief, Section of Pediatric
    Cardiology
Medical College of Georgia
Augusta, GA 30912-3710

"Adolescents are less physically fit as a group than they were twenty years ago."

"It is likely this deterioration in adolescent physical fitness will not change."

"And there is little we can do to change this decline in adolescent fitness."

These three statements paint a bleak picture of the current and future status of physical fitness among adolescents in the United States. Whether or not one agrees with these statements depends on one's definition of physical fitness and one's professional or anecdotal experience with adolescents. Anecdotal information, however, may not reflect the actual status of adolescent physical fitness. Both scientific journals and the lay literature tout the increased prevalence of fitness among more affluent, better educated adults. Evidence suggests that adolescents do not participate in this national trend.

Over the past decade numerous reports have cited the health benefits associated with physical activity and regular exercise. Physical fitness also confirms similar benefits. Table 1 summarizes the potential benefits associated with being active and physically fit. A goal of this chapter is to distinguish physical activity from physical fitness, although the two are closely linked.

Additional purposes of this chapter are: (1) to review the current status of adolescent physical fitness; (2) to review the benefits of

ADOLESCENT MEDICINE: State of the Art Reviews—Vol. 2, No. 1, February 1991
Philadelphia, Hanley & Belfus, Inc.

65

TABLE 1. Potential Benefits of Physical Fitness

Emotional/Mental	General Health
Release of endorphins	Increased likelihood of proper nutrition
Improved self-esteem	Increased likelihood to promote similar health
Reduced anxiety and tension	pattern in one's children
Reduced depression	Reduced likelihood of abusing tobacco, alcohol,
Increased mental acuity	illicit drugs
Musculoskeletal	**Economic**
Increased muscular strength	Reduced number and severity of illnesses
Increased muscular endurance	Reduced absence from school or work
Increased flexibility	Reduced use of health insurance
Increased balance	Reduced loss of employer's work force
Increased agility	
Increased bone density	
Reduced risk of joint injury	
Reduced risk of osteoporosis	
Cardiovascular	
Increased cardiorespiratory endurance	
Increased cardiac output	
Reduced incidence/degree of obesity	
Reduced incidence/degree of hypertension	
Reduced low-density lipoprotein level	
Reduced triglyceride level	
Increased high-density lipoprotein level	
Increased coronary artery caliber	
Reduced risk for lethal arrhythmias	
Reduced incidence of risk for developing	
cardiovascular disease	

physical fitness; and (3) to suggest methods the physician can use to improve adolescent physical fitness. In order to accomplish these objectives, it will be necessary to: (1) differentiate between physical activity and physical fitness; (2) define the components of physical fitness, distinguishing between motor- and health-related physical fitness; and (3) present current tests that measure physical fitness and understand their strengths and weaknesses.

Physical activity is any activity that requires use of any muscle group within the body. Physical activity and physical fitness are not synonymous. Blair describes physical activity as a behavior that is a significant determinant of physical fitness, an attribute.[6] He further states that physical fitness is "an objective marker for habitual physical activity." Physical fitness is the ability to accomplish work (exercise) without undue discomfort or prolonged fatigue.[65] Fitness cannot be defined so generically when evaluating its presence in adolescents. The differences between motor (athletic) fitness and health-related physical fitness must also be understood. This can be accomplished by reviewing the evolution of physical fitness assessment in the United States which became more uniform in the late 1950s.

President Dwight D. Eisenhower created the President's Council on Physical Fitness to improve physical fitness among children as a response to a report by Kraus and Hirschland in 1954.[33] That paper concluded that American children were less physically fit than European children of the same age. Shortly thereafter, the American Alliance for Health, Physical

Education, and Recreation (AAHPER) developed their Youth Fitness Test (1958).[49]

The AAHPER Youth Fitness Test (1958) assessed motor fitness, often referred to as "athletic fitness" because the components of motor fitness can be important to athletic performance. These components include cardiorespiratory endurance, muscular strength and endurance, body composition, flexibility, speed, balance, power, and agility. Pate refers to this "military approach to physical fitness" as a residual effect of the nation's wartime health emphasis. He accredits this definition of physical fitness along with an expansion of school athletic programs with sending a message to the youth of the late 1950s to early 1970s: "If you want to be physically fit, you must be fast, agile, and powerful as well as strong and enduring."[49]

During the past 15 years, the definitions of fitness and fitness testing have evolved with the emphasis placed on areas of conditioning that promote overall health and lifelong physical activity. This concept is called health-related physical fitness.[37,49] Figure 1 compares the components of health-related fitness and motor fitness. The components of health-related physical fitness include cardiorespiratory endurance, muscular strength and endurance, flexibility, and body composition. Cardiorespiratory endurance is required to meet our original definition of physical fitness—the ability to accomplish work without undue discomfort or prolonged fatigue.[65,74] Muscular strength is the ability of muscles to exert or apply a force; it includes both static (isometric) and dynamic contractions. Muscular endurance reflects resistance to local muscle fatigue. Flexibility is a measure of body suppleness. More specifically, it is a measure of the range of motion across joints, reflecting the interrelationship

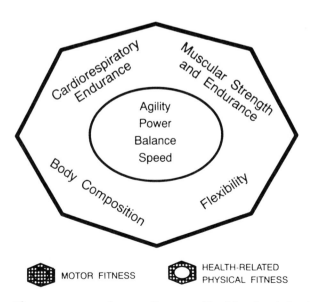

FIGURE 1.   The components of motor fitness and health-related physical fitness.

of muscle, ligaments, and tendons. Body composition is an assessment of total body mass, and shape and distribution of that mass, and specifically assesses percent body fat.

A battery of tests has been developed to measure health-related physical fitness. Some tests measure only one of the four components, such as the Canadian Aerobic Fitness Test or the Modified Harvard Step Test (cardiorespiratory fitness).[30] Others attempt to assess all four components. These include the American Alliance for Health, Physical Education, Recreation, and Dance (AAHPERD) Youth Fitness Test (1980) and the Council of Europe's Eurofit.[24,45] The Eurofit additionally assesses power, speed, and balance, which are more appropriately defined under motor fitness.[24] Many other countries have developed youth fitness tests similar to those presented at the First International Conference on Nutrition and Fitness held in May 1988, in Ancient Olympia, Greece, emphasizing the increased worldwide interest in assessing youth physical fitness.[18,20,24,55,67,69]

The wide variety of fitness tests identifies the lack of agreement as to what constitutes physical fitness. Defining physical fitness and selection of testing methods may be related to investigator bias rather than to actual differences in physical fitness. There is no perfect test that is "fair" to all sizes and shapes of youth, as exemplified by the sit and reach test, which assesses flexibility and is used in the AAHPERD Youth Fitness Test (1980) and Eurofit.[4,24] This test favors the individual with long arms and short legs.[4,74] Also, although most experts agree that maximal aerobic power, as measured by maximal oxygen uptake, is the best index of cardiovascular fitness,[29,74] they disagree on the means of measurement. Techniques vary from a timed distance run to sophisticated ergometry and expired gas measurements.[4,29,30,74] Many tests make assessments strictly on the basis of age. Adolescents, however, mature at different rates. Studies indicate that maturational age measured by Tanner staging, rather than chronological age, may correlate more accurately with strength and flexibility.[52] In spite of these variables, interpretations of overall fitness trends can be gleaned from studies of large populations. For practicality, the authors arbitrarily accept the health-related physical fitness tests of the AAHPERD to be a reasonable, although not perfect instrument to measure youth fitness.[4,68]

CURRENT STATUS OF ADOLESCENT PHYSICAL FITNESS

Interpretations of overall fitness trends can be gleaned from studies of large populations. The Centers for Disease Control (CDC) published in 1989 the progress over the preceding 10 years in achieving the 1990 National Objectives for Physical Fitness and Exercise.[54] Three of eleven objectives pertain directly to children and adolescents.

The first of these three was that by 1990, greater than 90% of children and adolescents would be participating regularly in appropriate physical activities, particularly cardiorespiratory fitness programs, which can be carried into adulthood. The 1984 National Children Youth Fitness Study (NCYFS) found that only 66% of this group was participating at the recommended level of at least three 20-minute sessions of exercise using at least 60% of cardiorespiratory capacity and involving dynamic contractions of large muscle groups.[54,57] The CDC stated it was unlikely that this objective would be met by 1990.

The second objective was to have greater than 60% of children ages 10–17 years participating in daily school physical education classes. In 1974–1975 approximately 33% of this group had daily classes.[3] By 1984, the NCYFS reported 36% had daily classes. However, although more than 90% of children and adolescents in grades 5–8 were enrolled in physical education classes, less than half attended classes daily. The 1984 NCYFS also reported that enrollment in daily physical education classes varied from 81% in grade 9 to 52% in grade 12.[59] The CDC predicted that this objective also would not be achieved by 1990.

The third objective for children and adolescents has two components. The first was to have adequate methods to assess the fitness of children and adolescents ages 10–17 years. This goal has been achieved through tests such as the AAHPERD Health-Related Physical Fitness Test (1980) and the President's Council on Physical Fitness and Sports Test (1985).[1,53,54,60,63] The second component—to have at least 70% of this group participating in such an assessment—has not been achieved.[54] Other studies have presented both better and worse descriptions of overall health of American children and adolescents.[17,26,68]

A nationwide fitness testing of children that was sponsored by the Amateur Athletic Union and the Chrysler Fund also found fitness deficiencies among children and adolescents.[17] Almost 120,000 students aged 6–17 years were sampled from millions of participants between 1980 and 1989. Distance-run time averages decreased by almost 10% over the decade. Weight also increased over the decade without a concomitant increase in height, which is indicative of an increased incidence of obesity. There was some encouraging evidence, however, of increased upper body flexibility in males and both upper and lower body flexibility in females.

THE BENEFITS OF PHYSICAL ACTIVITY

The health benefits of exercise are numerous. When evaluating these benefits critically, three questions must be addressed before the evaluation can be considered complete: (1) what is the relationship between physical activity, physical fitness, and health? (2) is it important to understand the benefits in non-adolescents? and (3) what is the amount of physical activity necessary to induce the desired level of physical fitness and health? One must also realize that physical activity and fitness taken to an extreme can be associated with health risks such as overuse injuries, arthritis, Osgood-Schlatter disease, and even depression.[9,36,43,52,57] Certain physical activities can lead to physical fitness, which in turn improves health in a cause-and-effect fashion. Physical activity may lead to independent but concomitant improvement in physical fitness and health. Other physical activity may improve physical fitness

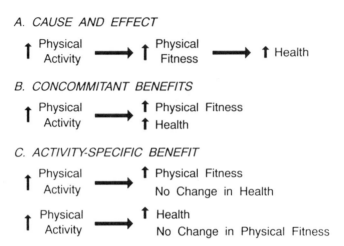

FIGURE 2. Possible relationships between physical activity, physical fitness, and health. (Modified from Haskell WL: Physical activity and health: Need to define the required stimulus. Am J Cardiol 55:4D–9D, 1985.)

without having an effect on an individual's health. The converse may also be true.[28] Figure 2 summarizes these relationships between activity, fitness, and health. This discussion emphasizes studies in which health benefits are associated with some component of physical fitness, whether the relationship is dependent or independent.

When evaluating health benefits associated with physical fitness, one must also examine the evidence in studies of adults and children, understanding that fitness and health habits at each age can affect an individual's future well-being. Dennison et al. documented a significant relationship between adult physical activity levels and performance as children on physical fitness tests, particularly with scores on the 600-yard run.[16] Dennison proposes that it is possible to use youth fitness testing as a predictor of physical activity during adulthood. Paffenbarger has also found that physical activity during college may be protective against risk factors for cardiovascular disease during adulthood, but only if the activity is continued habitually.[48]

The amount of physical activity required to achieve a desired benefit depends on the individual and the particular parameter being assessed. Encouraging studies suggest, however, that even small amounts of regular physical activity may significantly improve an individual's overall health. Blair et al. support this statement after evaluating the level of physical fitness as measured by maximal treadmill exercise test in a prospective study of healthy, Caucasian, middle-class adults.[6] They concluded that even the lowest fitness group (first quintile) had significant protection from all-cause mortality compared with the sedentary population studied. A brisk walk of 30–60 minutes daily may be sufficient to produce this fitness standard. Figure 3 summarizes deaths and mortality rates documented by fitness group.

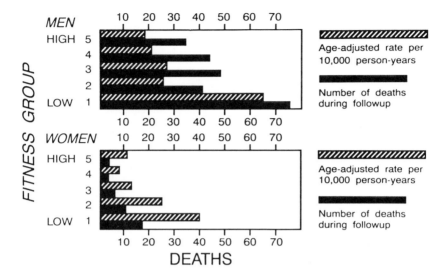

FIGURE 3. Deaths and age-adjusted death rates (all causes) during follow-up of fitness groups in men and women in the Aerobics Center Longitudinal Study. Highest number represents the most physically fit group. (From Blair SN, Kohl HW, Paffenbarger RS, et al: Physical fitness and all-cause mortality: A prospective study of healthy men and women. JAMA 262:2395–2401, 1989, with permission.)

Physical activity is associated with many potential benefits: mental, emotional, musculoskeletal, cardiovascular, and economic. The mental and emotional health benefits of exercise surpass the individual's subjective observation of "feeling good" after exercise.[41,57] A consensus panel of the National Institute of Mental Health concluded that exercise (1) reduces anxiety and tension, (2) is associated with a significant increase in self-esteem, and (3) in moderately depressed individuals, is associated with a decrease in depression.

These findings are supported by McMahon and Gross, who documented a concomitant but independent improvement in both physical fitness and self-esteem among delinquent adolescent males participating in an aerobic exercise program.[37] Aerobic exercise has specifically been shown to improve emotional outlook and mood among adult populations.[40,42]

Perhaps less well documented but equally important is the association of increased mental sharpness in physically fit individuals. Although not a health care professional, one of our greatest fitness advocates, President John F. Kennedy, said: "The relationship between the soundness of the body and the activities of the mind is subtle and complex. Much is not yet understood. But we do know what the Greeks knew: That intelligence and skill can only function at the peak of their capacity when the body is healthy and strong; that hardy spirits and tough minds usually inhabit sound bodies." Despite insufficient evidence to provide scientific proof of a correlation between physical fitness and academic excellence, a belief in that correlation has been promoted and even led to the development of programs such as the Cincinnati Academy of Physical Education—a public high school whose underlying goal is "sound mind, sound body."[44]

Physical and metabolic health benefits are also associated with physical fitness. Moderate physical fitness, particularly that which enhances muscle strength, reduces the risk of musculoskeletal injuries by reducing localized weakness around a joint.[7,8,38,43,56] Consistent physical activity may also increase bone density, reducing the risk of osteoporosis.[57,62,64]

Perhaps the most important and well-documented health benefits are the reduction of risk factors associated with the likelihood of developing cardiovascular diseases.[6,19,47] Obesity has many causes, which include genetics, inactivity, poor nutrition, and pathologic processes.[10] Obesity has been recognized as a risk factor in coronary heart disease, hypertension, non-insulin dependent diabetes mellitus, gout, arthritis, and musculoskeletal problems of the back and lower extremities.[2,22,26,32,39] Although some of these diseases may not predominate in adolescents, habits promoting obesity developed at this age may contribute to their occurrence during adulthood. Exercise promoting physical fitness can provide either prevention or therapeutic reduction of obesity, particularly when augmented by proper nutrition.

Hypertension is the strongest clinical predictor of coronary disease. A sedentary lifestyle with concomitant hypertension significantly escalates the risk of developing coronary disease.[47] Studies indicate that increased levels of physical fitness can reduce the incidence of hypertension in children, adolescents, and adults.[5,14,21,27,31]

There is correlation in most studies assessing lipid profiles consistent with increased risk for cardiovascular disease[34] that the level of physical fitness is inversely proportionate to an undesirable lipid profile.[23,25,51,70–73] Routinely scheduled physical activity can reduce low-density lipoproteins and serum triglycerides, and increase protective high-density lipoproteins. Evidence indicating reduction of serum cholesterol levels is less clear.

The level of activity required to achieve this health benefit is questionable. Several studies have failed to show significant improvement in serum lipid profiles in males age 6.5–40 years participating in exercise training programs.[35,63] There is evidence, however, to suggest that both aerobic exercise and resistance weight-training can produce beneficial changes in serum lipid profiles.[23,25,46,73] Physical fitness augments the cardiovascular benefits of activity alone by increasing cardiac output, enhancing coronary artery development and caliber, and by increasing parasympathetic tone, which may reduce the risk of lethal dysrhythmias.[51]

RECOMMENDATIONS FOR IMPROVING ADOLESCENT PHYSICAL FITNESS

The first step in improving physical fitness in adolescents is physician education and role modeling. Physicians need additional training and continuing medical education regarding the physiologic and psychologic benefits of exercise. Physicians also need to develop and use physical activity assessment, prescription, and follow-up protocols for the developing child and adolescent. Physicians should be role models, allowing actions to set the example for physical fitness and other healthy habits.

Physicians should work within the school system to promote aerobic activities at least three times a week. Examples of aerobic activities include swimming, running, bicycling, fast walking, and soccer. Physicians need to be aware of potential financial strains that may lead to reductions in physical education budgets. They must appeal to their local school boards to continue to support physical education programs that promote lifetime physical activities over team sports for the majority of young people.[13,50] Competitive activities should be dependent upon maturational age rather than chronological age, particularly in the young adolescent.

Physicians also need to be aware of the difference between a child's and adolescent's view of physical activity. The child and pre-adolescent should participate in physical activities that promote fun, physical fitness, basic motor skills, and positive self-image, and a balanced perspective on sports as they relate to school and other activities. These goals should be espoused to directors of school and extracurricular organized athletics.[11] The American Academy of Pediatrics encourages parents, coaches, and officials to emphasize the self-image and mastery of the sport over winning or pleasing others.[11] Ideally a coach's lifestyle and behavior should reflect the health values desired in the child and adolescent.

At home, young children should be encouraged to be physically active after school, having spent most of their day sedentary at a desk. Parents should be encouraged to be role models for their children. Physicians should encourage family physical activities.[66] All of these efforts can produce habits that will be carried through adolescence and beyond.

Children respond to enthusiastic and involved leadership when participating in physical activities.[60] This is also true for adolescents. As the fun derived from participation becomes less important to adolescents, the physician should educate them about the health benefits of exercise. This is particularly true for the adolescent female, who often becomes much less physically active than her male counterpart. Verbal encouragement, particularly of adolescent females, by physicians, parents, and teachers may counteract a decrease in physical activity during adolescence.[15] Emphasis should be placed on indications that small amounts of regular activity may be sufficient to improve overall health. Physical fitness is attainable and does not necessarily require a high level of athleticism.

The physician should assist parents of mentally and physically handicapped children in finding appropriate opportunities for physical activity, equipment, facilities, and selected competition. Often the local Association for Retarded Citizens or United Way can assist with locating this information. On a national level, information about programs for the mentally handicapped can be obtained through the American Alliance of Health, Physical Education,

TABLE 2. Promotion of Physical Activity and Physical Fitness

Objective	Targets	Strategy
To make the parents aware of the benefits of physical activity	Parents	Increase parental involvement (1) Ask about their physical activity patterns. (2) Encourage them to be physically active. (3) Recommend specific activities based on their circumstances and environment.
To teach young children motor skills appropriate for their neuromotor development	Parents and preschool and early school-aged children	Recommend to parents that they should play actively with their children and encourage them to be physically active (e.g., roll a ball to the child, teach them to catch and to throw). Encourage free play or organized activities after school.
To demonstrate to the child and preadolescent the joy of physical activity and sports	Elementary and middle school children	Recommend to the parents and to one's local school free play or organized sports after school. Discourage watching TV after school or doing homework immediately following school. Encourage parents to be role models.
To teach the youth sports and physical activities that can be enjoyed for a lifetime	Junior high and high school	Promote physical activity by emphasizing: (1) The physiologic benefits of being active, e.g., less obese, lower blood pressure, more attractive appearance to opposite sex. (2) It helps to relieve stress and get rid of anger. (3) It makes one feel better and more alert.
To ensure physical education which develops physical fitness and encourages activities with known health benefits	Physical education teachers and school board	Promote physical activity and physical fitness by providing: (1) daily organized physical education with age-appropriate activities (2) emphasis on health-related fitness activities over athleticism for the majority of children and adolescents (3) safe equipment necessary for these activities and imaginative use of available resources
To assess physical fitness as an intergral component of a child's and adolescent's health	Physicians and school system	Physician education of health benefits of exercise and physical fitness assessment. Annual preparticipation sports physicals for adolescents. Organized periodic fitness testing for children and adolescents.

and Recreation, and Dance, and the Special Olympic Program (Joseph P. Kennedy, Jr. Foundation).[12] Table 2 summarizes recommendations for promoting physical activity and physical fitness.

SUMMARY

There would appear to be a consensus that adolescents are less physically fit than they were 10–20 years ago. There also appears to be a consensus that they are less physically fit than they should be. The benefits of health-related physical fitness have been presented and include improved muscular strength and endurance, flexibility, body composition, and cardiorespiratory endurance, as well as mental, emotional, general health and economic benefits. Finally, recommendations have been made as to how the physician can improve the physical activity and physical fitness of adolescents. This effort should include education, verbal encouragement, role-modeling, adequate facilities, fitness assessment, and development of scholastic and community programs that promote health-related physical fitness for all adolescents. Such programs also establish a foundation for adolescents who wish to pursue competitive athletic endeavors. The physician who enhances health-related physical fitness among children and adolescents is helping to establish habits that will potentially improve the health of those individuals into adulthood.

References

1. American Alliance for Health Physical Education, Recreation and Dance: AAHPERD Health-related Fitness Test Manual. Reston, VA, American Alliance for Health, Physical Education, Recreation and Dance, 1980.
2. Aristimuno GG, Foster TA, Voors AW, et al: Influence of persistent obesity in children on cardiovascular risk factors: The Bogalusa Heart Study. Circulation 69:859–904, 1984.
3. Berenson GS, Foster TA, Frank GC, et al: Cardiovascular disease risk factor variables at the preschool age: The Bogalusa heart study. Circulation 57:603–612, 1978.
4. Blair SN, Falls HB, Pate RR: A new physical fitness test. Phys Sportsmed 11(4):87–95, 1983.
5. Blair SN, Goodyear NN, Gibbons LW, et al: Physical fitness and incidence of hypertension in healthy normotensive men and women. JAMA 252:487–490, 1984.
6. Blair SN, Kohl HW, Paffenbarger RS, et al: Physical fitness and all-cause mortality: A prospective study of healthy men and women. JAMA 262:2395–2401, 1989.
7. Brooks WH, Young AB: High school football injuried: Prevention of injury to the central nervous system. South Med J 69:1258–1260, 1976.
8. Burkett LN: Causative factors in hamstring strain. Med Sci Sports Exerc 2:39, 1970.
9. Clain MR, Hershman EB: Overuse injuries in children and adolescents. Phys Sportsmed 17(9):111–123, 1989.
10. Comerci GD, Kilbourne KA, Harrison GG: Eating disorders: Obesity, anorexia nervosa, and bulima. In Hofmann AD, Greydanus DE (eds): Adolescent Medicine, 2nd ed. Norwalk, CT, Appleton and Lange, 1989, pp 441–444.
11. Committee on Sports Medicine and Committee on School Health: Organized athletics for preadolescent children. Pediatrics 84:583–584, 1989.
12. Committee on Sports Medicine, Committee on Children with Disabilities: Exercise for children who are mentally retarded. Pediatrics 80:447–448, 1987.
13. Committee on Sports Medicine, Committee on School Health: Physical fitness and the schools. Pediatrics 80:449–450, 1987.
14. Cooper KH, Goodyear NN, Gibbons LW, et al: Physical fitness levels vs selected coronary risk factors: A cross-sectional study. JAMA 236:166–169, 1976.
15. DeMarco T, Sidney K: Enhancing children's participation in physical activity. J School Health 59:337–340, 1989.
16. Dennison BA, Straus JH, Mellits ED, et al: Childhood physical fitness tests: Predictor of adult physical activity levels? Pediatrics 82:324–330, 1988.
17. Dreyfuss IJ: Youths termed slower, stronger than in 1980. Phys Sportsmed 17(12):20–21, 1989.
18. Dwyer T: Policies and programs in nutrition and physical fitness in Australia. Am J Clin Nutr 49:1030–1034, 1989.
19. Ekelund LG, Haskell WL, Johnson JL, et al: Physical fitness as a predictor of cardiovascular mortality in asymptomatic North American men: The Lipid Research Clinic's mortality follow-up study. N Engl J Med 319:1379–1384, 1988.
20. Fidanza F: Policies and programs in nutrition and physical fitness in Italy. Am J Clin Nutr 49:1035–1038, 1989.
21. Fraser GE, Phillips RL, Harris R: Physical fitness and blood pressure in school children. Circulation 67:405–411, 1983.
22. Fripp RR, Hodgson JL, Kwiterovich PO, et al: Aerobic capacity, obesity, and atherosclerotic risk factors in male adolescents. Pediatrics 75:813–818, 1985.
23. Fripp RR, Hodgson JL: Effect of resistive training on plasma lipid and lipoprotein levels in male adolescents. J Pediatr 111:926–931, 1987.
24. Georgiades G, Klissouras V: Assessment of youth fitness: The European prospective. Am J Clin Nutr 49:1048–1053, 1989.

25. Goldberg L, Elliot DL, Schultz RW, et al: Changes in lipid and lipoprotein levels after weight training. JAMA 252:504–506, 1984.
26. Gortmaker SL, Dietz WH, Sobol AN, et al: Increasing pediatric obesity in the U.S. Am J Dis Child 14:535–540, 1987.
27. Harshfield GA, Dupaul L, Alpert B, et al: Aerobic fitness and diurnal rhythm of blood pressure in adolescents. Read before the 43rd Annual Fall Conference and Scientific Sessions of the American Heart Associations Council for High Blood Pressure Research, Cleveland, September 1989.
28. Haskell WL: Physical activity and health: Need to define the required stimulus. Am J Cardiol 55:4D–9D, 1985.
29. Hergenroeder AC, Schwene RB: Predicting maximal oxygen uptake in adolescents. Am J Dis Child 143:673–678, 1989.
30. Hickenlooper GB, Sowan NA: Comparison of cardiorespiratory fitness tests for children. Pediatr Nurs 14:485–487, 1988.
31. Hofman A, Walter HJ, Connelly DA, et al: Blood pressure and physical fitness in children. Hypertension 9:188–191, 1987.
32. Kannel WB, Brand N, Skinner JJ, et al: The relation of adiposity to blood pressure and development of hypertension: The Framingham Study. Ann Intern Med 167, 1967.
33. Kraus H, Hirschland RP: Minimum muscular fitness tests in school children. Res Q Am Assoc Health Phys Educ 25:178–188, 1954.
34. Lauer RM, Connor WE, Leaverton PE, et al: Coronary heart disease risk factors in school children: The Muscatine Study. J Pediatr 86:697–706, 1975.
35. Linder CW, Durant RH, Mahoney OM: The effect of physical conditioning on serum lipids and lipoproteins in acute male adolescents. Med Sci Sports Exerc 15:232–236, 1983.
36. Lord RH, Kozar B: Pain tolerance in the presence of others: Implications for youth sports. Phys Sportsmed 17(10):71–77, 1989.
37. MacMahon JR, Gross RT: Physical and psychological effect of aerobic exercise in delinquent adolescent males. Am J Dis Child 142:1361–1366, 1988.
38. Maroon JC, Steele PB, Berlin R: Football head and neck injuries: An update. Clin Neurosurg 27:414–429, 1980.
39. Melby CL, Dunn PJ, Hyner GC, et al: Conelates of blood pressure in elementary school children. J School Health 57:375–378, 1987.
40. Morgan WP: Affective beneficence of vigorous physical activity. Med Sci Sports Exerc 17:94–100, 1985.
41. Morgan WP, Goldston SE (eds): Exercise and Mental Health. Washington, DC, Hemisphere Publishing, 1987.
42. Morgan WP, Roberts JA, Brand FR, et al: Psychological effects of chronic physical activity. Med Sci Sport Exerc 2:213–217, 1980.
43. Moskwa CA, Nicholas JA: Musculoskeletal risk factors in the young athlete. Phys Sportsmed 17(11):49–59, 1989.
44. Murphy P: The Cincinnati Academy of Physical Education: Using fitness to aid learning. Phys Sportsmed 15:173–178, 1987.
45. Natapoff JN, Essoka GC: Handicapped and able-bodied children's ideas of health. J School Health 59:436–440, 1989.
46. Nizankowska-Blaz T, Abramowicz T: Effects of intensive physical training on serum lipids and lipoproteins. Acta Pediatr Scand 2:357–359, 1983.
47. Paffenbarger RS, Hyde RT, Wing AL, et al: A natural history of athleticism and cardiovascular health. JAMA 252:491–495, 1984.
48. Paffenbarger RS, Hyde RT, Wing AL, et al: Physical activity, all-cause mortality, and longevity of college alumni. N Engl J Med 314:605–613, 1986.
49. Pate RR: A new definition of youth fitness. Phys Sportsmed 11(14):77–83, 1983.
50. Pate RR, Corbin CB, Simons-Morton BG, et al: Physical education and its role in school health promotion. J School Health 57:445–450, 1987.
51. Powell KE, Thompson PD, Caspersen CJ, Kendrick JS: Physical activity and the incidence of coronary heart disease. Am Rev Public Health 8:235–287, 1987.
52. Pratt M: Strength, flexibility, and maturity in adolescent athletes. Am J Dis Child 143:560–563, 1989.
53. President's Council on Physical Fitness and Sports: 1985 National School Population Fitness Survey. Washington, DC, U.S. Department of Health Service, Office of the Assistant Secretary for Health, 1986.
54. Progress toward achieving the 1990 national objectives for physical fitness and exercise. MMWR 38:449–453, 1989.

55. Prokop L: International Olympic Committee Medical Commission's policies and programs in nutrition and physical fitness. Am J Clin Nutr 49:1065, 1989.
56. Reider B, Marshall JL, Warren RF: Clinical characteristics of patellar disorders in young athletes. Am J Sports Med 9:270–274, 1981.
57. Rippe JM: The health benefits of exercise. Part 1 of 2: Phys Sportsmed 15(10):115–132, 1987. Part 2 of 2: Phys Sportsmed 15(11):121–131, 1987.
58. Ross JG, Dotson CO, Gilbert GG, Katz SJ: What are kids doing in school physical education? J Phys Educ Recreation Dance 56:73–76, 1985.
59. Ross JG, Gilbert GG: The National Children and Youth Fitness Study: A summary of findings. J Phys Educ Recreation Dance 56:45–50, 1985.
60. Rowland TW: Motivational factors in exercise training prognosis for children. Phys Sportsmed 14(2):122–128, 1986.
61. Safrit MJ: Health-related physical fitness levels of American youth. In Effects of Physical Activity on Children. Champaign, IL, Human Kinetics, 1986, pp 153–166.
62. Santora AG: Role of nutrition and exercise in osteoporosis. Am J Med 82(Suppl 1B):73–79, 1987.
63. Savage MP, Petratis MM, Thomson WH, et al: Exercise training effects on serum lipids of prepubescent boys and adult men. Med Sci Sports Exerc 18:197–204, 1986.
64. Smith EL, Reddan W, Smith PE: Physical activity and calcium modalities for bone mineral increase in aged women. Med Sci Sports Exerc 13:60–64, 1981.
65. Strong WB: Physical fitness of children: *Mens sana in corpore sano.* Am J Dis Child 141:488, 1987.
66. Strong WB, Wilmore JH: Unfit kids: An office-based approach to physical fitness. Contemp Pediatr April 1988, pp 1–7.
67. Stroot P: A priority for the World Health Organization: Promoting healthy ways of life. Am J Clin Nutr 49:1063–1064, 1989.
68. Summary of Findings from National Children and Youth Fitness Study II. JOPERD Nov-Dec 1987, pp 49–96.
69. Thairu K: Fitness and nutrition policy in developing nations: Kenya's example. Am J Clin Nutr 49:1054–1056, 1989.
70. Thorland WG, Gilliam TB: Comparison of serum lipids between habitually high and low active pre-adolescent males. Med Sci Sports Exerc 13:316–321, 1981.
71. Tran ZV, Weltman A, Glass GV, Mood DP: The effects of exercise on blood lipids and lipoproteins: A meta-analysis of studies. Med Sci Sports Exerc 15:393–402, 1983.
72. Tran ZV, Weltman A: Differential effect of exercise on serum lipid and lipoprotein levels seen in the changes in body weight: A meta-analysis. JAMA 254:919–924, 1985.
73. Weltman A, Janney C, Rians CB, et al: The effects of hydraulic-resistance strength training on serum lipid levels in prepubertal boys. Am J Dis Child 141:777–780, 1987.
74. Wilmore JH: Design issues and alternatives in assessing physical fitness among apparently healthy adults in a health examination survey of the general population. Assessing Physical Fitness and Physical Activity in Population-Based Surveys. National Center for Health Statistics. Washington, DC, U.S. Dept. of Health and Human Services (DHHS Pub. # 89-1253), 1990.

Suggested Reading

1. Bar-Or O: Pediatric Sports Medicine for the Practitioner. New York, Springer-Verlag, 1983.
2. Hulse E, Strong WB: Preparticipation evaluation for athletics. Pediatr Rev 9:173–182, 1987.
3. Jopling RJ: Health-related fitness as preventive medicine. Pediatr Rev 10:14–148, 1988.
4. Rooks DS, Micheli LJ: Musculoskeletal assessment and training: The young athlete. Clin Sports Med 7:641–677, 1988.
5. Rowland TW: Exercise and Children's Health. Champaign, IL, Human Kinetics Books, 1990.
6. Sallis JF, Nader PR: Family exercise: Designing a program to fit everyone. Phys Sportsmed 18(9):130–136, 1990.
7. Smith NJ (ed): Common Problems in Pediatric Sports Medicine. Chicago, Year Book Medical Publishers, 1989.
8. Squire DL: Female athletes. Pediatr Rev 9:183–190, 1987.

Steroids

MIMI D. JOHNSON, M.D.

Clinical Instructor
Division of Adolescent Medicine
Department of Pediatrics
University of Washington
Seattle, Washington

Private Practice
Pediatric and Young Adult
  Sports Medicine
Washington Sports Medicine
Kirkland, Washington

Team Physician
Department of Athletics
University of Washington
Seattle, Washington

Reprint requests to:
Mimi D. Johnson, M.D.
Division of Adolescent Medicine
Department of Pediatrics
CDMRC, Mail Slot WJ-10
University of Washington
Seattle, WA 98195

Anabolic steroids have been used by athletes for more than three decades in an attempt to improve athletic performance in those sports requiring great strength and size.[35] Within the last decade, use of these drugs has spread, involving not only elite athletes, but recreational athletes as well.[35,59] In the last several years, it has become apparent that adolescents are using anabolic steroids.[8,29,62,65] As primary care physicians, it is important that we understand the physiologic effects and side effects of steroids, how and why they are used by the adolescent, and what role we can play in screening for and preventing steroid use.

ANABOLIC/ANDROGENIC EFFECTS OF TESTOSTERONE

Anabolic-androgenic steroids, as they are properly called, are derivatives of the natural male sex steroid hormone, testosterone. Testosterone and other endogenously produced androgens are responsible for the androgenic and anabolic effects noted during male adolescence and adulthood. The androgenic effects involve the growth of the male reproductive tract and the development of secondary sexual characteristics. In the pubertal male, these effects include the increase in length and diameter of the penis, appearance of pubic, axillary and facial hair, and the development of the prostate and scrotum.[53] The anabolic effects involve non-reproductive tract tissues and include the stimulation of long bone growth with

ADOLESCENT MEDICINE: State of the Art Reviews—Vol. 2, No. 1, February 1991
  Philadelphia, Hanley & Belfus, Inc.

79

subsequent induction of epiphyseal closure at puberty, enlargement of the larynx and thickening of the vocal cords, increased skeletal muscle mass and strength, increase in protein synthesis, and decrease in body fat.[53] The androgenic and anabolic effects of testosterone are not due to different actions of the hormone, but rather to the same action in different tissues.[64] Therefore, these effects cannot be totally separated.[34,64]

EFFECTS OF STEROIDS ON MUSCLE STRENGTH AND SIZE

Over the last several decades, numerous studies have been performed to determine the effects of anabolic steroids in humans. The results have been controversial, with half of the studies showing an increase in strength and size with steroid use, and the other half showing no increase.[2,23] In 1984, several authors reviewed the literature on anabolic steroids, looking at differences in study protocols and how they influenced results.[2,23] It appeared that improvements in muscle strength and size could result from steroid use in persons who (1) had been intensively trained in weight lifting immediately before using anabolic steroids, and who continued intensive weight lifting during the steroid regimen, (2) maintained a high-protein, high-calorie diet, and (3) used the single repetition, maximal weight technique (i.e., bench press) for measurement of improvement (testing with the same exercises used in training).[2,23] There was no evidence that steroids improved aerobic capacity.[2,23]

Anabolic steroids appear to increase muscle strength and size through several mechanisms:

1. Intense weight training can lead to a catabolic state or negative nitrogen balance.[23] Steroids convert a negative nitrogen balance to a positive one by improving the use of ingested protein and increasing nitrogen retention.[34,64] They have the ability to induce protein synthesis in skeletal muscle cells.[46]

2. Anabolic steroids compete for glucocorticosteroid receptor sites, blocking the glucocorticosteroid-induced depression of protein synthesis during stressful events, such as training.[23,34]

3. Athletes using steroids claim to experience a state of euphoria, increased aggressive behavior and diminished fatigue, all of which can have a positive effect on weight training.[57,64] They report the ability to train more frequently and intensively while using the drugs, and to recover more rapidly from workouts.[36,64]

In growing adolescents, exogenous testosterone has been shown to promote an increase in the amount and number of growth hormone secretory bursts.[13] A 5- to 60-fold increase in serum growth hormone concentration has been seen in some power athletes who use steroids, but this has not been a consistent finding.[1] An increase in growth hormone might accentuate the anabolic effect of the steroids.

HOW ANABOLIC STEROIDS ARE USED

Anabolic steroids are available as oral and injectable agents. Testosterone undergoes rapid degradation following both oral and parenteral administration;

therefore, molecular changes have been made to increase the oral bioavailability and the half-life of the drugs.[46,64] Because the androgenic effects of testosterone are unwanted, modifications of the molecule have been made to decrease androgenicity.[46] All steroids do, however, have some androgenic effect.[34,64]

Most of the oral steroids are alkylated at the 17-alpha position, rapidly absorbed, and associated with an increased risk of hepatotoxicity.[34,46,64] The parenteral steroids, which include the testosterone esters and the 19-nortestosterone derivatives, are taken intramuscularly and slowly absorbed. The testosterone esters have the highest androgenic potency (androgenic:anabolic ratio of 1:1), whereas many of the 19-nortestosterone esters and the oral steroids have decreased androgenicity.[21,34] Commonly used anabolic steroids are listed in Table 1.

In an attempt to maximize the anabolic effects of steroids and minimize the side effects, steroid users have developed several patterns by which to take the drugs. When increases in strength and size are no longer being attained through weight lifting (sometimes called a "plateau"), a decision to stop, add, change, or increase the dose of a drug may be made.[15,59] When more than one steroid is being used at a time, it is referred to as "stacking."[15,17] The stack or "array" of drugs often includes at least one oral and one injectable agent. The drugs may be started at low doses, increased gradually, and then tapered[15,17] (sometimes called "pyramiding"). The dosages of an individual drug may be 2–40 times greater than those used for medical purposes.[15,35,43] Most users cycle the steroids by taking them for 4–18 weeks, then undergo a drug-free period that averages 2–3 months.[8,17] An example of a steroid cycle is given in Table 2. Some users take the drugs year-round.[15] There are handbooks available that describe the different steroids and offer suggestions on how to use them.[15,43]

The majority of anabolic steroid users obtain the drugs from black market sources in gyms or health clubs.[15,17] Some of the drugs are manufactured in the United States, but many are smuggled into the country from Europe or

TABLE 1.   Anabolic Steroids Used by Athletes

Oral Anabolic Steroids		Injectable Anabolic Steroids	
Generic name	**Trade name**	**Generic name**	**Trade name**
Oxymetholone*	Anadrol	Nandrolone decanoate[†]	Deca-Durabolin
Oxandrolone*	Anavar	Nandrolone phenpropionate[†]	Durabolin
Methandrostenolone*	Dianabol	Testosterone cypionate[‡]	Depotestosterone
Ethylestrenol*	Maxibolan	Testosterone enanthate[‡]	Delatestryl
Stanozolol*	Winstrol	Testosterone propionate[‡]	Oreton
Fluoxymesterone*	Halotestin	Methenolone enanthate	Primobolan Depot
Norethandrolone	Nilevar	Boldenon undecyclenate	Equipoise
Methenolone acetate	Primobolan	Trenbolone acetate	Finajet
Mesterolone	Proviron	Trenbolone	Parabolan
Testosterone undecanoate		Stanozolol	Winstrol V

From Johnson MD: Pediatr Clin North Am 37:1111–1123, 1990, with permission.
* 17-alpha alkylated steroids.
[†] 19-nortestosterone esters.
[‡] testosterone esters.

TABLE 2.　An Example of a Steroid Cycle

Week	Testosterone cypionate 200 mg/cc injection	Testosterone enanthate 200 mg/cc injection	Oxandrolone 2.5 mg/tab
1	2 cc/wk	2 cc/wk	10 tab/day
2	2 cc/wk	2 cc/wk	9 tab/day
3	1½ cc/wk	1½ cc/wk	8 tab/day
4	1½ cc/wk	1½ cc/wk	7 tab/day
5	1 cc/wk	1 cc/wk	6 tab/day
6	1cc/wk	1 cc/wk	5 tab/day
7	½ cc/wk	½ cc/wk	4 tab/day
8	½ cc/wk	½ cc/wk	3 tab/day
9	¼ cc/wk	¼ cc/wk	2 tab/day
10	¼ cc/wk	¼ cc/wk	1 tab/day

Therapeutic doses of testosterone cypionate and enanthate range from 50–400 mg every 2–4 weeks.[46] The therapeutic dose of oxandrolone is 5–10 mg/day.[46]

Mexico.[15] "Counterfeit" steroids, which may contain unknown ingredients, are being sold on the black market today.[15,43] The safety of these drugs is questionable, since they are often manufactured in underground labs.[15,43] Steroid users may attempt to counter the side effects of steroids by using drugs available on the black market.[15,59] For example, they may use human chorionic gonadotropin (HCG) to stimulate natural testosterone production, anti-estrogenic agents (tamoxifen) to decrease gynecomastia, isotretinoin (Accutane) to treat severe acne, and diuretics to lose excess fluid and increase muscle definition.[15,19,59]

STEROID USE IN ADOLESCENTS

Use of anabolic steroids by adolescents has been documented in the medical literature since 1988. Published reports of self-reported surveys have revealed steroid use in 5–11% of male high school students[8,29,62,65] and 0.5–2.5% of female high school students.[29,62,65] Popular opinion among many sports medicine physicians is that the prevalence of steroid use may range from 10–20% in some high schools, but may vary from one geographical region to the next, and between large schools and small schools.[8,29] One study of adolescent steroid users revealed that use was significantly greater in high school districts with students of predominantly upper socioeconomic status.[65] Another found that 77% of users in their study were Caucasian, 9% Black, 5% Hispanic, and 4% Asian.[8]

Recent studies of adolescent steroid users have found that the majority (65–84%) were involved in sports,[8,29,62] and many reported using steroids to improve athletic performance. The sports with the highest prevalence of steroid use were football, wrestling, and track and field,[8,62] but steroid use was present in all sports.[62] Many elite athletes have used steroids, trying to achieve a winning edge. The values and behaviors demonstrated by these role models may reinforce similar values and behaviors in young athletes. In addition, the pressure to win placed on athletes by parents, coaches, and peers may motivate them to look for an advantage in their sport. Some young athletes perceive that their only chance to compete with steroid-using peers is to use steroids themselves.

Sixteen to thirty-five percent of the adolescent steroid users were not involved in organized sports activities, and several studies found that many were using steroids to improve appearance.[8,29] This is not surprising when one considers the importance society places on appearance, in addition to the adolescent's heightened concern about body image. As male adolescents become increasingly aware of their bodies and compare themselves with others, they may become impatient with the normal rate of muscle development. Their concern about appearance may motivate them to pursue a shortcut toward increased size. The experience of being "big" seems to carry special significance in making some adolescents feel good about themselves. In this way, use of anabolic steroids may become a method of improving self-esteem. This underlying agenda may be prevalent in many adolescent steroid users, even those involved in sports.

Another reason that adolescents may use steroids is peer pressure. Achieving independence from parents and adopting peer codes and lifestyles are normal developmental tasks during adolescence. Peer pressure is known to be a strong force in illicit drug and alcohol use.[52] In the previously mentioned studies, some teens were found to use steroids because friends were using them.[8,29]

Finally, the adolescent's characteristic perception of his or her own invincibility can lead to risk-taking behavior, such as using anabolic steroids, without considering the long-term consequences.

ADVERSE EFFECTS OF STEROID USE

The adverse effects that one might experience from using steroids are dependent on the age, sex, and health of the user, the particular drugs and doses being used, and the frequency of use.[64] Although many of the short-term effects of steroids are known, the long-term effects are not. In the prepubertal and pubertal steroid user, the long-term effects might prove to be more serious than those in the adult because of the developing endocrine/reproductive systems.[45] Many of the short-term effects are reversible once steroids are discontinued; however, they have the potential to lead to deleterious long-term effects if steroids are used chronically. Presently, it appears that there are very few life-threatening effects of steroid use, and these are rarely seen. Potential complications of anabolic steroid use are discussed in the following section (Table 3).

Endocrine Effects

In the male, excessive amounts of exogenous androgens in the serum cause a decrease in the secretion of follicle-stimulating hormone (FSH) and luteinizing hormone (LH),[1,37] resulting in decreased testosterone production, testicular atrophy, and a decrease in spermatogenesis. These changes are reversible; however, abnormal sperm and decreased numbers of sperm have been noted for up to 6 months following discontinuation of steroids.[22,34,37]

TABLE 3. Potential Complications of Anabolic Steroid Use

Endocrine	**Cardiovascular**
Male	Decreased HDL cholesterol
Decreased reproductive hormones	Increased LDL cholesterol
Testicular atrophy	Hypertension
Oligospermia/azospermia	Clotting abnormalities
Gynecomastia	
Prostatic hypertrophy	**Hepatic**
Prostatic carcinoma*	Elevated liver function test values
Priapism	Cholestatic jaundice
Female	Tumor formation*
Masculinization	Peliosis hepatitis*
Hirsutism*	
Deepening of voice*	**Psychological**
Clitoral hypertrophy*	Aggressive behavior
Menstrual irregularities	Mood swings
Adolescent	Increased or decreased libido
Accelerated maturation*	Dependency
Altered glucose tolerance	Acute psychosis
	Manic and/or depressive episodes
Renal	
Elevated BUN, creatinine	**Subjective Effects**[†]
Wilms' tumor*	Edema
	Muscle spasm
Musculoskeletal	Nervous tension
Adolescent:	Increased urine output
Premature epiphyseal closure*	Headache
Increased risk of musculotendinous injury	Dizziness
	Nausea
Dermatologic	Euphoria
Acne	Skin rash
Alopecia*	Urethritis
Temporal hair recession*	Scrotal pain
	Irritability

Table adapted from Johnson MD: Pediatr Clin North Am 37:1111–1123, 1990.
* Considered irreversible.
[†] Adapted from Haupt HA, Rovere GD: Anabolic steroids: A review of the literature. Am J Sports Med 12:477, 1984.

Gynecomastia resulting from the aromatization of some androgens (i.e., the testosterone esters) to estradiol may be caused by excessive use of anabolic steroids.[19,34] Gynecomastia may be pronounced in persons with liver disease, probably because of decreased hepatic clearance of the parent steroid or estrogenic metabolites.[19,32] The breast tissue becomes less prominent once steroids are stopped; however, it may not disappear entirely.[19]

Prostatic hypertrophy,[53] priapism[34,53] and, rarely, carcinoma of the prostate[51] can be associated with steroid use.

In prepubertal or pubertal males, steroid use accelerates maturation, with the development of secondary sexual characteristics and changes in physique.[34,53,64]

In females, excess androgens result in irreversible signs of masculinization, including hirsutism, deepening of the voice, and clitoral hypertrophy.[34,64] Menstrual irregularities or amenorrhea may also occur during steroid use.[21,34]

Increased insulin resistance with altered glucose tolerance has been reported in athletes using anabolic steroids.[10] A decrease in serum concentrations of thyroxine (T4), triiodothyronine (T3), free thyroxine (FT4), and thyroid-stimulating hormone (TSH) may also be seen,[1,34] and is believed to be due to a decrease in thyroid-binding globulin (TBG), because triiodothyronine uptake (T3U) is increased.[1,34] Thyroid hormone is apparently available at the cellular level, and clinical thyroid function is normal.[1]

Cardiovascular Effects

Anabolic steroid use results in a decrease in the HDL-cholesterol level, and may result in an increase in the LDL-cholesterol level.[11,27] Cholesterol levels return to baseline once steroid use is discontinued.[11] Hypertension, which is reversible, is also associated with the use of steroids.[40] There have been two reported cases of myocardial infarction in young steroid users,[5,39] but long-term atherogenic effects have not been studied. Increased left ventricular wall thickness, with impaired diastolic function, has been reported in steroid-using bodybuilders.[63]

Anabolic steroids may increase red blood cell mass, therefore elevating the hemoglobin and hematocrit in users.[46,57] A decrease in clotting factors, an increase in fibrinolytic activity, and enhanced platelet aggregation have been associated with the use of specific steroids.[16,18,34] There have been several reports of cerebrovascular accidents in young steroid users.[18,44]

Edema, due to the retention of fluid and sodium, is common during steroid use.[34,46]

Hepatic Effects

Hepatotoxicity is most commonly associated with the 17-alpha-alkylated steroids.[34,46] Steroid use may result in an elevation in liver function test values.[23,64] The muscle damage incurred by weight lifting alone can cause an elevation in serum aspartate aminotransferase (AST, formerly SGOT) and alanine aminotransferase (ALT, formerly SGPT).[23,57] Therefore, liver isoenzymes of lactate dehydrogenase, alkaline phosphatase, and conjugated bilirubin should be used to follow liver status in the steroid user.[23] These values typically reverse following cessation of the drugs.[23,35]

Cholestatic jaundice may occur with steroid use and typically resolves within several months of discontinuing the drugs.[34,35] Rarely, liver tumors, both benign and malignant, have been associated with taking anabolic steroids.[28,58] Several athletes with histories of extensive steroid use have died of hepatocellular carcinoma,[20,47] and one from hepatic rupture.[14] There is an increased, but rare, risk of developing peliosis hepatitis with steroid use.[3]

Renal Effects

An increase in serum creatinine may be seen in steroid-free weightlifters because of the increase in skeletal muscle mass.[57] However, steroid use itself may cause an increase in BUN, creatinine, and uric acid.[21,36] These values typically return to normal once the drugs are discontinued. There is evidence suggesting that steroids may be weak carcinogens, and capable of initiating tumor growth or promoting tumor growth in the presence of other carcinogens.[35] Wilms' tumor, uncommon in adults, has been reported in several adult athletes using steroids.[50,57]

Musculoskeletal Effects

Children with poorly controlled diseases of androgen excess become relatively short adults.[45,53] This can result from accelerated advancement of bone age relative to acceleration in height velocity and from early onset of puberty with premature closure of the epiphyses.[45] The prepubertal or pubertal adolescent using excessive amounts of steroids for a prolonged period of time may experience premature epiphyseal closure with resulting stunted growth.[45,46,53]

Anabolic steroid use may result in an increased risk of musculotendinous injuries.[25,33,42] There have been several reported cases of atypical spontaneous tendon ruptures in bodybuilders using steroids.[25,33] An elevation of creatine phosphokinase, above that expected in bodybuilders, has been noted in steroid users.[38]

Dermatologic Effects

Acne is a common side effect of steroids owing to the androgenic stimulation of the sebaceous glands.[31,34] Acne lesions, commonly on the chest and back, do not always respond to routine treatment. In addition, the use of tetracycline or isotretinoin could have adverse consequences in a steroid user who has decreased hepatic clearance.

Temporal hair recession and alopecia may be seen in men and women using steroids for a prolonged period of time.[26]

Infections and Immune Response

Because steroid users may share needles, the risk of transmitting infections, such as hepatitis B and acquired immune deficiency syndrome (AIDS), is present. Two cases of AIDS have been reported in steroid users who were sharing needles with HIV-infected cohorts.[54,56] Infections may also be caused by dirty injection apparatus or impure drugs. A decrease in immunoglobulins, particularly IgA, has been reported in steroid-using bodybuilders.[9]

Psychological Effects

Anabolic steroid use has been associated with increased aggressive behavior, mood swings, and irritability.[23,48,57] One study of weightlifters with a history of steroid use revealed that 90% reported episodes of overaggressiveness and violent behavior they believed were induced by steroids ("roid rage").[59] There have been several legal cases involving previously nonviolent persons who committed violent acts, and even murder, while using steroids.[49] Overt psychotic symptoms and manic or depressive episodes have been reported during steroid use in persons who were symptom-free prior to initiating steroids.[48] Steroid use has been associated with suicide.[6] Other psychological changes that may result from steroid use include increased self-esteem and changes in libido.[57] A neurochemical basis for some of these psychoactive effects has been suggested by the discovery of neuronal androgen receptors in the brain.[55]

There is evidence that anabolic steroid use can result in dependency.[7,59] Steroid users report that they have difficulty discontinuing the drugs and have a strong desire to reinitiate use once they have discontinued.[7,24] Following cessation of steroids, users may experience fatigue, depression, anorexia, dissatisfaction with body image, and decreased self-esteem.[7,24] Some steroid users fulfill the Diagnostic and Statistical Manual, 3rd edition, revised criteria for psychoactive substance dependence.[7] Physical withdrawal symptoms, such as those seen in opiate withdrawal, have occurred upon cessation of extremely high doses of steroids.[60]

The psychological effects of steroids on adolescents may be the most devastating of all the side effects. The developing nervous system of the teen could be especially vulnerable to these effects. The adolescent may lack the maturity to handle drug-induced mood changes. In addition, the development of the appropriate social skills and controls necessary to deal with pubertal changes may be made more difficult when the changes are occurring more rapidly than usual. Signs of steroid habituation have been noted in adolescents.[66] One study found that, despite knowledge of possible dire health consequences, one quarter of adolescent steroid users were unwilling to discontinue steroid use, even if everyone else did.[8,66] These "heavy users" were characterized by initiation of steroid use at a younger age than most and by increased length and number of cycles.[66]

SCREENING THE ADOLESCENT FOR STEROID USE

At the present time, steroid use is considered unethical and illegal by many sports organizations. For this reason, it is unusual for an adolescent to approach a physician about information on steroids or for monitoring during steroid use. The adolescent steroid user may come to the physician's attention because of side effects caused by steroids (acne, hypertension, etc.), but he or she often will not offer the information that steroids are being used. The steroid user may also come to the physician because parents have discovered drug use and want a physical checkup for the adolescent and guidance on how to handle the problem. Most often, the physician will come into contact with the steroid user during the sports preparticipation examination; therefore, the index of suspicion should be high at this time. If steroid use in a teenager is suspected or confirmed, an appropriate history, physical examination, and laboratory evaluation can be performed to detect evidence of complications (Table 4).

Taking the History

It is important to be knowledgeable, yet nonjudgmental, when inquiring about steroid use. One might ask the patient if he or she is involved in weight

TABLE 4.   Approach to Patient with Suspected or Confirmed Steroid Use

History	Physical Examination	Laboratory Studies
When steroids used	Full exam including wt, ht, BP	Urinalysis
Names of steroids used	Tanner stage	Liver function tests
Doses of steroids used	Testicular volume	Complete blood count
Duration of use	Liver size and tenderness	Glucose
Weight gain	Gynecomastia	HDL/LDL cholesterol
Physical maturation	Prostate examination	BUN/creatinine
Side effects	Signs of masculinization	Bone age

From Johnson MD: Pediatr Clin North Am 37:1111–1123, 1990, with permission.[30]

training. Inquire as to whether the patient knows anyone who uses steroids, then ask if he or she has ever thought about using them or has tried them. If so, the last time steroids were used, what was used, how much was used, and the duration of use should be ascertained. Information about weight gain and physical maturation should be obtained. Is the patient maturing at an earlier age than expected by family history? Have the patient or parents noted puffy face or extremities, severe acne, yellow coloring of the eyes or skin, urinary dribbling, mood changes, increased aggressiveness, or other symptoms of steroid complications?

Physical Examination

The complete physical examination should include blood pressure, height, weight, and pubertal staging. Acne and gynecomastia, both possible signs of steroid use, can be normal occurrences during puberty. Testicular volume should be assessed and liver size and tenderness noted. A prostate examination could reveal evidence of hypertrophy. Because steroids have been associated with prostate cancer, irregularity of the prostate warrants further evaluation. Signs of masculinization should be noted in females.

Laboratory Studies

Laboratory studies to screen for possible steroid complications include urinalysis, liver function tests including alkaline phosphatase, liver isoenzymes of LDH, or conjugated bilirubin, complete blood count, serum glucose, HDL and LDL cholesterol levels, blood urea nitrogen, and creatinine. Indication of liver dysfunction in a long-term user might be reason to consider a liver sonogram. Blood urea nitrogen, uric acid, and creatinine may be elevated due to steroid use; an elevated creatinine should be followed by a 24-hour creatinine clearance. A radiographic bone age can aid in evaluating epiphyseal maturation in the peripubertal user.

Drug Testing

Drug testing for anabolic steroids is expensive, and few laboratories have the equipment necessary to perform accurate testing. Testing at the primary care level is often impractical and usually unnecessary. Testing for the purpose of proving use will alienate the adolescent and make anticipatory guidance difficult. If testing must be performed, it should be done with a reputable lab.

Screening the urine for anabolic steroids is accomplished by using radioimmunoassay.[22] If screening is positive, the drug or its metabolites are identified by performing gas chromatography with mass spectometry.[22] The testosterone to epitestosterone ratio is used to screen for exogenous testosterone use. This ratio is normally 1:1, and considered positive for steroid use at 6:1.[22] The oral steroids are usually detectable for several weeks after discontinuation, and parenteral agents for up to 3 months, although detectability at 6 months has been reported.[22]

Monitoring the Steroid User

It is unusual for the young adolescent to ask to be monitored during steroid use. College students and adults will more typically ask for this service. The physician must make a personal decision about monitoring steroid use. Some physicians feel that by monitoring use, one is supporting it. Others feel that monitoring steroid use is no different from monitoring the alcoholic for cirrhosis. It is claimed that the patient will use steroids anyway, and that testing periodically for serious effects is preferred to no testing at all. If one chooses to monitor the adolescent using steroids, it is important that neither physician nor patient develops a false sense of security, for the long-term side effects of steroid use cannot be predicted.

If the option of monitoring steroid use is chosen, it has been suggested that the steroid user be evaluated every 6 months or before each new cycle is begun.[36] At that time, a physical examination and repeat laboratory studies would be performed, and the results of all findings discussed with the user. Obviously, the main task of the physician would be to dissuade the user from further use.

INTERVENTION

Physicians

Physicians can provide anticipatory guidance to the adolescent at risk for steroid use. The information obtained through history-taking during the office visit can be used to provide educational feedback. If the adolescent does not use steroids, the physician can answer any questions he or she might have about their use. With the adolescent who admits to steroid use, the physician might inquire as to why he or she chose to use them. This is a nonjudgmental way to assess fund of knowledge, and will allow the physician to correct any false information about physiologic effects or complications. It is not helpful to attempt to talk a teenager out of using steroids by saying they do not work; this will only result in alienation and decreased physician credibility. Instead, the teen can be encouraged to think of alternatives to steroid use, not only in the areas of appropriate nutrition and weight training, but also in areas that might improve self-esteem.

The physician can educate parents about anabolic steroid use, and encourage them to support fair play in their teenagers' sports activities. The physician can also help to educate coaches about the effects of anabolic steroids, and teach them how to recognize steroid use in their teenage athletes.

Schools

A recent study on the effectiveness of educational intervention in steroid use revealed that high school athletes showed a higher potential for steroid use following education in a lecture/handout format than before education was given.[4] Informational approaches to education on illicit drugs and alcohol have failed to result in a decrease in their use.[12] Programs that use these approaches assume that teenagers use drugs and alcohol because they are not aware of the side effects and social consequences of such use; they do not address the reasons that teenagers use the drugs.[12] More recently, programs have incorporated activities designed to increase self-esteem, promote responsible decision-making and problem-solving, and decrease social anxiety.[12] These programs might be effective in addressing some of the issues surrounding anabolic steroid use.

Society

Anabolic steroids are used by elite athletes trying to gain the winning edge. As long as high school athletes perceive an increasing pressure to win (i.e., with growing national media coverage of high school athletic events), the impetus to follow the lead of their role models will continue. When random drug testing and genuine penalties for steroid use are implemented in college, professional, and Olympic athletics, these role models may reconsider their use of the drugs. Until that time, there will be little deterrence to steroid use in the adolescent age group.

Society places a tremendous importance on several values that influence anabolic steroid use in today's adolescents—those of winning and appearance. If, through the concerted efforts of the members of society, these values can be deemphasized, anabolic steroid use in our adolescents will likely decrease.

References

1. Alen M, Rahkila P, Reinila M, et al: Androgenic-anabolic steroid effects on serum thyroid, pituitary and steroid hormones in athletes. Am J Sports Med 15:357–361, 1987.
2. American College of Sports Medicine: Position stand on the use of anabolic-androgenic steroids in sports. Sports Med Bull 19:13–18, 1984.
3. Bagheri SA, Boyer JL: Peliosis hepatitis associated with androgenic-anabolic steroid therapy—a severe form of hepatic injury. Ann Intern Med 81:610–618, 1974.
4. Bents R, Trevisan L, Bosworth E, et al: The effect of teachng interventions on knowledge and attitudes of anabolic steroids among high school athletes. Med Sci Sports Exerc 21:S26, 1989.
5. Bowman S: Anabolic steroids and infarction. Br Med J 300:750, 1990.
6. Brower KJ, Blow FC, Eliopulos GA, et al: Anabolic androgenic steroids and suicide. Am J Psychiatry 146:1075, 1989.
7. Brower KJ, Eliopulos GA, Blow FC, et al: Evidence for physical and psychological dependence on anabolic androgenic steroids in eight weight lifters. Am J Psychiatry 147:510–512, 1990.
8. Buckley WE, Yesalis CE, Friedl KE: Estimated prevalence of anabolic steroid use among male high school seniors. JAMA 260:3441–3445, 1988.

9. Calabrese LH, Kleiner SM, Barna BP, et al: The effects of anabolic steroids and strength training on the human immune response. Med Sci Sports Exerc 21:386–392, 1989.
10. Cohen JC, Hickman R: Insulin resistance and diminished glucose tolerance in powerlifters ingesting anabolic steroids. J Clin Endocrinol Metab 64:960–963, 1987.
11. Cohen JC, Noakes TD, Benade AJ: Hypercholesterolemia in male power lifters using anabolic-androgenic steroids. Phys Sportsmed 16:49–56, 1988.
12. Comerci GD, Macdonald DI: Prevention of substance abuse in children and adolescents. In Strasburger VC, Greydanus DE (eds): The At-Risk Adolescent. Philadelphia, Hanley & Belfus, 1990.
13. Cowart VS: If youngsters overdose with anabolic steroids, what's the cost anatomically and otherwise? JAMA 261:1856–1857, 1989.
14. Creagh TM, Rubin A, Evans DJ: Hepatic tumours induced by anabolic steroids in an athlete. J Clin Pathol 41:441–443, 1988.
15. Duchaine D: Underground Steroid Handbook II. Venice, CA, HLR Technical Books, 1989.
15a. Dyment PG: Steroids: Breakfast of champions. Pediatr Rev 12:103–105, 1990.
16. Ferenchick GS: Are androgenic steroids thrombogenic? N Engl J Med 322:476, 1990.
17. Frankle MA, Cicero GJ, Payne J: Use of androgenic anabolic steroids by athletes. JAMA 252:482, 1984.
18. Frankle MA, Eichberg R, Zachariah SB: Anabolic androgenic steroids and a stroke in an athlete: Case report. Arch Phys Med Rehabil 69:632–633, 1988.
19. Friedl KE, Yesalis CE: Self-treatment of gynecomastia in bodybuilders who use anabolic steroids. Phys Sportsmed 17:67–79, 1989.
20. Goldman B: Liver carcinoma in an athlete taking anabolic steroids. J Am Osteopath Assoc 5:25, 1985.
21. Gribbin HR, Matts SG: Mode of action and use of anabolic steroids. Br J Clin Pract 30:3–9, 1976.
22. Hatton CK, Catlin DH: Detection of androgenic anabolic steroids in urine. Clin Lab Med 7:655–668, 1987.
23. Haupt HA, Rovere GD: Anabolic steroids: A review of the literature. Am J Sports Med 12:469–484, 1984.
24. Hays LR, Littleton S, Stillner V: Anabolic steroid dependence. Am J Psychiatry 147:122, 1990.
25. Hill JA, Suker JR, Sachs K, et al: The athletic polydrug abuse phenomenon: A case report. Am J Sports Med 11:269–271, 1983.
26. Houssay AB: Effects of anabolic-androgenic steroids on the skin including hair and sebaceous glands. In Kochakian CD (ed): Anabolic-Androgenic Steroids. New York, Springer-Verlag, 1976.
27. Hurley BF, Seals DR, Hagberg JM, et al: High-density-lipoprotein cholesterol in bodybuilders vs. powerlifters—negative effects of androgen use. JAMA 252:507–513, 1984.
28. Johnson FL, Lerner KG, Siegel M, et al: Association of androgenic-anabolic steroid therapy with development of hepatocellular carcinoma. Lancet 2:1273–1276, 1972.
29. Johnson MD, Jay MS, Shoup B, et al: Anabolic steroid use by male adolescents. Pediatrics 83:921–924, 1989.
30. Johnson MD: Anabolic steroid use in adolescent athletes. Pediatr Clin North Am 37:1111–1123, 1990.
31. Kiraly CL, Alen M, Rahkila R, et al: Effect of androgenic and anabolic steroids on the sebaceous gland in power athletes. Acta Derm Venereol (Stockh) 67:36–40, 1987.
32. Kley HK, Strohmeyer G, Kruskemper HL: Effect of testosterone application on hormone concentrations of androgens and estrogens in male patients with cirrhosis of the liver. Gastroenterology 76:235, 1979.
33. Kramhoft M, Solgaard S: Spontaneous rupture of the extensor pollicis longus tendon after anabolic steroids. J Hand Surg 11:87, 1986.
34. Kruskemper HL: Anabolic Steroids. New York, Academic Press, 1968.
35. Lamb DR: Anabolic steroids in athletics: How well do they work and how dangerous are they? Am J Sports Med 12:31–38, 1984.
36. Lombardo JA, Longcope C, Voy RO (JP Crawshaw, ed): Recognizing anabolic steroid abuse. Patient Care 19:28–47, 1985.
37. Mauss J, Borsch G, Bormacher K, et al: Effect of long-term testosterone oenanthate administration on male reproductive function: Clinical evaluation, serum FSH, LH, testosterone, and seminal fluid analyses in normal men. Acta Endocrinol 78:373–384, 1975.
38. Mckillop G, Ballantyne FC, Borland W, et al: Acute metabolic effects of exercise in bodybuilders using anabolic steroids. Br J Sports Med 23:186–187, 1989.
39. McNutt RA, Ferenchick GS, Kirlin PC, et al: Acute myocardial infarction in a 22-year-old world class weight lifter using anabolic steroids. Am J Cardiol 62:164, 1988.

40. Messerli FH, Frohlich ED: High blood pressure—a side effect of drugs, poisons, and food. Arch Intern Med 139:682–687, 1979.

42. Michna H, Stang-Voss C: The predisposition to tendon rupture after doping with anabolic steroids. Int J Sports Med 4:59, 1983.

43. Mile High Publishing (author unknown): Anabolic Reference Guide, 4th ed. Golden, CO, 1989.

44. Mochizuki RM, Richter KJ: Cardiomyopathy and cerebrovascular accident associated with anabolic-androgenic steroid use. Phys Sportsmed 16:109–114, 1988.

45. Moore WV: Anabolic steroid use in adolescence. JAMA 260:3484–3486, 1988.

46. Murad F, Haynes RC: Androgens. In Gilman AG, Goodman LS, Rall TW, et al (eds): The Pharmacological Basis of Therapeutics, 7th ed. New York, Macmillan, 1985.

47. Overly WL, Dankoff JA, Wang BK, et al: Androgens and hepatocellular carcinoma in an athlete. Ann Intern Med 100:158–159, 1984.

48. Pope HG, Katz DL: Affective and psychotic symptoms associated with anabolic steroid use. Am J Psychiatry 145:487–490, 1988.

49. Pope HG, Katz DL: Homicide and near-homicide by anabolic steroid users. J Clin Psychiatry 51:28–31, 1990.

50. Prat J, Gray GF, Stolley PD, et al: Wilms' tumor in an adult associated with androgen abuse. JAMA 237:2322–2323, 1977.

51. Roberts JT, Essenhigh DM: Adenocarcinoma of prostate in 40-year-old body-builder. Lancet 2:742, 1986.

52. Robinson JT, Killen JD, Taylor B, et al: Perspective on adolescent substance use: A defined population study. JAMA 258:2072–2076, 1987.

53. Rogol AD: Drugs to enhance athletic performance in the adolescent. Semin Adolesc 1:317–324, 1985.

54. Scott MJ, Scott MJ Jr: HIV infection associated with injections of anabolic steroids. JAMA 262:207–208, 1989.

55. Sheridan PJ: Androgen receptors in the brain: What are we measuring? Endocrinol Rev 4:171–178, 1983.

56. Sklarek HM, Mantovani RP, Erens E, et al: AIDS in a bodybuilder using anabolic steroids. N Engl J Med 311:1701, 1984.

57. Strauss RH, Wright JE, Finerman GA, et al: Side effects of anabolic steroids in weight-trained men. Phys Sportsmed 11:87–96, 1983.

58. Sweeney EC, Evans DJ: Hepatic lesions in patients treated with synthetic anabolic steroids. J Clin Pathol 29:626–633, 1976.

59. Taylor WN: Synthetic anabolic-androgenic steroids: A plea for controlled substance status. Phys Sportsmed 15:140–150, 1987.

60. Tennant F, Black DL, Voy RO: Anabolic steroid dependence with opioid-type features. N Engl J Med 319:578, 1988.

62. Terney R, Mclain LG: The use of anabolic steroids in high school students. Am J Dis Child 144:99–103, 1990.

63. Urhausen A, Holpes R, Kindermann W: One- and two-dimensional echocardiography in bodybuilders using anabolic steroids. Eur J Appl Physiol 58:633–640, 1989.

64. Wilson JD, Griffin JE: The use and misuse of androgens. Metabolism 29:1278–1295, 1980.

65. Windsor R, Dumitru D: Prevalence of anabolic steroid use by male and female adolescents. Med Sci Sports Exerc 21:494–497, 1989.

66. Yesalis CE, Streit AL, Vicary JR, et al: Anabolic steroid use: Indications of habituation among adolescents. J Drug Educ 19:103–116, 1989.

Death on the Playing Field

RICHARD C. McFAUL, M.D., F.A.A.P., F.A.C.C.

Director, Pediatric and Adolescent
  Cardiology
Maine Medical Center
Portland, Maine

Reprint requests to:
Richard C. McFaul, M.D.
Maine Medical Center
22 Bramhall St.
Portland, ME 04102

Sudden death during activity in children and adolescents is a rare event, considering the larger number of hours spent by this population in recreational and organized physical activities. It is estimated that an average community of 100,000 people encounters one unexpected death yearly in their child and adolescent population.[8] The shock that follow such an occurrence frequently results in the family and physician's questioning whether the death could have been avoided. Invariably, misconceptions surface. The most common are (1) that the physical fitness of a child correlates with the condition of the heart, and (2) that cardiac disorders responsible for sudden death give ample symptoms or clues to forecast these tragedies.

Sudden death from a cardiac disorder follows loss of consciousness usually from an abrupt alteration in cardiac rhythm. Changes in heart rate that are excessively slow, extremely rapid, or disorganized can profoundly alter the forward flow of blood and interrupt normal physiological processes. Without spontaneous resumption of normal activity or emergency intervention, these rhythm disturbances threaten life within minutes.

This article discusses the more common disorders that cause sudden death during activity (Table 1), and addresses what, if any, practical measures can be taken to prevent it.

PROPERTIES OF THE HEART

Cardiac function is a composite of both electrical and mechanical events. Its durability

ADOLESCENT MEDICINE: State of the Art Reviews—Vol. 2, No. 1, February 1991
Philadelphia, Hanley & Belfus, Inc.

93

TABLE 1.   Causes of Sudden Death During Exercise

Cardiomyopathies
    Dilated
    Hypertrophic
    Dysplastic
Coronary Artery Anomalies
    Anomalous coronary artery origin
    Post-Kawasaki's illness
Valve Defects
    Mitral valve prolapse
    Aortic stenosis
    Ebstein's malformation
    Aortic aneurysm in Marfan syndrome
Primary Rhythm Disorders
    QT prolongation
    WPW syndrome
    Complete heart block
Pulmonary Hypertension

is evident given that 2½ billion impulses and 41 million gallons of blood pass through the heart within an average life span of 70 years. These processes result from complex interactions of membranes and intercellular channels, active and inactive transport of electrolytes, and the coupling of intracellular proteins. Within this myriad of interrelationships, problems arise.

MYOCARDIAL DISORDERS

The majority of young patients who die during activity have abnormalities within the heart muscle brought about by inflammation, fibrosis, or hypertrophy of normal tissue.[2] All of these changes may occur silently or be overshadowed by other symptoms. For instance, in acute myocarditis, cardiac involvement may be overshadowed by fever, myalgia, or other influenza-like symptoms. In chronic inflammatory conditions, the slow damage within the heart muscle might be masked by the heart's compensatory processes, thereby delaying the onset of symptoms or diagnosis. In young children, only a small segment of the myocardium may be defective and become the source of a life-threatening rhythm disturbance. Similarly, the heart can become markedly hypertrophied without creating symptoms or cardiac murmurs.

Dilated Cardiomyopathy

The heart can dilate in the presence of inflammation or when normal myocardium becomes substantially replaced by other tissue. At autopsy, the heart will appear pale and often there is a decrease in wall thickness (Fig. 1). Cell inflammation may be found but in fewer cases than previously estimated; in other words, the histologic evidence often does not support the diagnosis of myocarditis when cardiac enlargement is found during postmortem examination.[17] In such cases, the term "idiopathic dilated cardiomyopathy" has been applied.

These young patients may be diagnosed clinically if heart function deteriorates to the extent that exercise fatigue or signs of congestive failure

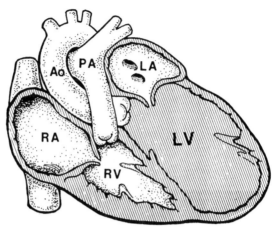

FIGURE 1. Dilated left ventricular cardiomyopathy (RA = right atrium, LA = left atrium, RV = right ventricle, LV = left ventricle, AO = aorta, PA = pulmonary artery).

develop. Unfortunately, changes in cardiac rhythm precipitated by these weakened hearts can cause death before this damage becomes recognized. Also, these changes are silent on physical examination unless mitral valve insufficiency develops as a consequence of left ventricular enlargement.

Hypertrophic Cardiomyopathy

A feature common in athletes who die unexpectedly is abnormal cardiac hypertrophy.[11] As a primary disorder, this muscle enlargement usually involves the ventricular septum more than other regions of the heart (Fig. 2). The severity may vary with respect to the degree of hypertrophy and obstruction to flow from the left ventricle. Histology shows large, disorganized myocytes primarily, but not exclusively, within the thickened septum. The etiology of this strongly familial disorder is unknown. The term

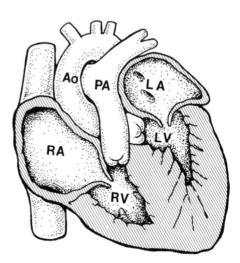

FIGURE 2. Hypertrophic cardiomyopathy (RA = right atrium, LA = left atrium, RV = right ventricle, LV = left ventricle, AO = aorta, PA = pulmonary artery).

idiopathic hypertrophic subaortic stenosis (IHSS) has been used to describe this disorder.

Some young athletes are asymptomatic even with significant obstruction, whereas others may have exertional chest pain, palpitations, or dizziness. The exact cause of these symptoms is not entirely clear but probably relates to increasing obstruction and coronary insufficiency created by exercise.

The physician examining an athlete with a blowing systolic murmur at the left sternal border or apex must consider hypertrophic cardiomyopathy as the source for this sound, especially if a Valsalva maneuver or a change to the sitting position intensifies the murmur.

Myocardial Dysplasia

The heart may be structurally normal except for small areas that have been altered by previous infection or developmental abnormalities. These scarred or dysplastic regions, more commonly found within the right ventricle (Fig. 3), are sources of ventricular ectopy and, in extreme cases, tachycardia or fibrillation.[19] Histologic inspection often shows fibrous or lipomatous infiltrates within spare myocardial tissue rather than cellular changes of a recent infection.

These dysplastic areas are usually silent on physical examination so premortem detection can be made only if the patient seeks medical advice for

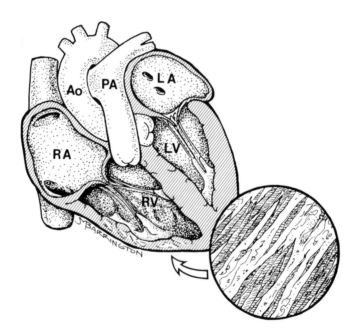

FIGURE 3. Diminished myocytes and fibrous tissue infiltration within dysplastic right ventricular segment (RA = right atrium, LA = left atrium, RV = right ventricle, LV = left ventricle, AO = aorta, PA = pulmonary artery).

palpitations, dizziness, or syncope, and echocardiographic scans show wall motion abnormalities within either the right or left ventricle.

HEART VALVE DISORDERS

Serious rhythm changes may occur in children or adolescents with defects that involve the mitral, aortic, or tricuspid valve.

Mitral Valve Prolapse

Two percent of adolescents have mitral valve prolapse that can be detected by physical examination. The valve becomes enlarged and redundant from collagen disruption and mucopolysaccharide deposition within the valve leaflets or the supporting chordae tendineae, and prolapses during systole into the left atrium (Fig. 4). Although these changes rarely produce significant mitral valve impairment at a young age, studies show that the incidence of cardiac dysrhythmias, primarily of ventricular origin, is much higher compared with normal patients.[7] The available natural history studies, however, indicate that sudden death during activity is rare.[14] Nevertheless, physicians examining these young patients for athletic participation or evaluating symptoms of palpitations and dizziness must be mindful of the arrhythmogenic nature of this valve disorder.

The systolic ejection sounds heard on cardiac auscultation result from sudden expansion of these redundant areas or elongated chordae. When the valve is incompetent, a blowing apical murmur of mitral insufficiency can be detected as well. Variation in these physical findings with body position relates to the changes in left ventricular size in relationship to this redundant valve. Classically, these ejection clicks or murmurs are best heard in the upright position. The cause of chest pain and light headedness commonly noted remains unknown. Orthostatic dizziness may occur from vasovagal factors, although cardiac rhythm disorders must be suspected if syncope occurs.

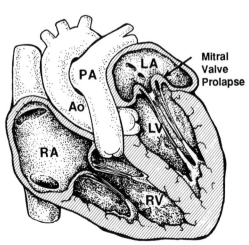

FIGURE 4. Prolapse of redundant mitral valve leaflets during systole (RA = right atrium, LA = left atrium, RV = right ventricle, LV = left ventricle, AO = aorta, PA = pulmonary artery).

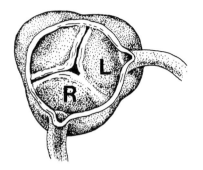

FIGURE 5. Fusion of right (R) and left (L) coronary commissure creating stenotic, bicuspid aortic valve.

Aortic Valve Stenosis

The most common congenital cardiac abnormality is a bicuspid aortic valve (Fig. 5). Because of commissural fusion, 1% of the population have only two, rather than the usual three, aortic valve leaflets. Obstruction to blood flow out of the left ventricle occurs when congenital changes substantially decrease the size of the valve orifice. The pressure increase within the left ventricle causes myocardial hypertrophy. In young patients with severe narrowing, this adaptive response eventually results in fibrosis of myocardium. The hypertrophied muscle and the need for increased coronary flow during activity are factors responsible for rhythm changes that have resulted in sudden death.[20]

The loud and harsh sounding murmur created by the obstructed valve is usually heard on physical examination. Minor valve changes that can be more difficult to detect by the untrained ear do not create the myocardial changes that predispose young athletes to sudden death.

Ebstein's Malformation

An enlarged and displaced tricuspid valve (Ebstein's malformation) may be a source of rhythm disorders that lead to syncope and sudden death.[15] The heart rate abnormalities in this uncommon congenital defect usually originate within the atrium or involve accessory conduction pathways between the atrium and right ventricle.

The physical findings may be subtle if the degree of tricuspid insufficiency is mild, because these soft murmurs located along the left lower sternal border sound like innocent or functional sounds. The large, anterior leaflet may create an ejection click during systole, which distinguishes tricuspid valve insufficiency from a functional murmur.

Ascending Aortic Aneurysm of Marfan's Syndrome

An aortic aneurysm of Marfan's syndrome may go unrecognized when the obvious musculoskeletal or eye lens abnormalities of this connective tissue disorder are lacking. The aortic root enlargement may be silent unless aortic valve insufficiency occurs and the murmur of this incompetent valve is noted on physical examination. The collagen and elastic tissue disruption within the ascending aorta can create a large aneurysm by early adolescence that has the potential to rupture or tear during periods of exercise when an elevation in systolic blood pressure increases wall stress.[13] The internal blood loss and hypotension from aortic rupture preclude successful resuscitation, whereas intimal tears within this artery have been surgically managed when the diagnosis is made promptly after the onset of excruciating back or neck pain.[5]

Tall individuals with mitral valve prolapse or other stigmata of this connective tissue disorder should have a complete echocardiographic scan so that the ascending aorta can be viewed before they are given permission to participate in competitive athletics.

THE CORONARY CIRCULATION

Several congenital and acquired coronary artery abnormalities that alter normal coronary flow have been documented in young athletes who have died unexpectedly during vigorous exercise.[10] The two small vessels that supply blood to both conduction tissues and myocardium originate within separate aortic valve sinuses. The right coronary artery supplies the sinus and atrioventricular nodes, right atrium, right ventricle, and posterior portion of the ventricular septum. The two major branches of the left coronary trunk supply the left ventricle and left atrium. During intense exercise, coronary artery flow must increase three to five times to adequately meet metabolic requirements of the myocardium. When coronary perfusion is inadequate, the oxidative processes responsible for stabilizing cell membrane potentials become altered and this creates an environment wherein conduction and impulse abnormalities develop.

Anomalous Coronary Artery

The two coronary arteries may arise adjacent to each other within the same aortic valve sinus. The congenitally displaced vessel en route to its normal area of distribution forms an acute angle at its point of origin and courses between the pulmonary artery and aorta (Figs. 6 and 7). The vigorous cardiac contractions that occur during intense exercise may compress the malpositioned artery at a time when coronary blood flow requirements are at their highest.

Another recognized abnormality responsible for sudden death is when the left coronary artery originates off the main pulmonary artery (Fig. 8).[21] The coronary blood supply to the left ventricle then depends on the adequacy of collateral vessels from the right coronary system. When these connections are grossly inadequate, acute ischemia will develop shortly after birth. By contrast, young patients may remain asymptomatic for years because the supply of blood from the right coronary into the displaced left coronary trunk is adequate under most circumstances.

The physical clues may include murmurs created by flow through collateral arteries or through mitral insufficiency when chronic ischemia leads

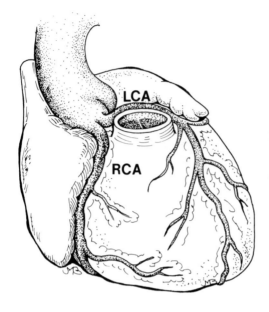

FIGURE 6. Entrapped left coronary artery (LCA) originating from right coronary sinus (RCA = right coronary artery).

to left ventricular enlargement. Exertional chest pain noted in these patients results from inadequate coronary supply to the left ventricle.

Post-Kawasaki's Coronary Occlusion

A growing number of patients are being followed for coronary artery abnormalities following Kawasaki's syndrome. Although gamma globulin infusions have reduced the number of patients with coronary artery involvement from 25% to less than 10%, a growing number of active youngsters

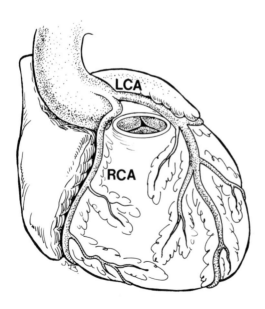

FIGURE 7. Entrapped right coronary artery (RCA) originating from left coronary sinus (LCA = left coronary artery).

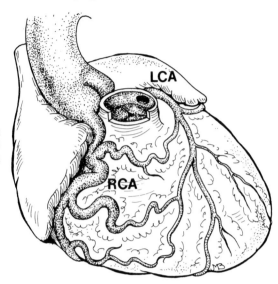

FIGURE 8. Anomalous origin of left coronary artery (LCA) from main pulmonary trunk (LCA = left coronary artery).

continue to have aneurysms or develop coronary obstruction beyond the acute and subacute phase of this illness. The impediment to coronary flow created by these changes has resulted in early symptoms of angina and sudden death during physical activity.[9]

PRIMARY RHYTHM DISORDERS

In a small percentage of athletic adolescents who have died unexpectedly, there is no obvious cause for death on postmortem examination. Death is assumed to result from a sudden and irreversible alteration in heart rate or conduction. Several disorders known to cause sudden death may apply in such instances.

Prolonged QT Interval

Patients with congenital prolongation of the QT interval are at increased risk for syncope or sudden death with physical activity.[1] In the presence of this repolarization abnormality, premature ventricular beats may propagate into extended ventricular tachycardia or fibrillation. Early sudden death or deafness in other family members are clues to these inherited conduction disorders. The diagnosis can be made with a standard electrocardiogram or an exercise treadmill study.

Complete Heart Block

Disruption of normal conduction from acquired or congenital causes that results in a slow ventricular rate places a person at risk for sudden death. Third-degree heart block with rates fewer than 45 beats per minute or slow rates with a wide QRS pattern have been considered poor prognostic features and indication for pacemaker implantation.[16]

Wolff-Parkinson-White Syndrome

Normally, the conduction tracts of the atria and ventricles are connected through only the junctional tissue (atrioventricular node and bundle of His). In some young patients, extra strands of tissue, distant from this normal area of conduction, bridge these two chambers and carry impulses rapidly into the ventricles (Wolff-Parkinson-White syndrome).[4] These extra pathways predispose young individuals to tachycardias, which in many circumstances are well tolerated or effectively altered with medication. In some instances, especially in association with atrial fibrillation, conduction through these extra pathways becomes so rapid that syncope or death occurs from ventricular tachycardia.

The physical examination is normal but the electrocardiogram shows accelerated conduction into the ventricles with a short PR interval and widened QRS pattern.

THE POSTOPERATIVE CARDIAC PATIENT

During the first two decades of life, 1 in 1000 young people will undergo palliative or corrective cardiac surgery for congenital heart disease. These operations are offered to improve function or decrease the hypoxemia created by congenital defects.

Palliative procedures are performed during infancy to avoid the higher risks associated with early total repair. Even though these procedures may be deemed successful, these young patients continue to have cardiac enlargement from persistent shunts and/or subnormal oxygen delivery.

Although corrective surgery restores oxygenation by eliminating intra- and extracardiac communications or blockage of blood flow through the cardiac chambers and great arteries, followup studies increasingly reveal that the term "corrective" is a misnomer.[3] Even when intracardiac shunts and obstructions are removed, many postoperative patients have residual abnormalities that cause chamber hypertrophy or dilatation and create the potential for rhythm disturbances.[12] These also result when conduction pathways are disrupted or from scars forming around synthetic material placed within the heart (Table 2).

The uncertainties for these postoperative patients have increased because recent advances in surgical and interventional techniques are now applied regularly to patients who previously were considered to be inoperable, including infants born with hypoplastic ventricles or small and developmentally

TABLE 2.   Postoperative Congenital Cardiac Defects Associated
with Sudden Death

Aortic valvar and subaortic stenosis
Tetralogy of Fallot
Transposition of great arteries
Hypoplastic left ventricle
Ebstein's anomaly
Any repaired condition with residual pulmonary hypertension

---

abnormal pulmonary arteries or older patients with cardiomyopathies who benefit from cardiac transplantation.

Except for the patient who has had surgical ligation of a patent ductus arteriosus, the postoperative congential heart patient may continue to be at risk for cardiac problems during intense exercise. Because many of these youngsters express interest in competitive athletics, the pediatrician and cardiologist must carefully match the desired activity with the present cardiac condition, as determined by regular clinical, echocardiographic, and treadmill examinations.

PULMONARY HYPERTENSION

Sudden death can occur in young patients with abnormally high pulmonary artery pressure.[6] The most common cause is Eisenmenger's syndrome, a cyanotic cardiac condition created by irreversible vascular damage within small arteries in the lung produced by some surgically uncorrected congenital heart defects. These patients may die suddenly during activity from an abrupt decrease in oxygen created by changes in either pulmonary or systemic pressure.

Primary pulmonary hypertension is a term reserved for elevated pulmonary artery pressure for which there is no explanation. These young people show diffuse vascular changes within the lungs. The pressure within the pulmonary arteries and right ventricle rises steadily as more and more small vessels become obstructed. The associated hypertrophy within the heart eventually creates the potential for serious rhythm disturbances.

Elevated pulmonary artery pressure can be suspected on physical examination by abnormal cardiac pulsation resulting from the enlarged right ventricle and from the loud second heart sound brought about by the high pulmonary pressure.

IS SUDDEN DEATH PREVENTABLE?

Many young athletes who have died suddenly have had few, if any, complaints or symptoms that caused them to seek medical attention. In those circumstances, these tragedies seem unavoidable. Other patients with recognized disorders or previous cardiac surgery may have regular and thorough examinations and still die unexpectedly—reminders that close monitoring and treatment is not always successful. Despite these facts and uncertainties, the primary care physician should be acquainted with the disorders responsible for sudden death and seek to clarify symptoms and signs that could result from cardiac conditions known to cause sudden changes in cardiac rhythm or coronary or cerebral blood flow.

The Cardiac Examination

All cardiac murmurs detected on physical examination should be precisely defined before any young person is allowed to participate in competitive athletics. Although a slow heart rate with an increased stroke volume in a well-conditioned athlete may result in a functional murmur, this sound might also be the only clue to an underlying cardiac disorder. Usually murmurs created by intracardiac defects have harsh or blowing qualities and localize over one area of the precordium in contrast to the low-pitched and diffusely transmitted functional sounds. A click or diastolic murmur increases the likelihood that the sound is organic in origin.

Palpation of the precordium may be difficult to interpret because many young patients are anxious during these physical examinations and have increased heart rates. Often these athletes are thin from the rigors of regular training, which also accentuates chest wall pulsations. A thrill felt over the anterior precordium or within the suprasternal notch is always an abnormal sign.

Palpitations

Active youngsters who notice irregularities or a rapid heart beat should have a thorough cardiac evaluation to exclude primary or secondary cardiac disorders. Although extrasystoles are noted on routine extended ECG monitoring in normal children, most patients are unaware of these infrequent extrasystoles or pauses. Dizziness, pallor, or nausea indicates the cardiac rhythm is exceedingly rapid or disorganized, compromising both cardiac output and cerebral blood flow.

A standard electrocardiogram may depict the accessory conduction pathway of Wolff-Parkinson-White syndrome, the prolonged QT interval responsible for ventricular tachycardia or the conduction delays that predispose to complete heart block. Hypertrophy might be the first clue to an underlying cardiomyopathy.

An effort should also be made to correlate accurately these young patients' symptoms to their cardiac rhythms. The Holter device allows constant ECG monitoring for 24–48 hours. This rather short monitoring period often fails to detect any abnormalities, especially when symptoms occur infrequently. Under these circumstances, a home telemetry device can be given to the patient or family that allows ECG recordings when symptoms or heart rate changes develop. Recordings are transmitted by telephone to assure rapid interpretation and correlation.

Chest Pain

The vast majority of children or adolescents with chest pain do not have an underlying cardiac explanation for their complaint. Nevertheless, disorders that produce coronary insufficiency can result in angina even in this young population. The history must probe the relationship of these symptoms to exercise and explore whether the patient ever had a Kawasaki-like illness. Family history may disclose other family members who died unexpectedly from a cardiomyopathy or primary rhythm disorder.

The physical examination should include a careful search for an ejection click or murmur. When chest pain develops during or shortly following physical exertion, treadmill studies are recommended to reproduce this pain and note its relationship to cardiac rhythm and the ST segments. Echocardiography can view the origins of the coronary arteries, all four heart valves, as well as the myocardium for evidence of an underlying heart muscle disorder. These studies are usually unnecessary in children complaining of chest pain if a thorough medical history is obtained.

Unexplained Syncope

Unexplained unconsciousness must be explored from both a neurologic and cardiac perspective.[18] If this occurs during exercise, the physician in all circumstances must make every effort to assure the patient that the heart is normal and free from defects that may cause a serious, if not life-threatening, dysrhythmia. Vasovagal and orthostatic events can usually be identified by careful review of the circumstances preceding the syncope. When doubt remains, standard and extended EGC tracings should be obtained, looking for abnormalities that are known to cause sudden alteration in cardiac output. In the rare youngster requiring resuscitative efforts to restore consciousness, electrophysiologic and head-tilt maneuvers must be considered to elicit cardiac rhythm or blood pressure disturbances. Arrhythmogenic valve disorders such as mitral valve prolapse or Ebstein's malformation and right ventricular dysplasia are detectable by echocardiography.

USE OF CARDIOLOGY STUDIES

A thorough history and physical examination are the best guides in directing the physician to appropriate laboratory studies. If the primary care physician is unfamiliar with the newer technology, consultation with a pediatric cardiologist is advised.

The standard electrocardiogram identifies patients with WPW syndrome, prolonged QT interval, heart block, and patterns of hypertrophy. Physicians interpreting pediatric ECGs must be mindful of the differences in conduction intervals and voltage measurements compared with standards applied to adult tracings.

Chest roentgenograms rarely identify abnormalities that predispose to sudden and life-threatening cardiac events. However, they do allow the physician to identify pulmonary causes of chest pain such as pneumonia or spontaneous pneumothorax.

Echocardiography, which includes Doppler and color flow studies, allows cardiologists to make an accurate anatomic and hemodynamic assessment of the heart. Both the technician performing these studies and the physician interpreting the data must be familiar with congenital and postoperative conditions. All too frequently, studies done outside pediatric cardiac centers are incomplete or inconclusive so that, when possible, final interpretations should be made by a cardiologist trained and experienced in congenital heart defects.

In this cardiologist's opinion, adolescents who desire to participate in vigorous, competitive athletics should have treadmill studies if they have residual abnormalities following open heart surgery or if they have recognized arrhythmogenic disorders, including mitral valve prolapse. The efforts in many sports often require sustained aerobic and anaerobic stresses. Treadmill studies performed to maximum exertion (greater than 95% predicted maximum heart rate) can detect rhythm changes that might be provoked by such activity and, importantly, provide the patient and parents reassurance that the activity is indeed safe. Because both the patient and level of exertion change with age, yearly studies may be necessary in some individuals.

CONCLUSION

Because sudden death is an event for which family, friends, and community are unable to prepare, the resolution of grief requires discussion with the pediatrician or pediatric cardiologist. These cases rarely involve oversight on the part of parents or physicians, and thus the difficulty of making a diagnosis beforehand, the silent nature of these disorders, and the disparity between physical fitness and cardiac health must be stressed. Genetic counselling and studies of other family members are warranted in some cases such as hypertrophic cardiomyopathy or inherited conduction disorders.

References

1. Burchell HB: The QT interval historically treated. Pediatr Cardiol 4:138, 1983.
2. Denfield SW, Garson A Jr: Sudden death in children and young adults. Pediatr Clin North Am 37:215, 1990.
3. Garson A Jr, McNamara DG: Sudden death in a pediatric cardiology population, 1958 to 1983: Relation to prior arrhythmias. J Am Coll Cardiol 6:221, 1985.
4. Gillette RC, Garson A Jr, Kugler JD: Wolff-Parkinson-White syndrome in children: Electrophysiologic and pharmacologic characteristics. Circulation 60:1487, 1979.
5. Gott VL, Pyeritz RE, Magovern GJ Jr, et al: Surgical treatment of aneurysms of the ascending aorta in the Marfan syndrome. N Engl J Med 314:1070, 1986.
6. Grossman W, Braunwald E: Pulmonary hypertension. In Braunald E (ed): Heart Disease: A Textbook of Cardiovascular Medicine. Philadelphia, W.B. Saunders, 1988, p 793.
7. Kavey RW, Blackman MS, Sondheimer HM, Byrum CJ: Ventricular arrhythmias and mitral valve prolapse in childhood. J Pediatr 105:885, 1984.
8. Kennedy HL, Whitlock JA: Sudden death in young persons—an urban study (abstract). J Am Coll Cardiol 3:485, 1984.
9. Kohr RM: Progressive asymptomatic coronary artery disease as a late fatal sequelae of Kawasaki's disease. J Pediatr 108:256, 1986.
10. Kragel AH, Roberts WC: Anomalous origin of either right or left main coronary artery from the aorta with subsequent coursing between aorta and pulmonary trunk. Am J Cardiol 62:771, 1988.
11. Maron BJ, Roberts WC, McAllister HA, et al: Sudden death in young athletes. Circulation 62:218, 1980.
12. McNamara DGL, Bricker JT, Galiota FM Jr, et al: Task Force I: Congenital Heart Disease. J Am Coll Cardiol 6:1200, 1985.
13. Murdoch JL, Walker BA, Halpern BI, et al: Life expectancy and causes of death in Marfan's syndrome. N Engl J Med 286:804, 1972.
14. Nishimure RA, McGoon M, Shub C, et al: Echocardiographically documented mitral valve prolapse—long term followup of 237 patients. N Engl J Med 313:1305, 1985.
15. Oh JK, Holmes DR Jr, Hayes DL, et al: Cardiac arrhythmias in patients with surgical repair of Ebstein's anomaly. J Am Coll Cardiol 6:1351, 1985.
16. Pinsky WW, Gillette PC, Garson A Jr, McNamara DG: The diagnosis, management and long term results with congenital complete atrioventricular block. Pediatrics 69:728, 1982.

17. Roberts WC, Siegel RJ: Idiopathic dilated cardiomyopathy: Analysis of 152 necropsy patients. Am J Cardiol 60:1340, 1987.
18. Ross BA: Evaluation and treatment of syncope in children. Learning Center Highlights 5:7, 1990.
19. Thiene G, et al: Right ventricular cardiomyopathy and sudden death in young people. N Engl J Med 318:129, 1988.
20. Wagner HD, Ellison RC, Keane JF, et al: Clinical course of aortic stenosis. Circulation 56(Suppl 1):47, 1977.
21. Wilson CL, Diabal RW, Holeyfield RW, et al: Anomalous origin of left coronary artery from the pulmonary trunk. J Thorac Cardiovasc Surg 73:887, 1977.

Epidemiology of Sports Injuries in Adolescents

WILLIAM L. RISSER, M.D.

Director, Division of Community
and General Pediatrics
Professor of Pediatrics
University of Texas Medical
School at Houston
Houston, Texas

This chapter discusses the epidemiology of injuries in organized sports in adolescents from junior high school through college age. Epidemiology includes the study of the distribution, causes, and prevention of disease. Epidemiologic data on sports injuries can help pediatricians to counsel families about the risks of specific sports, to know what injuries to expect in a given activity, to help athletic programs plan for medical care, and to advise athletes and coaches on injury prevention.

Two kinds of musculoskeletal injuries are common in sport. The first is acute traumatic injuries such as ankle sprains ("macrotrauma"). The second is overuse injuries that usually begin insidiously following repetitive minor injury ("microtrauma"). Sports vary in the proportion of these two kinds of injury, but both can be disabling.

Investigations differ in the way they define the occurrence and severity of an injury. Most often, athletes are considered to be injured if they lose time from participation. The severity of injury is determined by the amount of time lost. This measure has its drawbacks, because it is affected by such factors as the motivation of the athlete, the sport, and the position played. For example, a fracture of the dominant hand may sideline a football quarterback but not affect the participation of a football lineman or a distance runner. In addition, relatively severe injuries may not be counted. A concussion may not be called an injury if

ADOLESCENT MEDICINE: State of the Art Reviews—Vol. 2, No. 1, February 1991
Philadelphia, Hanley & Belfus, Inc.

109

a football player returns to practice on Monday after his concussion in Friday's game.

Incomplete ascertainment of the number of injuries is another potential methodologic problem in sports epidemiology research. If the injury is defined by the need to see a physician or the filing of an insurance claim, some injuries will be missed. If there is an athletic trainer in the sports program who is determining and recording injuries as they happen, the data will be more complete than if a researcher depends on coaches to send in periodic injury reports, or on coaches and athletes to remember previous injuries. These sorts of problems probably influence the reporting of mild injuries more than severe ones.

Incidence of injury is reported in two ways. Most commonly, the cumulative incidence is given, which is the number of injuries among a specific group of athletes, e.g., a team, followed for a defined period of time, e.g., a season. This measure gives the individual's risk of injury. The incidence of *first* injuries may be given, which gives the risk of any one athlete being injured. At other times, the total number of injuries is divided by the total number of athletes. Because some athletes will be injured more than once, this approach overestimates the risk of injury to any one athlete. It is often not clear which approach a given author is using.

Occasionally the incidence density is reported, which is the number of injuries per person-time of participation. This value gives less information about individual risk, but indicates how fast injuries are occurring, and can be adjusted for the fact that individuals on a team are at risk for varying amounts of time.

Incidence values are often inaccurate because the determination of the number of athletes at risk is imprecise. If the cumulative incidence of injury is calculated using the number of athletes on the team at one defined point in the season, for example the beginning, individuals who leave the team will be counted as being at risk, as will injured athletes who at least temporarily are nonparticipants. In addition, this measure is not usually adjusted for the fact that athletes on a team have varying levels of participation. As the most obvious example, those who rarely play in games are exposed to injury only during practice, and should not be counted equally in the denominator of an incidence calculation with those who *do* play in games. Both of these problems result in underestimation of the risk of injury, especially for the more active participants.

Authors of case series often draw conclusions about incidence or relative incidence of injury that are not justifiable. If an orthopedist in 5 years of practice sees twice as many female as male basketball players with anterior cruciate ligament injuries, he is likely to state that these injuries are twice as common in females. This conclusion is not warranted if, as is usually the case, he has no information on how many basketball players of each sex are at risk for injury in his area, and if he does not know if he is seeing all athletes of each sex who have this problem.

The physician wants to prevent injuries: this requires an understanding of their causes. Case series of injured athletes may provide clues to causes, but these can only be carefully studied in case-control or cohort studies that have been designed for this purpose. Proving causation usually requires consistent results from several investigations. Articles on sports injury frequently present plausible or commonly accepted causal factors, but surprisingly few of these have been confirmed by good research.

The following discussion of injury epidemiology uses, unless noted otherwise, this definition of injury incidence: the percent of athletes on the team who, because of injury, missed at least part of a practice or game during one season. Injuries are classified as "mild" if the athlete was out for < 8 days, or "significant" if disability was ≥ 8 days. Significant injuries are further subclassified as moderate, 8–21 days of disability; and major, > 21 days. The incidence of *first* injuries will be presented if possible. When the results of more than one study are discussed for a given sport, reports of injury incidence, type, location, and severity vary. This is a result of differences in methodology among the studies, the natural season-to-season variability in injury occurrence, and dissimilarities among sports programs.

Good data are not always available on athletes in junior high school and college. The discussion below often emphasizes high-school programs.

OVERALL INCIDENCE OF INJURY

The only good data are available for interscholastic high school sports. For boys, the yearly injury incidence for all sports combined was 27%[37] to 39%,[23] and for girls, 12% to 22%. Of all the above injuries, 25–35% were significant.

Football

Football has one of the highest injury rates of all sports. This is true in all age groups.

Among young adolescents playing youth football, Goldberg et al.[26] found that 5.2% of boys 11–14 years old in the two heaviest weight classes had moderate injuries; 3.3% had major ones. The most commonly injured areas were the hand/wrist (28%), knee (17%), and shoulder/humerus (15%), and the most common injury type was a fracture (38%).

In 1986, using the injury experience of a probability sample of schools to project national data, Powell[44] estimated that, among the one million boys who played interscholastic high-school football, 28% had mild, 5.9% moderate, and 3.3% major injuries. An average of one athlete per team required hospitalization within 18 hours of injury, and one per team required surgery, usually to the knee (70%). Twenty-nine percent of injuries were contusions or lacerations, 28% sprains, 21% strains, 7% fractures, and 6% concussions or other injuries to the nervous system.

Garrick and Requa[23] found that 81% of high-school players had an injury that caused 1–4 days of missed participation, whereas 30% were out for at least 5 days. Blyth and Mueller[9] found that 31% had injuries resulting in 1–6 days of disability, and 17% missed at least 7 days. The knee (19%) and ankle (15%) were the most frequently injured areas. Slightly fewer than 1% of athletes had injuries severe enough to disqualify them from contact sports.

In college players, Alles et al.[2] established that approximately 27% per season had significant injuries. About two players per team required knee surgery. As in high-school athletes, the knee (34%) and foot/ankle (19%) were the areas most often injured. Sprains (50%), contusions/lacerations (21%), and strains (12%) were the most common types; 11% were fractures and 4% neurotrauma.

Entrepreneurs have developed knee braces designed to prevent medial collateral ligament injuries in the knees of football players. There have been a number of studies of the efficacy of these braces. Although no study is without flaws, taken together the evidence indicates that the knee brace does *not* effectively prevent injury, and may even make it more likely. The American Academy of Pediatrics has recently issued a position statement[3] recommending that these braces "*not* be considered standard equipment for football players."

Injuries or other problems causing death or serious central nervous system injury are of particular concern in football. These are discussed in the chapter on catastrophic head and neck injuries. In the years 1983–1987, among high-school and college athletes, the number of intracranial hemorrhages ranged from 11–21 per year. During this period, the number dying yearly from cranio-cerebral injury varied from 1–9; 32–69 had cervical spine fracture, dislocation, or subluxation; and 5–11 had permanent cervical quadriplegia.[60] Heat stroke and heart disease resulted in the death of a few more.[39] Quadriplegia from spinal cord trauma has decreased significantly since the use of top of the head as a point of contact ("spearing") in blocking and tackling was outlawed in 1976.[60]

Concussion, including recurrent concussion, is a relatively common injury in football. The studies cited above, without defining a concussion, reported seasonal cumulative incidences of approximately 2% (high school),[44] 2.6% (high school),[9] and 5.7% (high school and college combined);[2] however, one study that clearly defined a concussion reported a dramatically higher incidence: 19% among football players at 103 high schools in one season.[24]

Do injuries in high school and college cause permanent disability? The only data concern knee injuries. Pritchett found that 25% of a group of high school athletes who had significant knee injuries were restricting their activity 10 years later.[47]

Ice Hockey

Because injuries to the face and head were found to be common in ice hockey,[55] amateur athletes in Canada and the U.S. through the college level are now required to wear helmets and face protectors. Following the requirement, Pashby found that eye injuries have decreased significantly in frequency but have not disappeared.[43] In a retrospective study that may have had incomplete ascertainment of injury in its earlier years, Tator and Edmonds[57] demonstrated an apparent increase in spinal cord injuries. They ascribe this to more aggressive play by helmet-users; this theory is unproven, but the incidence and causes of this problem need careful prospective study.

In the only comprehensive study since the advent of helmets and face guards, Gerberich et al.,[25] who included concussion and dental trauma in their injury count even if no time was lost from participation, found that 41% of 251 interscholastic high school players were injured, some more than once, at a rate of one injury per 200 player-hours. Nineteen percent of athletes had moderately severe injuries or concussions, dental trauma, or fractures; 7% had major ones. The head and neck (22%), shoulder (16%), arm/hand (13%), and back/chest/ribs (12%) were the most often injured areas. Contusions, lacerations, and sprains/strains comprised 51% of injuries, but fractures of the arm or hand (7%) and separations, dislocations, or torn ligaments in the shoulder (12%) were also relatively common.

Concussion accounted for 12% of injuries; many athletes reported blows to the head that made them dizzy (34%) or caused a headache (30%). Of athletes with injuries to the head, neck, or back, 5–10% reported transient paresthesia and/or weakness in the extremities, and a few described persistent weakness.

Soccer

The growing popularity of soccer in the U.S. apparently results in part from its reputation for causing fewer serious injuries than football. Although these can occur, the available data do indicate that soccer is a relatively safe sport.

A representative study of soccer injury incidence is that of McCarroll et al.,[36] who evaluated a youth soccer league during one season. This was a mix of recreational and competitive teams; the latter played twice as many games and participated in tournaments. The overall risk of injury by age was: 12–13 years, 5.3%; 14–15, 6.0%; and 16–18, 8.7%. The competitive teams in each age group had about twice the incidence of injury as the recreational ones. The majority of these injuries were apparently mild ones.

Garrick and Requa[23] found a yearly incidence of 30% in male interscholastic high school players. Ten percent of players missed > 4 days.

Nilsson and Roass[41] reported incidence densities as well as types and locations of injury for elite adolescent soccer players aged 11–18 years participating in a 5-day tournament in which 25,000 players on 1,549 teams played 2,987 matches. Most injuries were mild, with 9 of 10 athletes returning to play in one day. Injuries occurred at a rate of 14/1000 hours of play among boys and 32/1000 hours in girls. These rates were similar across different age subgroups. Fifty-nine percent of injuries were contusions; 33% sprains and strains; 6% fractures; and 2% concussions. Sixty-eight percent were to the lower and 15% to the upper extremity; 10% to the head and face; and 7% to the trunk. The injuries to the lower extremity were approximately evenly divided between the hip/thigh, knee, shin, ankle, and foot. Of the knee injuries, 12 of 72 (69%) were contusions, 15 of 72 (21%) sprains, 2 of 72 (3%) complete ligament tears, 3 of 72 (4%) meniscus tears, and 2 of 72 (3%) fractures.

It has been alleged that serious knee injuries happen as commonly in high-school soccer as in football. Pritchett[45] asserts this in his study of insurance claims for soccer injuries; however, his data show that internal derangement of the knee, the only serious knee injury reported for soccer players, occurred in 0.66/1000 soccer players compared with 2.2/1000 football players.[46] Football players had additional kinds of serious knee injuries as well. During one season of youth league soccer,[36] 6/4018 players required knee surgery; the ages of the six were not given, but 2015 players were $\geq$ 12 years old and therefore in the age group in which knee surgery is most likely. Powell[44] found that approximately 1 of 70 high-school football players required knee surgery during the 1986 season. Thus the available data do not support the claim that the two sports have equal risk of serious knee injury.

Concussion can occur in soccer but is uncommon. There has been concern[62] about cumulative damage to the brain from repeated heading of the ball; there are case reports of acute problems, but no convincing evidence of chronic injury is yet available.

Eye injuries can be severe and eye protection has been advocated.[12] No good data establish the risk of serious injury, although this has been estimated to be 1/1000 participants per season.[12]

Wrestling

Wrestling vies with football for the highest injury rate in organized sports. In high-school athletes, Requa and Garrick[49] found that 70% had mild, 62% moderate (out for > 4 days), and 18% major injuries each season. Among college wrestlers, Roy[54] found that 63% had mild, 11% moderate, and 6% major injuries per season.

Requa and Garrick[49] demonstrated that the majority of injuries were sprains and strains (75%), equally distributed between the upper and lower extremities and the trunk. The spine and trunk were most commonly strained, whereas the knee was most often sprained. Acromioclavicular sprains were common as well. The incidence of surgical injuries (1.7%) in wrestling was second only to football among high-school sports. In Roy's study,[54] 2 of 40 college athletes per season required surgery, usually to the knee. Other serious injuries included fractures of the hand and ankle, subluxation of the shoulder, dislocations of the shoulder and elbow, severe ankle sprains, and nonsurgical meniscus injuries of the knee.

Spread of skin infections between wrestlers is a problem relatively unique to this sport. Among 115 athletes during three seasons, Roy identified 56 staphylococcal or herpes simplex infections that he attributed to wrestler-to-wrestler transmission.

Wrestlers sometimes use starvation or acute dehydration to "make weight" in a given weight class. These practices may have acute and chronic complications such as heat illness and impaired growth. As have other organizations, the American College of Sports Medicine has published a position paper condemning these behaviors and making recommendations on how they can be avoided.[7]

Baseball

Garrick and Requa[23] found an injury rate of 18% per season among high-school players, with 5% missing > 4 days. McLain and Reynolds[37] established that 15% of a high-school team was injured; the proportion with more than mild injuries is not given, but the mean number of days lost per injury was 21.5. Few data are available on the types and locations of injury in baseball players above Little League age.

Although baseball players can be injured in a variety of ways, injuries to the shoulder and elbow, especially among pitchers, have received much of the attention of researchers. The occurrence of serious elbow and shoulder injuries among Little League pitchers has led to limitations on the amount they are allowed to pitch. It is not known if pitching at an early age predisposes athletes to problems in high school and college. The available evidence suggests that, although many high-school pitchers complain of elbow or shoulder pain, few have significant problems.[27] Those few that have persistent symptoms need careful evaluation to rule out the uncommon serious injuries and to establish an accurate diagnosis and an appropriate rehabilitation plan.

Of all sports in the U.S., baseball causes the largest number of serious eye injuries among junior high-school athletes, and one of the largest in high-school and college players.[63] Vinger[63] and other experts have recommended that baseball players wear protective eye wear, especially if the athlete has uncorrectable poor vision in one eye. The recent "Recommendations for Participation in Competitive Sports" of the American Academy of Pediatrics also advocate eye protection for the latter group of athletes in high-risk sports such as baseball.[4]

Rarely, a player dies from cardiac arrhythmia caused by a blow to the chest from a baseball.[15] Because of the very small risk to any individual player, chest protection is not currently recommended.

Softball

In one study,[23] 44% of high-school girls playing softball were injured, with 15% missing > 4 days; in another, 13% were injured, with a mean of 9.4 days lost/injury.[37]

The only comprehensive data on injury incidence, type, and location are in young adults playing recreational softball in the U.S. Armed Services.[64] Injuries occurred from collisions between players, falls, sliding into a base, and jamming of fingers by the ball. Injuries to the batter were unusual. Sliding caused the most injuries, including ankle and knee sprains, ankle and lower leg fractures, and, when the athlete slid head first, injuries to the upper extremity. Follow-up studies[30] showed that the use of break-away bases (bases not anchored firmly to the ground) significantly reduced the number and severity of sliding injuries. The authors also suggested that using recessed bases, outlawing sliding, and teaching proper sliding technique would also probably decrease these injuries.

Swimming

In Garrick and Requa's study,[23] 1.2% of male high-school swimmers were injured, with none missing > 4 days of participation; for girls, these values were 9% and 6%. In McClain and Reynolds' report,[37] no male or female high-school swimmers were injured.

In studies of the prevalence of shoulder injuries in elite swimmers of high-school age, as many as 82% complained of shoulder pain.[14] This most commonly occurs in butterfly and freestyle swimmers and is usually caused by impingement of the rotator cuff on surrounding structures. Less frequent concomitant injuries include subluxation, labral tears, and acromioclavicular joint disruption. Rotator cuff irritation usually responds to conservative management with rest, ice, anti-inflammatory drugs, and rehabilitative exercises.

Other injuries[19] include, among breaststroke swimmers, knee pain that is usually caused by medial collateral ligament sprain, patellofemoral pain, or synovitis. Breaststroke swimmers are also at risk for low back pain, often caused by muscle strain. but sometimes resulting from spondylolysis or spondylolisthesis. The butterfly stroke and breaststroke may cause lateral epicondylitis ("tennis elbow"). All types of swimmers may have foot or ankle pain, usually caused by tendinitis of the extensor tendons of the ankle.

Tennis

In one study,[23] 3% of male and 7% of female high-school tennis players were injured, with 2% of males and 3% of females missing > 4 days. In a second report, 3.3% of girls and no boys were injured.[37]

Much of the information about tennis injuries has come from studies of elite adolescent and young adult players.[34] Low back strain is relatively common, as are ankle sprains and overuse problems such as shin splints, plantar fasciitis, patellar tendinitis, and patellofemoral stress syndrome. Strains of the Achilles tendon and the gastrocnemius, quadriceps, hamstring, and thigh adductor muscles occur, as do ulnar nerve dysfunction from compression at the medial epicondylar groove, tendinitis of the hand and wrist, and lacerations, contusions, and abrasions of the skin of the hand.

Although it is more common in older players, adolescents may also develop "tennis elbow," an overuse injury resulting from microtrauma at the insertion of tendons on the medial or lateral epicondyle of the humerus or on the olecranon.[33] Significant intra-articular disease is unusual. In the shoulder,[33] supraspinatus or biceps tendinitis or rotator cuff irritation may occur, as may microtrauma at the insertion of tendons on the greater or lesser tuberosities of the proximal humerus. More significant injuries such as a slipped capital epiphysis are rare.

Eye injuries in tennis and other racquet sports, especially racquetball and squash, are common enough that eye protection is strongly recommended, especially for athletes with uncorrectable poor vision in one eye.[63]

Horseback Riding

A variety of injuries are possible in horseback riding; the most common are to the upper and lower extremities.[8] Of greatest concern, however, are head injuries (cerebral contusions, concussions, or skull fractures), which constitute 20% of injuries to riders less than 21 years of age and which occasionally are fatal.[8] Almost all can be prevented by the use of appropriate headgear.[34] In

1988 the American Society for Testing and Materials passed new standards (ASTM F-1163) for equestrian helmets. Helmets meeting these standards are certified by the Safety Equipment Institute, which affixes its seal to the inside of the helmet. The United States Pony Club now requires these helmets for all of its activities. During *all* riding activities, riders should wear these helmets, secured by appropriate chinstraps.

Basketball

In one study,[23] 30.5% of male and 25% of female high-school basketball players were injured during one season; 10% of boys and 7% of girls missed > 4 days. In a second,[37] 37% of boys and 31% of girls had injuries; the mean number of days lost/injury were 12 for boys and 29 for girls. In a third,[38] 14% of boys and 53% of girls were injured, with 8% of boys and 13% of girls having significant injuries.

Whiteside[65] used National Athletic Injury/Illness Reporting System (NAIRS) data to determine that, during three seasons, male college basketball players had 11.1 significant injuries/1000 exposures, whereas females had 6.0 (an exposure was participation in a practice or game).

In all these studies, sprains and strains in the lower extremity constituted most of the injuries. Ankle sprain was the most common problem.

Gray et al.[28] have alleged, based on cases seen at a sports medicine clinic, that female basketball players have a higher incidence of anterior cruciate ligament injuries than males. The above studies do not confirm this finding, nor do they generally support the idea that girls have a higher rate of other significant injuries.

Basketball has a relatively high risk of serious eye injuries. Eye protection is advisable, especially for athletes with uncorrectable poor vision in one eye.

Track and Distance Running

Requa and Garrick[48] found injury rates of 33% among male and 35% among female high-school track and field athletes. These rates were similar in cross country runners. Most injuries were musculotendinous, and 85% were to the lower extremity. These injuries resulted in greater time loss than those in almost all other sports. Ten percent of boys missed > 5 and 2.3% missed > 10 days. Fourteen percent of girls missed > 5 and 6.6% > 10 days. Strains of the muscles of the thigh were the most common injuries; shin splints, muscle and tendon injuries of the lower leg, and various inflammatory problems of the knee made up most of the rest. Sprains, even of the ankle, were relatively infrequent. Eighty percent of injuries occurred in track as opposed to field athletes. Girls were most often injured running distances of 440 yards or less, whereas boys were most often injured when hurdling.

There has been concern that distance running, particularly for the youngest adolescent athlete, may cause serious, possibly permanent musculo-skeletal damage. Few good studies of this question are available. Most injuries in this age group are of the overuse type, and can include such relatively serious problems as epiphyseal plate injuries and stress fractures. Although they can lead to permanent disability, this appears to be rare with appropriate treatment.[42]

Distance running is sometimes associated with heat illness, which will be discussed below. Distance runners often attempt to maintain a low percent body fat, which sometimes contributes to delayed menarche or secondary amenorrhea (discussed elsewhere in this issue).[20]

Women's Gymnastics

Among all women's sports, gymnastics has one of the highest injury rates. The risk of injury increases with the level of competition. Garrick and Requa[22] found that 39% of high-school gymnasts were injured, with 16% missing > 4 days. Among 33 college athletes, the injury incidence was 71%. In one study of elite performers, in a year there were 530 injuries per 100 athletes.[35]

In a variety of studies, the majority of injuries (50–66%) are to the lower extremities, with the upper extremities (25–31%) and the trunk and spine (12–19%) less often affected. Injury types are sprains and strains (47–58%), contusions (11–30%), and fractures and dislocations (5–12%). Overuse injuries represent 33–42% of the total.[35]

The knee and the ankle are the sites of the most common disabling injuries. Injuries to the elbow, wrist, back, shoulder, and foot are also relatively common.[35]

Some gymnastic injuries have potential for long-term complications. Tertti et al.[58] found that 3 of 35 athletes with chronic back pain had disc degeneration, and a relatively large number had spondylolysis and spondylolisthesis.[35] There have been recent reports of stress changes, possibly fractures, of the distal radial epiphysis,[35] which on occasion result in premature closure of the epiphysis and shortening of the radius.[1]

Elite gymnasts sometimes use the trampoline and mini-trampoline as training tools. Unfortunately, even experienced participants who are well supervised have suffered catastrophic cervical spine injuries when using these devices. Recommendations have been made that trampoline use be discontinued.[59]

Gymnasts, like distance runners, typically attempt to maintain a low percent body fat. This may lead to menstrual disorders.

Weight Use

Weight training ("strength training"), which is the use of weights as a conditioning method to improve sports performance, has become a part of many interscholastic high-school, and virtually all college, sports programs. Weight and power lifting, which involve thousands of adolescents, are competitive sports in which the goal is to lift the maximum amount of weight in several specific exercises. From case series, it is clear that serious injury can result from weight use, including ruptured intervertebral discs, severe meniscus and ligament injuries in the knee, avulsion fractures of the cervical spine, and epiphyseal fractures of the radius and ulna.[10]

There are only two reports of the incidence of injuries resulting from weight use. In a study of power lifters,[11] 71 adolescents with a mean age of 16 years and a mean duration of participation of 17 months sustained 98 musculoskeletal injuries, causing discontinuance of training for a total of 1126 days.

Among 354 junior and senior high-school football players training with weights for conditioning,[50] the incidence of significant injury (disability of > 7 days) was 7.6%, with 0.082 injuries/person-year of participation. In both of these studies, the most common injury type was a strain, and the most common site was the back, particularly the lower back.

The American Academy of Pediatrics[5] will soon issue a position statement advocating that strength training programs be supervised by *well-trained* adults. A home study program for coaches is offered by the National Strength and Conditioning Association in Lincoln, Nebraska. The position statement also recommends that adolescents avoid the sports of weight lifting, power lifting, and body building, as well as the repetitive use of maximal amounts of weight in strength training programs, until they have reached Tanner stage 5 of maturity.

Eye Injuries

The above discussion has mentioned several sports in which eye protectors are recommended. These are particularly important for athletes who have corrected vision of 20/200 or less in one eye; because eye protection does not always work, such individuals should seriously consider avoiding altogether sports with a relatively high risk of eye injury. Athletes with corrected vision of less than 20/40 in the poorer eye also may suffer significant disability if the better eye is seriously injured.[63]

Sports in addition to those mentioned above in which eye protection may be advisable for athletes with uncorrectable poor vision include lacrosse (men's and women's), field hockey, horseback riding, skiing (cross country and downhill), softball, cycling, motorcycling, auto racing, snowmobiling, polo, cricket, fencing, surfing, and golf. Eye protectors should be worn underneath the face mask in sports such as football and ice hockey. Because eye protection in wrestling and boxing is not practical, these sports should be avoided by athletes who have unilateral uncorrectable poor vision.[63]

Dental Injuries

Injuries to the face and oral structures are common in some sports. This has led experts to recommend appropriate mouth guards for at least the following sports: ice hockey; field hockey; rugby; wrestling; boxing; basketball; lacrosse; skiing; horseback riding; and weight lifting, shot putting, and discus throwing (to prevent injuries during clenching of the teeth).[32]

Males Versus Females

There has been concern that, in the same sport at the same level of competition, female athletes are at greater risk of injury than males. From the information presented above, it appears that females have a greater injury incidence in some sports, but there is no compelling evidence that there is much difference in the number of significant as opposed to mild injuries. Two studies that specifically compared injury incidence between males and females found similar values in high-school and college sports.[21,65]

OTHER "INJURIES"

Injury epidemiology mostly concerns itself with musculoskeletal problems, but other medical complications can result from sports participation. A few of these are discussed below.

Iron Deficiency

Iron deficiency is relatively common in young women following menarche. The National Health and Nutrition Survey II in 1976–80[18] determined that, based on low serum ferritin concentrations, the following proportions of young women in the U.S. have iron deficiency (the percent with iron deficiency *anemia* is in parenthesis): age 11–14 yrs., 16% (2.7%); 15–19 yrs., 30% (2.5%); and 20–44 yrs., 15% (4.2%). For males, only those 11–14 yrs. old are at relatively high risk: 16% have iron deficiency, and 5.4% iron deficiency anemia.

A number of studies confirm that adolescent and young adult athletes have a prevalence of iron deficiency that is at least as great as, and occasionally greater than, that of the general population.[51] A number of factors that may place athletes at increased risk have been studied, including decreased gastrointestinal absorption of iron and increased loss of iron in the sweat, urine, or stool. These factors appear to have some effect on iron balance in some but not all athletes.[40]

It is uncertain whether iron deficiency without anemia or mild iron deficiency anemia has an effect on sports performance. One recent study in female high-school runners suggests that they do.[53] Other evidence suggests that they do not.[13] The research in this area is inadequate. Meanwhile, it seems reasonable to identify and treat iron deficiency in all adolescents and young adults, not just athletes; a possible improvement in athletic performance is one of several benefits.

Heat Illness

A potentially lethal complication of athletic activity is heat stroke, but good data on its incidence are unavailable. This is an avoidable medical emergency, and yet it is not receiving the attention is should in some athletic programs.

Heat illness and heat stroke are most likely to occur in the first 1–2 weeks of sports participation in a hot climate, particularly in dehydrated individuals. A period of acclimatization is important for all athletes, coupled with frequent, *supervised* water breaks. Special risk groups have been identified: these include athletes who have obesity; a fever; a gastrointestinal infection; mental deficiency; a previous, especially a recent, episode of heat illness; and several chronic diseases, including, among others, cystic fibrosis, diabetes mellitus, and anorexia nervosa.[6,52]

A recent report[31] suggested that black army recruits with sickle-cell *trait* are at increased risk for sudden death during basic training, apparently due to a sickling crisis induced by dehydration and heat illness. This raised the concern that such individuals are at particular risk in athletic programs, especially at high altitudes. The weight of evidence suggests that no excessive risk exists for athletes with sickle-cell trait. They, like all others, require good hydration and careful acclimatization.

Pediatricians have an obligation to educate their patients about the avoidance of heat illness, particularly through good hydration, and to make sure that athletic programs in their community, especially those in which heat stroke has occurred, observe appropriate principles of prevention.

Infectious Diseases

Concern has arisen that human immunodeficiency virus (HIV) infection can be transmitted in bloody contact sports such as football and wrestling. There is one report of alleged transmission between soccer players in Italy,[61] but the available data are not conclusive. Because the likelihood of infection of health personnel after exposure to contaminated needlesticks is no more than 1:250,[21] transmission in the athletic setting seems likely to occur extremely rarely, if at all. It appears inappropriate at this time to exclude infected athletes from contact sports, until cases of unequivocal transmission between athletes are detected.[56]

Hepatitis B is an infection that is more readily contracted from contact with infected blood. There are two reports of transmission in the athletic setting.[56] It is probably reasonable to exclude chronic carriers of hepatitis B, especially those who are e-antigen positive, from sports such as football and wrestling. Screening of all athletes is not cost-effective, although evaluation of those from high-risk areas, such as Southeast Asia and Subsaharan Africa, is more reasonable.[56]

Spontaneous rupture of the spleen may occur in as many as 0.1% of individuals who have recently had infectious mononucleosis. This almost always occurs within 3 weeks of the onset of symptoms. It seems reasonable that, if an athlete no longer has symptoms or a palpable spleen, he may return to full athletic participation 4 weeks after he first became ill.[17]

INJURY PREVENTION

Goldberg[16] has summarized steps in injury prevention that have reasonable support through good research:
- proper conditioning and acclimatization,
- the avoidance of training excesses,
- a safe environment,
- resolution of previous injuries,
- good supervision,

- enforcement of rules concerned with safety, with continued revision as new risk factors are identified,
- instruction in proper technique,
- appropriate safety equipment,
- a careful preparticipation medical assessment, and
- matching of competitors by age, weight, and stage of maturation.

ACKNOWLEDGMENTS

I thank Dr. Barry Goldberg, whose previous work[16] was of major assistance.

References

1. Albanese SA, Palmer AK, Kerr DR, et al: Wrist pain and distal growth plate closure of the radius in gymnasts. J Pediatr Orthop 9:23–28, 1989.
2. Alles WF, Powell JW, Buckley W, et al: The National Athletic Injury/Illness Reporting System 3-year findings of high school and college football injuries. J Orthop Sports Phys Ther 1:103–107, 1979.
3. American Academy of Pediatrics, Committee on Sports Medicine: Position statement on knee brace use by athletes. Pediatrics 85:228, 1990.
4. American Academy of Pediatrics, Committee on Sports Medicine: Position statement on recommendations for participation in competitive sports. Pediatrics 81:737–739, 1988.
5. American Academy of Pediatrics, Committee on Sports Medicine. Position statement on strength training, weight and power lifting and body building by children and adolescents. Pediatrics, in press, 1991.
6. American Academy of Pediatrics, Committee on Sports Medicine: Position statement on climatic heat stress and the exercising child. Pediatrics 69:808–809, 1982.
7. American College of Sports Medicine: Position statement on weight loss in wrestlers. Med Sci Sports Exerc 8:xi–xiii, 1976.
8. Bixby-Hammett D, Brooks WH: Common injuries in horseback riding: A review. Sports Med 9:36–47, 1990.
9. Blyth CS, Mueller FO: Football injury survey. I. When and where players get hurt. Phys Sportsmed 9:45–52, 1974.
10. Brady TA, Cahill BR, Bodner LM: Weight-training-related injuries in the high school athlete. Am J Sports Med 10:1–5, 1982.
11. Brown EW, Kimball RG: Medical history associated with adolescent powerlifting. Pediatrics 72:636–644, 1983.
12. Burke MJ, Sanitato JJ, Vinger PF, et al: Soccerball-induced eye injuries. JAMA 249:2682–2685, 1980.
13. Celsing F, Blomstrand E, Werner B, et al: Effect of iron deficiency on endurance and muscle enzyme activity in man. Med Sci Sports Exerc 18:156–161, 1986.
14. Ciullo JV: Swimmer's shoulder. Clin Sports Med 5:115–137, 1986.
15. Dickman GL, Hassan A, Luckstead EF: Ventricular fibrillation following baseball injury. Phys Sportsmed 6(7):85–86, 1978.
16. Dyment PG (ed): Sports Medicine: Health Care for Young Athletes, 2nd ed. Elk Grove Village, IL, American Academy of Pediatrics, in press.
17. Eichner ER: Infectious mononucleosis: Recognition and management in athletes. Phys Sportsmed 15(12):61–70, 1987.
18. Expert Scientific Working Group: Summary of a report on assessment of the iron nutritional status of the United States population. Am J Clin Nutr 42:1318–1330, 1985.
19. Fowler PJ, Regan WD: Swimming injuries of the knee, foot and ankle, elbow, and back. Clin Sports Med 5:139–148, 1986.
20. Gadpaille WJ, Sanborn DF, Wagner WW Jr: Athletic amenorrhea, major affective disorders, and eating disorders. Am J Psychiatry 144:939–942, 1987.
21. Garrick JG, Requa RK: Girls sports injuries in high school athletics. JAMA 239:2245–2248, 1978.
22. Garrick JG, Requa RK: Epidemiology of women's gymnastics injuries. Am J Sports Med 8:261–264, 1980.
23. Garrick JG, Requa RK: Injuries in high school sports. Pediatrics 61:465–469, 1978.

24. Gerberich SG, Priest JD, Boen JR, et al: Concussion incidences and severity in secondary school varsity football players. Am J Public Health 73:1370–1375, 1983.
25. Gerberich SG, Finke R, Madden M, et al: An epidemiological study of high school ice hockey injuries. Child Nerv Syst 3:59–64, 1987.
26. Goldberg B, Rosenthal PP, Robertson LS, et al: Injuries in youth football. Pediatrics 81:255–261, 1988.
27. Grana WA, Rashkin A: Pitcher's elbow in adolescents. Am J Sports Med 8:333–336, 1978.
28. Gray J, Taunton JE, McKenzie DC: A survey of injuries to the anterior cruciate ligament of the knee in female basketball players. Int J Sports Med 6:314–316, 1985.
29. Henderson DK, Saah AJ, Zak BJ, et al: Risk of nosocomial infection with human T-cell lymphotropic virus type III/lymphadenopathy-associated virus in a large cohort of intensively exposed health care workers. Ann Intern Med 104:644–647, 1986.
30. Janda DH, Wojtys EM, Hankin FM, et al: Softball sliding injuries. JAMA 259:1848–1850, 1988.
31. Kark JA, Posey DM, Schumacher HR, et al: Sickle-cell trait as a risk factor for sudden death in physical training. N Engl J Med 317:781–787, 1987.
32. Kerr IL: Mouth guards for the prevention of injuries in contact sports. Sports Med 3:415–427, 1986.
33. Lehman RC (ed): Racquet sports: Injury treatment and prevention. Clin Sports Med 7:233–452, 1988.
34. Lloyd RG: Riding and other equestrian injuries: Considerable severity. Br J Sports Med 21:22–24, 1987.
35. McAuley E, Hudash G, Shields K, et al: Injuries in women's gymnastics: The state of the art. Am J Sports Med 16(Suppl 1):S124–S131, 1988.
36. McCarroll JR, Meaney C, Sieber JM: Profile of youth soccer injuries. Phys Sportsmed 12(2):113–117, 1984.
37. McLain LG, Reynolds S: Sports injuries in a high school. Pediatrics 84:446–450, 1989.
38. Moretz A III, Grana WA: High school basketball injuries. Phys Sportsmed 6(10):92–95, 1978.
39. Mueller FO, Blyth CS: An update on football deaths and catastrophic injuries. Phys Sportsmed 14(10):139–143, 1986.
40. Newhouse IJ, Clement DB: Iron status in athletes. Sports Med 5:337–352, 1988.
41. Nilsson S, Roaas A: Soccer injuries in adolescents. Am J Sports Med 6:358–361, 1978.
42. Orava S, Saarela J: Exertion injuries in young athletes. Am J Sports Med 6:68–74, 1978.
43. Pashby TJ: Eye injuries in Canadian amateur hockey. Am J Sports Med 7:254–257, 1979.
44. Powell J: 636,000 injuries annually in high school football. Athletic Training 22:19–22, 1987.
45. Pritchett JW: Cost of high school soccer injuries. Am J Sports Med 9:64–66, 1981.
46. Pritchett JW: High cost of high school football injuries. Am J Sports Med 8:197–199, 1980.
47. Pritchett JW: A claims-made study of knee injuries due to football in high school athletes. J Pediatr Orthop 8:551–553, 1988.
48. Requa RK, Garrick JG: Injuries in interscholastic track and field. Phys Sportsmed 9(3):42–49, 1981.
49. Requa R, Garrick JG: Injuries in interscholastic wrestling. Phys Sportsmed 9(4):44–51, 1981.
50. Risser WL, Risser JMH, Preston D: Weight training injuries in adolescents. Am J Dis Child 144:1015–1017, 1990.
51. Risser WL, Lee EJ, Poindexter HB, et al: Iron deficiency in female athletes: Its prevalence and impact on performance. Med Sci Sports Exerc 20:116–121, 1988.
52. Risser WL: Exercise for children. Pediatr Rev 10:131–139, 1988.
53. Rowland TW, Deiroth MB, Green GM, et al: The effect of iron therapy on the exercise capacity of nonanemic iron-deficient adolescent runners. Am J Dis Child 142:165–169, 1988.
54. Roy SP: Intercollegiate wrestling injuries. Phys Sportsmed 7(11):83–94, 1979.
55. Sims FH, Simonet WT, Melton LJ III, et al: Ice hockey injuries. Am J Sports Med 16(Suppl I):586–596, 1988.
56. Landry GL: Some serious viral infections and high school sports. In Smith NJ (ed): Common Problems in Pediatrics Sports Medicine. Chicago, Year Book, 1989, pp 210–215.
57. Tator CH, Edmonds VE: National survey of spinal injuries in hockey players. Can Med Assoc J 130:875–880, 1984.
58. Tertti M, Paaganen H, Kugala VH, et al: Disc degeneration in young gymnasts. Am J Sports Med 18:206–208, 1990.
59. Torg JS, Das M: Trampoline and minitrampoline injuries to the cervical spine. Clin Sports Med 4:45–60, 1985.
60. Torg JS, Vegso JJ, O'Neill MJ, et al: The epidemiologic, pathologic, biomechanical, and cinematographic analysis of football induced cervical spine trauma. Am J Sports Med 18:50–57, 1990.

61. Torre D, Sampietro C, Ferraro G, et al: Transmission of HIV-1 infection via sports injury (letter). Lancet 335:1105, 1990.
62. Tysvaer AT, Storli OV: Soccer injuries to the brain. Am J Sports Med 17:573–578, 1989.
63. Vinger PF: Eye injuries in sports. Phys Sportsmed 15(2):48–52, 1987.
64. Wheeler BR: Slowpitch softball injuries. Am J Sports Med 12:237–240, 1984.
65. Whiteside PA: Men's and women's injuries in comparable sports. Phys Sportsmed 8(3):130–140, 1980.

Management of Soft Tissue Injuries

GREGORY L. LANDRY, M.D.
JORGE E. GOMEZ, M.D.

Gregory L. Landry, M.D.
Associate Professor of Pediatrics
University of Wisconsin Medical
    School
Head Medical Team Physician
University of Wisconsin Athletic
    Teams
Madison, Wisconsin

Jorge E. Gomez, M.D.
Nathan Smith Fellow in
    Adolescent and Sports
    Medicine
Department of Pediatrics
University of Wisconsin Medical
    School
Madison, Wisconsin

Reprint requests to:
Gregory L. Landry, M.D.
600 Highland Ave. H6/440
Madison, WI 53792

Sporting and recreational activities are among the leading causes of injuries among adolescents.[11,31,35] Of injuries reported in the adolescent age group, injuries to soft tissues are by far the most common. In an emergency department in Massachusetts, minor soft tissue injuries accounted for nearly three-fourths of all visits for patients 0–19 years.[13] Sprains, strains, and contusions together accounted for 75% of all sports-related injuries in a Chicago high school.[26] These three types of injuries accounted for 82% of injuries among teenage soccer players in another study in Georgia.[2]

Because soft tissue injuries are common, adolescents are likely to go to their primary care physicians for diagnosis and management. This chapter is intended to help primary care physicians and other providers of health care to adolescents to become more knowledgeable about the management of soft tissue injuries. Discussion includes the pathophysiology of injury, the assessment of the degree of injury, and the rationale for the RICE method of acute treatment. Principles of rehabilitation are also discussed along with the objective criteria that can be used to make return-to-play decisions following a soft tissue injury.

PATHOPHYSIOLOGY AND ASSESSMENT

Soft tissue injury is common because the forces applied to the tendons, ligaments, and

ADOLESCENT MEDICINE: State of the Art Reviews—Vol. 2, No. 1, February 1991
Philadelphia, Hanley & Belfus, Inc.

125

muscles during sporting activity can be quite large. For example, the force applied to the ground generated by a high jumper has been estimated to be greater than five times the weight of the body.[10] Normally, the ligaments, tendons, and muscles are able to sustain large forces in one direction while producing smooth, stable motion at the joint in another direction. Injury occurs when the forces that these structures must bear become too great.

The unique composition of ligaments, tendons, and muscles allows them to withstand tremendous loads during athletic activity.[3] Tendons and ligaments are sparsely vascularized, dense connective tissues containing about 20% cellular material and 80% extracellular matrix. The chief cell in these tissues is the fibroblast, which produces collagen, elastin, ground substance, and other proteins. Collagen is the predominant constituent of the extracellular matrix, and is primarily responsible for the strength of connective tissue. Newly synthesized, immature, collagen fibers are laid down in a random orientation, with few intermolecular cross-links. This material is inherently weak. As the collagen matures, the cross-links become more numerous and stable. Stress applied to this collagen structure in the course of normal movement induces the collagen fibers to align themselves parallel to directions of greatest stress. Mature (type 1) collagen owes its strength primarily to its extensively cross-linked character and the parallel orientation of essentially all the fibers in the direction of greatest stress. The other components of the extracellular matrix are present only in small amounts in tendons, ligaments, and muscle, and add little to their mechanical properties.

Tendons and ligaments differ somewhat in their ultrastructure. The fibers composing tendons have a uniformly parallel arrangement that enable tendons to withstand high unidirectional (uniaxial) stress. Ligaments may sustain smaller loads in directions other than the predominant one, and have collagen fibers that are not as completely parallel as in tendon, but are tightly woven in a strong mesh.

The structure of muscle differs significantly from that of tendon or ligament. Muscle is predominantly cellular, more elastic than ligamentous tissue, and more vascular. The structural unit of skeletal muscle is the muscle fiber, which is the muscle cell itself. The muscle cells are arranged in parallel along the axis of force. The collagen fibers of the muscle cells are continuous with those in the tendons, permitting transmission of forces to the adjacent bones.

SPRAINS

A sprain is defined as an injury to a ligament or joint capsule. Ligaments connect adjacent bones across the joint. Because of the multidirectional orientation of the collagen fibers, ligaments are well suited to resist forces in several directions. For example, the medial collateral ligament resists separation of the medial surfaces of the femur and tibia when a valgus force is applied and resists rotation of these bones when a torsion is applied (Fig. 1). Injury results from stretching beyond the physiologic limit to recover, causing

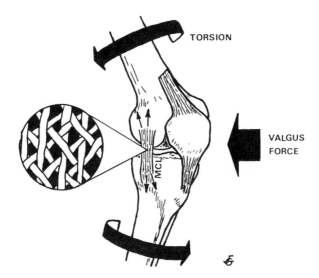

FIGURE 1. Example of multidirectional stress on the medial collateral ligament. Collagen fibers are aligned along axes of stress. Injury may result in instability in more than one direction.

various amounts of tearing of the ligament fibers in the direction of stress, followed by bleeding and inflammation. A sprain may produce instability of a joint in more than one direction.

Sprains can be assessed using a grading system that reflects the degree of injury (Table 1). A grade I sprain is one in which few fibers are torn. There is mild pain and swelling, full range of motion, and no increased joint laxity. In grade II sprain, a significant number of fibers are torn and there is detectable increase in joint laxity, but the ligament retains some strength. There is significant pain and swelling, with impairment of range of motion. In a grade III sprain, the joint is clearly unstable when the ligament is stressed. In this case, the ligament has been grossly disrupted, and the ligament can no longer sustain loading.[19] Clinically, severe pain and swelling are present, along with ecchymosis and significant loss of range of motion. Some grade III sprains may require surgical intervention.

Grading of sprains requires stress testing ligaments at a particular joint using specific maneuvers to isolate each ligament across a joint. The various maneuvers for testing ligamentous laxity at each joint is beyond the scope of this discussion.

TABLE 1.   Grading of Sprains

Grade	Pain and Swelling	Range of Motion	Laxity/Instability
I	Little	Full	None
II	Moderate	Impaired	Noticeable
III	Severe	Prevented by pain and spasm	Marked

STRAINS

Commonly called a "pull," a strain is an injury to a muscle or tendon. Muscles and tendons work in series to transmit the forces generated by muscle to the adjacent bone. Strain injuries occur not only when large external forces are applied, but also when muscle contracts forcefully in resisting applied forces. Strains involve tearing of collagen fibers, but usually do not result in joint instability. Similar to sprains, strains may diminish the range of motion at an adjacent joint because of the associated muscle spasm.

Grading of strain injuries is more difficult because abnormal motion is not prominent. Grading of strains requires assessing strength, which is more subjective than grading stability for sprains (Table 2). In a grade I strain, only a few fibers are torn, and clinically there is only mild pain or contraction of the muscle against resistance. Strength testing reveals little, if any, loss of strength. In a grade II strain, a significant number of muscle fibers have been injured, and clinically there is marked pain on palpation and on contraction against resistance, as well as significant loss in strength (due more to a protective inhibition of recruitment than to actual muscle injury). A grade III strain involves a complete rupture of the muscle. A palpable defect may be present. This rupture actually occurs most commonly at the muscle-tendon junction, and sometimes requires surgical repair.

CONTUSIONS

Contusions usually result from a direct blow that causes crushing of cells in the soft tissue and bleeding. Muscles, being more vascular than ligaments or tendons, are prone to extensive hematoma formation after a blow. Consequently, a muscle contusion can be quite disabling. For example, one of the most common contusions of muscle occurs in the quadriceps mechanism and is sometimes called a "charley horse." Although contusions are usually not graded in any objective manner, a grading system has been described for the quadriceps contusion based on the degree of flexion of the knee 2 to 3 days following the injury (Fig. 2).[17] Best examined with the athlete prone, the grade I quadriceps contusion is not severe enough to limit flexion of the knee or is mild enough that the knee can be flexed past 90 degrees. A grade II injury describes a contusion that limits knee flexion to between 45 and 90 degrees of knee flexion. A grade III quadriceps contusion limits knee flexion to less than 45 degrees.

TABLE 2. Grading of Strains

Grade	Pain on Palpation or Contraction	Loss of Strength	Palpable Defect
I	Little	Little or none ($> 4/5$)	−
II	Moderate	Significant ($3-4/5$)	+/−
III	Severe	Marked ($< 3/5$)	+/−

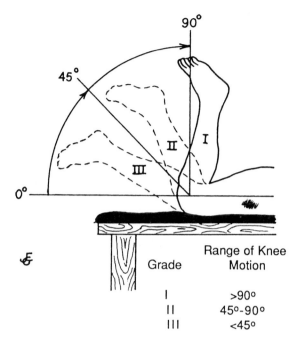

FIGURE 2.   Grading of quadriceps contusions.

THE INFLAMMATORY RESPONSE AND REPAIR

The inflammatory reaction that ensues after a soft tissue injury is nonspecific and can be excessive for the purpose of healing.[5] The reaction of the body toward any noxious stimuli is the same, regardless of the nature of the insult. The inflammatory process appears to be essentially the same whether there is a bacterial infection or an injury (Fig. 3).

Whether a sprain, strain, or contusion, there is initial bleeding into the tissue from broken blood vessels. There is a brief vasoconstrictor response of local blood vessels that may last up to several hours, depending on the volume of tissue damaged.[22] The exposed vascular endothelium comes in contact with factor XII (Hageman factor), which activates the intrinsic clotting cascade, the complement system, and the kinin system.[33] Bradykinin and the complement components C3a and C5a are produced, which markedly increase vascular permeability. Histamine is released from mast cells immediately after injury, and increases vascular permeability, as well as causes a transient local vasodilatation. Later on, prostaglandins, particularly PGE1 and PGE2, are produced by damaged tissues, platelets, and leukocytes, which maintain vasodilatation and vascular permeability.[22] The hyperemia causes redness and warmth. Within a few hours, leukocytes can be found marginating along vascular walls. These cells, predominantly mononuclear cells in the early stages of inflammation, migrate into the surrounding tissues.[33] Damaged cells and leukocytes spill lysosomal enzymes, many of them proteases, which

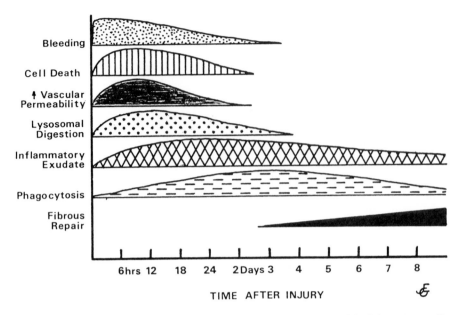

FIGURE 3. Timing of events in inflammation and repair. (Modified from Evans P: The healing process at cellular level: A review. Physiotherapy 66:256–259, 1980.)

degrade tissue constituents and cause liquefaction. The presence of extravasated blood, migrating leukocytes, fibrin, and other debris increases local tissue turgor and draws fluid into the tissues through the leaky capillary membranes, resulting in edema.[7] Damaged nerve endings become extra sensitive to noxious stimuli, which include pressure from edema and chemical irritation from histamine, bradykinin, and prostaglandins. Pain sets up a reflex arc mediated via spinal pathways which increases local muscle tone, resulting in spasm.[6] Muscle spindles also become hypersensitive, producing an exaggerated stretch reflex that also provokes spasm.

 Repair of soft tissues is primarily through formation of scar tissue, since human muscle, tendon, and ligament have little or no capacity to regenerate. Repair begins as the inflammatory reaction is subsiding. Repair can be delayed if damage and bleeding are extensive, prolonging the process of phagocytosis or "clean-up." Within 72 hours after a minor injury, activated fibroblasts can be seen elaborating collagen fibers within the injured area in a disorderly fashion.[9] The structural defect is filled with granulation tissue composed of capillary buds and collagen fibers. The healing process proceeds to the end of developing a scar that will allow the tissue to function optimally. Development of the scar in the absence of applied stress (external load or muscular contraction) results in a random orientation of collagen fibrils that conveys little tensile strength. In contrast, applied stress on the order of gentle muscle contractions or stretching induces orientation of collagen fibrils along axes of stress, resulting in a stronger scar. In addition, studies have demonstrated that early mobilization of injuries accelerates healing.[39,40]

The management of injuries is divided into two stages based on the previous discussion of pathophysiology. The immediate goal is to limit the degree of bleeding and the complications of the inflammatory response. The rehabilitation phase is designed to stress the tissue to form a stronger scar without causing more injury, while reconditioning the athlete for his or her athletic activity.

THE ACUTE TREATMENT OF SOFT TISSUE INJURIES

Acutely, that is, in the first 48–72 hours following a soft tissue injury, the aim of management is to limit the extent of bleeding and inflammation. This facilitates early healing and allows the athlete to proceed quickly with rehabilitation with less pain. The treatment applied to achieve this goal is easily remembered as RICE, an acronym for rest, ice, compression, elevation. Anti-inflammatory or analgesic medication may also be employed. This treatment helps to achieve the following goals:

1. Prevent further tissue injury
2. Prevent further bleeding and hematoma formation
3. Limit the amount of inflammatory exudate
4. Control edema
5. Reduce muscle spasm and relieve pain

Rest

Rest prevents further injury and relieves pain, and consists of cessation of activity, immobilization, and load relief. Continued movement after an injury may cause further disruption of connective tissue and blood vessels and may increase bleeding. Therefore, cessation of the activity is imperative. Usually, pain and loss of function serve a protective function by inhibiting voluntary movement. Immobilization and unloading prevent excitation of muscle spindles which reduces spasm, and prevent excitation of nerve endings, which reduces pain.

In general, injury at or near a joint, or any injury that is aggravated by movement, should require immobilization. If a fracture is suspected or a joint appears unstable, the extremity should be immobilized in the field using splints. These splints should be long enough to immobilize the joint above and below the injury. A variety of commercial splints are available, or splints can be made from items available on the scene.

Complete load relief is often necessary. Mildly to moderately injured lower extremities can be relieved from load-bearing using crutches. Treatment of back injuries often includes a period of bed rest. Injured upper extremities can be placed in a sling.

The length of time a body part is put to rest varies with the severity of the injury, but generally should be a minimum of 48–72 hours. Failure to rest the injured body part is one of the most common errors athletes make in caring for a soft tissue injury. Young athletes need frequent reassurance that rest is important in the process of healing and eventual return to athletic activity.

Ice (Cryotherapy)

The application of cold (rather than heat) is the mainstay of therapy of acute soft tissue injuries.[15,18,23,24,27,29,30] Cryotherapy has been shown to decrease bleeding and inflammation and reduce pain in injured tissues. Using heat acutely may have the opposite effect and cause more injury.

Cryotherapy has a direct vasoconstrictor effect on blood vessels at temperatures down to 15°C.[21] Minimizing bleeding into the injured area facilitates the healing process. Rapid and intense cooling of the skin and subcutaneous tissues may alternately produce vasoconstriction and vasodilatation, the "hunting reaction."[29] This is probably a reflex phenomenon to maintain tissue viability in apical structures (digits, nose, ears) at very low temperatures.[30] Vasodilatation has been seen in rapidly cooled muscle, but appears to be associated with tissue temperatures below 15°C.[29] Cold-induced vasodilatation probably does not occur during therapeutic application of cold.[21]

Cryotherapy has been shown to limit effectively the accumulation of inflammatory cells and exudate in acutely injured tissues.[8] Cooling probably protects healing tissue from further ischemic damage by lowering the local metabolic rate, allowing the tissue to function at lower oxygen tensions. Cooling may block the release of histamine, which would decrease edema by decreasing hyperemia. By decreasing bleeding and inflammation, it should follow that cryotherapy controls tissue edema. Surprisingly, experiments using animal models of soft tissue injury have reported increased swelling with the application of cold when the circumference of the injured limbs was measured.[8,25] However, the swelling occurred primarily in the skin and subcutaneous layers, whose lymphatic drainage was disrupted by the cold. In these studies, the anti-inflammatory effect of cryotherapy in the deeper structures was evident.

Cooling injured tissues reduces pain and spasm.[32] Cold depresses the excitability of free nerve endings and conduction of nerve impulses,[18] although complete conduction blockade does not occur until tissue temperature approaches 10°C.[23] Furthermore, cryotherapy decreases the concentration of inflammatory mediators and lowers tissue tension, both of which cause noxious stimulation of nerve endings. Cold may also act by overwhelming pain receptors with cold impulses so that pain impulses are obliterated.[30]

Temperature reduction must be sufficient to produce the above effects, but not so much as to be counterproductive. The deleterious effects of cold that have been reported, including cold vasodilatation, edema (associated with disintegration of lymphatic channels), and frostbite, appear to be associated with cooling tissues below 15°C. Thus the optimal therapeutic temperature range seems to be between 25 and 35°C, although this has not been firmly established experimentally.

Ice appears to be superior to other cooling agents in cooling sufficiently to provide therapeutic benefit, while not causing untoward effects. Ice, when wrapped, has the advantage over ethylchloride spray of producing less cooling of the skin with less risk of cold injury (frostbite), while cooling deeper structures more effectively.[23] Application of ice was found to achieve a greater overall reduction in muscle temperature than frozen gel, chemical ice pack, or refrigerant injected splint.[27] Reported muscle temperature reductions from 6.5 to 20.4°C with various forms of ice application represent a safe, therapeutic range.[29] Moreover, ice is inexpensive and easy to use.

Ice is usually applied in the form of crushed ice or ice chips placed in a plastic bag or wrapped in a wet towel, which is placed on the skin and covered with a towel. An elastic bandage can be used to hold the ice bag in place. Factors that affect the degree of cooling are the size of the area to be cooled, the length of application, and the thickness between the lesion and the surface. The ice pack should be large enough to cover the entire injured area.

The duration of application of ice varies with the type of injury. Skin begins to cool within the first 5 minutes of ice application, but significant reduction of muscle temperature does not take place until at least 10 minutes have elapsed.[28,38] Indeed, brief applications of ice have little effect on deep structures. Lesions deep below the surface, as in large muscle, or lesions underlying thick subcutaneous fat, which has poor thermal conductivity, require longer times of application.[24]

Although the thermal properties of different tissues (muscle, tendon, ligament, cartilage) vary, it has been shown that a standard application of covered ice for 20 minutes produces roughly the same amount of cooling in different tissues.[23] In general, ice therapy is most effective when applied immediately after injury.[15] Thereafter, it is recommended that ice be applied for 10–20 minutes, two to four times/day for the first 2 to 3 days for best results.[18]

Another form of ice therapy, ice massage, has been shown to be effective in the treatment of superficial conditions such as tendinitis and ligament sprains,[14] and is a good technique for application over a small area.[24] In this technique, ice is prepared by freezing water-filled paper cups, then pulling off the paper, or by placing a cylindrical block of ice in a hand towel. The ice is applied directly to the skin with a circular or back-and-forth massage motion. This massage is extended circumferentially about the painful area. The time required for ice massage may vary from 5 to 10 minutes, or longer if the lesion is extensive or deep.[12] The treatment is stopped when numbness is achieved. Ice massage has proved effective in reducing spasm associated with injury and spastic conditions, and is thus useful prior to stretching.[12,21]

Immersion in an ice bath or cold water bath may be desirable for extensive limb injuries. However, this form of cryotherapy is more uncomfortable than either ice pack or ice massage.

Any form of cryotherapy brings quick relief from pain and spasm. Within the first 5 minutes, the patient has the sensation of cold, which becomes progressively more uncomfortable. Between 5 and 12 minutes after application, the coldness is replaced by a burning sensation. Within reason, cryotherapy should be continued beyond the period of discomfort, as this is soon followed by numbness. At this point, the therapy can be continued for a short time, or the therapy can be stopped and followed by active range of motion exercises. The analgesic effect may last anywhere from 30 minutes to 3 hours after the cold application is stopped.[29] The risk of further injury during physical therapy under cold-induced analgesia is minimal when supervised by an experienced trainer or therapist.

Cryotherapy is relatively safe. When ice is properly applied, the risk of cold injury is low. There are few contraindications to using cryotherapy, including Raynaud's phenomenon, cold urticaria, cyroglobulinemia, and paroxysmal cold hemoglobinuria.

Compression

Compression limits swelling (edema) by a direct mechanical effect. Transudation of fluid across leaky capillary membranes depends on the hydrostatic pressure difference across the capillary membrane as well as the difference in oncotic pressure between the extravascular and intravascular spaces. Compression of an injured region increases the interstitial hydrostatic pressure, decreasing the pressure gradient across the capillary membrane. The increased tissue pressure may also aid in hemostasis by sealing off injured blood vessels.

Compression is usually achieved by wrapping the injured part with an appropriately sized elastic bandage. Specific techniques for bandaging different body parts appear elsewhere.[34] The compression bandage may be used immediately in conjunction with cryotherapy (to keep the ice bag in place), and left on following cryotherapy for a period of 4 to 6 hours until ice is re-applied.[37] Compression combined with cryotherapy may be more effective than either compression or cooling alone in controlling edema.[8,36]

By restricting the volume of the injured muscle or tendon compartment, compression also has the potential for significantly decreasing perfusion. Application of the elastic bandage must be done firmly, yet carefully, in order not to diminish peripheral pulses or venous return. Once the elastic bandage has been applied, the adequacy of peripheral perfusion should be checked periodically, as ongoing hemorrhage and tissue fluid production may further increase tissue pressure.

Elevation

Elevation is a means of controlling edema by facilitating venous and lymphatic drainage centripetally, away from the injured part. Blood and lymph flow toward the heart is determined primarily by the pressure difference between the peripheral and central circulations. The muscle pump (the increase in tissue pressure resulting from muscular contraction) increases the peripheral hydrostatic pressure. The other component of pressure is the potential energy difference, or pressure "head," which is a function of the height difference between two points. Elevating the injured part increases the pressure head between it and the central circulation, increasing the driving potential for the flow of blood and lymph. Similarly, elevation may diminish production of edema fluid by decreasing the peripheral intravascular pressure.

Elevation is done by raising the injured part on cushions or pillows or whatever else is handy. The injured part should remain elevated as much as possible for up to 72 hours, after which mobilization may be attempted.

MEDICATIONS

Application of the RICE regimen alone usually provides effective relief of pain and inflammation in most soft tissue injuries. Further relief may be achieved with a variety of medications, used most often in the acute stage of injury. Because the use of anti-inflammatory medication is controversial, the pros and cons will be discussed below.

Reduction of inflammation is important in the management of soft tissue injuries. Thus compounds with both analgesic and anti-inflammatory effects, such as aspirin or the nonsteroidal anti-inflammatory drugs (NSAIDs), may theoretically have an advantage over pure analgesics, such as acetaminophen or narcotics. This is true if therapeutic doses of a given anti-inflammatory/analgesic provide the same degree of pain relief as recommended doses of an analgesic. Aspirin is equal to acetaminophen as an analgesic on an equivalent-dose basis.[16] On the other hand, some studies have shown that some of the NSAIDs are more effective analgesics than aspirin or acetaminophen alone, or either aspirin or acetaminophen in combination with codeine.[16] NSAIDs have the advantage over opiates in being effective analgesics without having the potential for dependence from chronic use. Some NSAIDs require less frequent dosing intervals than aspirin or narcotics (bid or tid), therefore potentially increasing compliance (Table 3).

Aspirin and NSAIDs may be superior to acetaminophen for the management of soft tissue injuries because of their ability to inhibit the production of prostaglandins, which are integral to sustaining inflammation. Some physicians believe that NSAIDs should be started within 24 hours of the injury, because prostaglandin release is maximum in this time frame.[18]

Those who are hesitant to use aspirin or NSAIDs are often concerned about potential side effects, among which is the ability to inhibit platelet aggregation, an effect that theoretically could increase hemorrhage following

TABLE 3.   Doses of NSAIDs Commonly Used for Soft Tissue Injuries

Drug	Amount Usually Prescribed for Anti-inflammatory Effect
Aspirin	650–1000 mg qid
Ibuprofen	400–800 mg tid or qid
Naproxen	250–500 mg bid or tid
Indomethacin	25–50 mg tid or 75 mg bid*
Tolmetin	200–400 mg tid
Piroxicam	20 mg qd
Sulindac	150–200 mg bid

* Sustained release preparation.

TABLE 4.   Adverse Effects of NSAIDs

Gastritis
Headache
Mental status changes
Hypersensitivity
Impairment of platelet function
Impairment of renal function
Bronchospasm

acute injury. Gastritis and ulceration are also well-known side effects of both aspirin and NSAIDs. Other side effects are summarized in Table 4. Other than ibuprofen, NSAIDs have the disadvantage of being considerably more expensive than aspirin or acetaminophen.

The role of anti-inflammatory medications in acute soft tissue injuries is controversial. We believe that most mild to moderate injuries can be managed without medication. In addition, we are concerned that recommending a medication to an adolescent may make RICE seem less important, decreasing compliance with the RICE regimen. Several studies have compared the efficacy of aspirin and NSAIDs in the treatment of traumatic injury, with equivocal results. Most of these studies are plagued with methodologic problems, such as the absence of double blinding, inadequate controls, and the use of subjective criteria as measurements of outcome.[4] Further studies are needed to determine if medication speeds recovery time for soft tissue injuries.

MANAGEMENT AFTER THE ACUTE PHASE

Use of RICE immediately following injury results in cessation of bleeding and control of inflammation and swelling within 72 hours. After this period, the main goal of therapy is to resolve the hematoma and edema and emphasize rehabilitation. Rehabilitation should include activities such as non-ballistic stretching, active range of motion, and strengthening exercises. These should be started as soon as possible to ensure stronger healing and quicker return to full activity. It has long been held that the application of heat to injuries in the subacute phase increases blood flow and thereby speeds removal of cellular debris and increases delivery of nutrients to healing tissue. More recently, cryostretch or cryokinetics (physical therapy immediately following cryotherapy) is being favored over heat and exercise in rehabilitation for soft tissue injuries.[12,14,21,32] The application of cold has the advantage of temporarily decreasing both pain and spasm. At least one study demonstrated that use of cold is more effective than heat in speeding return to full activity after injury.[15] This issue remains somewhat controversial, but there is a trend toward use of ice during the rehabilitation process as well as during the acute phase of soft tissue injuries.

Although not necessary with most injuries, modalities such as ultrasound and electronic galvanic stimulation may be employed in treating some athletes with certain injuries, providing that the athletes have access to the necessary equipment and the appropriate professionals knowledgeable in their use.[1] Massage therapy and manipulations are also useful in selected cases if performed by professionals trained in these areas.

Principles of Rehabilitation

Rehabilitation of the injured extremity begins when the risk of further bleeding is minimal, usually 48–72 hours after the injury. With a mild injury, this may begin as early as 24 hours after the injury. The goals of treatment then shift to the following:

1. Resolve the hematoma
2. Resolve the edema
3. Regain full range of motion or flexibility
4. Regain full muscle strength and endurance
5. Regain agility and coordination
6. Regain cardiovascular endurance

Ideally, a certified athletic trainer or physical therapist should be consulted to direct the rehabilitation program on a daily basis. In fact, in collegiate and professional sports, injured athletes often work on a rehabilitation program two or three times a day. This is not practical for the majority of adolescent athletes. However, it is helpful to consult an athletic trainer or physical therapist to teach the athlete a proper rehabilitation program for the injury. Many physicians do not have the time or the expertise to teach rehabilitation techniques to an athlete, yet other than acute treatment with RICE, rehabilitation is probably the most important aspect of treatment of soft tissue injuries for the competitive athlete.

One of the first exercises the athlete can work on following an injury is range of motion. Range-of-motion exercises are usually simple, isolated movement patterns used to regain normal range of motion in the injured joint. Initially, even the limited range of motion should be maintained with active movement. As the condition improves, active stretching can be added in the form of isometric or isokinetic exercises. Performing these exercises as early as possible helps to control edema, promotes removal of cellular debris and resorption of hematoma, and prevents functional shortening due to spasm and scar contracture.

Once range of motion is nearly normal, strengthening exercises should be initiated. Muscle atrophy and weakness occur following most soft tissue injuries. Regaining strength is not only important to athletic function, but is also important for preventing re-injury. Generally, some type of progressive resistance exercises should be performed. When strength is approaching 80–90% of normal, i.e., the strength of the normal side, repetitions should be increased to build endurance of the muscle groups.

Early in the process of rehabilitation, cardiovascular endurance should be addressed. Rest of the injured part need not mean resting the entire body. When there is a lower extremity injury, for example, the athlete may not be able to run, but can swim or bike. Providing alternative exercises not only helps the athlete physiologically, but also helps him or her psychologically to cope with the injury. The injured athlete, who tends to focus on the disability, can be encouraged by discussing what he or she *can* do safely during the process of healing to prepare for return to competition. This may include some sport-specific exercises to regain agility and skills important to the athlete's particular sport.

Return to Play

Full tissue healing of most soft tissue injuries may take 6 to 8 weeks. Fortunately, most athletes do not have to wait that long to return to athletic activity. How does one determine playability after soft tissue injury? Without objective criteria for return to play, the athlete and coach will be tempted to shortcut the rehabilitation process and risk re-injury. In general, the injured body part should have the following:

1. Full range of motion
2. Full strength
3. No swelling
4. No evidence of joint instability
5. No tenderness or pain with motion

The athlete should be able to perform the athletic activity without limping or favoring the injured part. Objective criteria take the guesswork out of the playability decision. They also give the athlete goals to work toward during rehabilitation. For most lower extremity injuries, a progressive running program is particularly useful (Table 5). The running program should not be started until the five criteria are met for function of the body part. The athlete should be able to hop up and down eight to ten times on the injured extremity without pain or limp. Similar progressive functional rehabilitation programs can be devised for other injuries and are best taught by certified athletic trainers or certified physical therapists.

TABLE 5. The Running Program

---

1. Jog ½ to 1 mile. Stop immediately if you are limping or if there is pain. Wait until tomorrow to start the program again. If there is no pain or limp during your jog, you may proceed to:
2. Six to eight 80-yard sprints at half speed. If no pain or limp, then do:
3. Six to eight 80-yard sprints at three-quarter speed. If no pain or limp, then do:
4. Six to eight 80-yard sprints at full speed, followed by four to six full-speed starts. If no pain or limp, then do:
5. Six to eight 80-yard cutting (changing directions) every 10 yards at half-speed. Then do:
6. Six to eight 80-yard cutting at full speed.

Each day start at the beginning of the program. After every workout, ice should be applied immediately to the injured area. (Don't stand around.) Once you can perform all of the above tasks with no pain and minimal swelling, you may return to competition. If you short-cut this program, you are only fooling yourself, risking reinjury or possibly a more serious injury and a much longer time out of competition.

Adapted from Landry GL: Sports Medicine. In Oski FA (ed): Principles and Practice of Pediatrics. Philadelphia, J.B. Lippincott, 1990 p 933.

SUMMARY

Most grade I and II soft tissue injuries can be managed by the primary care physician. Soft tissue injuries are best treated acutely using RICE (rest, ice, compression, and elevation). The use of anti-inflammatory medication in the management of soft tissue injuries is controversial. Early rehabilitation is important for return to sports activity, and playability should be determined using functional criteria.

ACKNOWLEDGMENT

We would like to thank Dan Campbell, PT, ATC, for his helpful comments.

References

1. Arnhim DD: Therapeutic modalities. In: Modern Principles of Athletic Training. St. Louis, Times Mirror/Mosby College Publishing, 1985, pp 339–360.
2. Backous DD, Friedl KE, Smith NJ, et al: Soccer injuries and their relation to physical maturity. Am J Dis Child 142:839–842, 1988.
3. Carlstedt CA, Nordin M: Biomechanics of tendons and ligaments. In Nordin M, Frankel VH (eds): Basic Biomechanics of the Musculoskeletal System. Philadelphia, Lea & Febiger, 1989, pp 59–74.
4. Clyman B: Role of non-steroidal anti-flammatory drugs in sports medicine. Sports Med 3:242–246, 1986.
5. Cyriax J: Textbook of Orthopaedic Medcine, 8th ed. London, Balliere Tindall, 1982, pp 14–19.
6. DeVrieś H: Quantitative electromyographic investigation of the spasm theory of muscle pain. Am J Phys Med 45:119–134, 1966.
7. Evans P: The healing process at cellular level: A review. Physiotherapy 66:256–259, 1980.
8. Farry PJ, Prentice NG, Hunter AC, et al: Ice treatment of injured ligaments: An experimental model. NZ J Med 91:12–14, 1980.
9. Fisher BD, Baracos VE, Shnitka TK, et al: Ultrastructural events following acute muscle trauma. Med Sci Sports Exerc 22:185–193, 1990.
10. Frank CB, Woo SL: Clinical biomechanics of sports injuries. In Nahum AM, Melvin J (eds): The Biomechanics of Trauma. Norwalk, CT, Appleton-Century-Crofts, 1985, pp 181–203.
11. Gallagher SS, Finison K, Guyer B: The incidence of injuries among 87,000 Massachusetts children and adolescents: Results of the 1980–81 statewide childhood injury prevention program surveillance system. Am J Pub Health 74:1340–1346, 1984.
12. Grant AE: Massage with ice (cryokinetics) in the treatment of painful conditions of the musculoskeletal system. Arch Phys Med Rehab 45:233–238, 1964.
13. Guyer B, Berenholz G, Galagher SS: Injury surveillance using hospital discarded abstracts coded by external cause of injury (E Code). J Trauma 30:470–473, 1990.
14. Halvorson GA: Therapeutic heat and cold for athletic injuries. Phys Sports Med 18:87–94, 1990.
15. Hocutt JE, Jaffe R, Rylander CR: Cryotherapy in ankle sprains. Am J Sports Med 10:316, 1982.
16. Hodge NA: Athletic injuries and the use of medication. In Torg JS, Welsh RP, Shephard RJ (eds): Current Therapy in Sports Medicine. St. Louis, C.V. Mosby Co., 1990, pp 178–182.
17. Jackson DW, Feagin JA: Quadriceps contusions in young athletes. Relation of severity of injury to treatment and prognosis. J Bone Joint Surg 55A:95–105, 1973.
18. Kellett J: Acute soft tissue injuries—a review of the literature. Med Sci Sports Exerc 18:489–500, 1986.
19. Kennedy JC, Hawkins RJ, Willis RB: Tension studies in human knee ligaments. J Bone Joint Surg 58A:350–355, 1976.
20. Knight KL, Londeree BR: Comparison of blood flow in the ankle of uninjured subjects during therapeutic applications of heat, cold, and exercise. Med Sci Sports Exerc 12:76–80, 1980.
21. Knight KL: Cryotherapy: Theory, Technique, and Physiology. Chattanooga, Chattanooga Corp., 1985, chapters 7 and 10.
22. Lachman S: Soft Tissue Injuries in Sport. Boston, Blackwell Scientific, 1988, pp 7–32.
23. Laing DR, Dalley DR, Kirk JA: Ice therapy in soft tissue injuries. NZ Med J 78:155–158, 1973.

24. Lehman JF, de Lateur BJ: Cryotherapy. In Lehman JF (ed): Therapeutic Heat and Cold. Baltimore, Williams & Wilkins, 1990, pp 605–607.
25. Matsen FA, Questad K, Matsen AL: The effect of local cooling on post fracture swelling. A controlled study. Clin Orthop 109:201–206, 1975.
26. McLain LG, Reynolds S: Sports injuries in a high school. Pediatrics 84:446–450, 1989.
27. McMaster WC: A literary review on ice therapy in injuries. Am J Sports Med 5:124–126, 1977.
28. McMaster WC, Liddle S, Waugh TR: Laboratory evaluation of various cold therapy modalities. Am J Sports Med 6:291–294, 1978.
29. Meeusen R, Lievens P: The use of cryotherapy in sports injuries. Sports Med 3:398–414, 1986.
30. Olson JE, Stravino VD: A review of cryotherapy. PhysTher 52:840–853, 1972.
31. Paulson JA: The epidemiology of injuries in adolescents. Pediatr Ann 17:84–86, 1988.
32. Prentice WE: An electromyographic analysis of the effectiveness of heat or cold and stretching for inducing relaxation in injured muscle. J Orthop Sports Phys Ther 3:133–140.
33. Robbins SL, Cotran RS: Pathologic Basis of Disease, 2nd ed. Philadelphia, W.B. Saunders, 1979, pp 55–106.
34. Ryan AJ, Allman FL (eds): Sports Medicine. San Diego, Academic Press, 1989, pp 81–92.
35. Sheps SB, Evans GD: Epidemiology of school injuries: A 2-year experience in a municipal health department. Pediatrics 79:69–75, 1987.
36. Sloan JP, Giddings P, Hain R: Effects of cold and compression on edema. Phys Sportsmed 16:116–120, 1988.
37. Starkey JA: Treatment of ankle sprains by simultaneous use of intermittent compression and ice packs. Sports Med 4:142–144, 1976.
38. Thorsson O, Lilja B, Ahigren L: The effect of local cold application on intramuscular blood flow at rest and after running. Med Sci Sports Exerc 17:710–713, 1985.
39. Tipton CM: The influence of physical activity on ligaments and tendons. Med Sci Sports Exerc 7:165–175, 1975.
40. Vailas AC, Tipton CM, Matthes RD, et al: Physical activity and its influence on the repair process of medial collateral ligaments. Connect Tissue Res 9:25–31, 1981.

Minor Head Injuries in Sports

ROBERT C. CANTU, M.D., F.A.C.S., F.A.C.S.M.

Chief, Neurosurgery Service
Chairman, Department of
  Surgery
Director, Service of Sports
  Medicine
Emerson Hospital
Concord, Massachusetts

Reprint requests to:
Robert C. Cantu, M.D.
Emerson Hospital
Old Rd. to Nine Acre Corner
Concord, MA 01742

The brain and spinal cord are incapable of regeneration. Although many parts of the body now can be replaced by organ transplantation or artificial hardware, this is not possible for the brain. Brain injuries are one of the most common catastrophic athletic injuries and the leading cause of athletic death.

According to the catastrophic sports injury registry, sports that have the greatest chance of causing catastrophic head injury per 100,000 participants include football, gymnastics, ice hockey, and wrestling.[6] In football, the use of the head in making a tackle is the most common cause of head injury; in gymnastics, it is the dismount in which one accidentally lands on the head; in wrestling, it is landing on the head in the process of the take-down; and in ice hockey, it is striking the boards head first. Other school sports that entail a significant chance for head injury include the pole-vault in track and the head-first slide in baseball. Other sporting activities with significant risk for head injury include equestrian sports, especially horse racing,[3,4] as well as motorcycle, automobile, and boat racing,[5,7] sky diving,[19,28] boxing,[30] the martial arts,[25] and rugby.[24]

Sports that carry a risk for catastrophic head injury pose an even greater risk for minor head injuries. Football, because it is participated in by more than 1.5 million high-school and college athletes, causes more minor

ADOLESCENT MEDICINE: State of the Art Reviews—Vol. 2, No. 1, February 1991
Philadelphia, Hanley & Belfus, Inc.

141

head injuries than any other single sport. The incidence is estimated to be 250,000 per year or approximately 20%.[10]

MECHANISMS OF HEAD INJURY

Biomechanical Forces That Affect the Brain

An understanding of three principles is necessary in order to comprehend how biomechanical forces produce skull and brain injury. A forceful blow to the resting movable head usually produces maximal brain injury beneath the point of cranial impact (coup injury). This is the situation when the head in a resting state is forcibly struck by another object such as a left hook or an opponent's football helmet.[2] A moving head colliding with a nonmoving object usually produces maximal brain injury opposite the site of cranial impact (contra-coup injury). An example is an individual falling over backward, striking the head on the ground at the instant of impact. If a skull fracture is present, the first two dictums do not pertain, because the bone itself, either transiently (linear skull fracture) or permanently (depressed skull fracture), is displaced at the moment of impact and may directly injure brain tissue.

An understanding of the mechanisms of brain injury requires a realization that there are three distinct types of stresses that can be generated by an applied force. The first is compressive, the second is tensile (opposite of compressive and sometimes called negative pressure), and the third is shearing (a force applied parallel to a surface). Uniform compressive stresses are well tolerated by neural tissue but shearing forces are extremely poorly tolerated.

The brain has its own cushioning and protective shock absorber—the cerebrospinal fluid (CSF). The CSF essentially converts focally applied external stress to compressive stress because the fluid follows the contours of the sulci and gyri and distributes the force in a uniform fashion. Without CSF, compressive forces would be received by gyri crests but not in the depths of the sulci, thus potentiating a greater degree of the damaging shearing forces.

The CSF, however, does not totally prevent shearing forces from being imparted to the brain, especially when rotational forces are applied to the head and shearing forces occur at those sites where rotational gliding is hindered. Characteristically there are three such sites: (1) the dura mater–brain attachments impeding brain motion such as the midline falx cerbri and the tentorium cerebelli; (2) the rough irregular surface contacts between the brain and skull that hinder smooth movement and are especially prominent in the floor of the frontal and middle fossa; (3) dissipation of CSF between the brain and skull. This third condition explains the mechanisms of coup and contra-coup injuries. When the head is accelerated prior to impact, the brain lags toward the trailing surface, thus squeezing away the protective CSF and allowing excess CSF to accumulate in the opposite surface. This allows the shearing forces to be maximal at the site where CSF is thinnest and thus has its least cushioning effect, which is opposite the site of impact. On the other hand, when the head is stationary prior to impact, there is neither brain lag nor disproportionate distribution of CSF. In this situation, the shearing stresses are greatest at the site of cranial impact and explain the mechanism of the coup injury.

In understanding how acceleration forces are applied to the brain, it is important to keep in mind Newton's law: force = mass × acceleration, or, stated another way, force/mass = acceleration. An athlete's head can sustain far greater forces without injury if the neck muscles are tensed, such as when the athlete sees the collision coming. In the relaxed state, the mass of the head is essentially its own weight, whereas in the tensed state the mass of the head takes on an approximation of the mass of the body. Therefore, as the mass of the head increases, the forces must also increase to produce the same amount of acceleration. The athlete is at greatest risk for brain injury when the neck is limp, such as when one does not see the blow coming or when one is stunned (a boxer with concussion) and cannot maintain neck muscle rigidity.

TYPES OF HEAD INJURY

While the focus of this chapter is minor head injuries, no discussion of head injury is complete without mention of intracranial hemorrhage, malignant brain edema syndrome, and postconcussion syndrome. Intracranial hemorrhage is the leading cause of death in athletes today,[36] as shown by Schneider many years ago.[32-35] Acute subdural hematoma accounts for most athletic head injury deaths.[32,36]

Epidural Hematoma

Recognition of an epidural hematoma is especially important because usually there is no associated brain injury and death results from the mass effect of the rapidly expanding blood producing brain herniation. This condition most commonly occurs with a temporal skull fracture that crosses the middle meningeal groove and tears the middle meningeal artery in its course through the bony skull. This lesion may be associated with a brief period of unconsciousness, but there is usually a lucid period thereafter, before there is a precipitous deterioration in state of consciousness to coma and death, often only in a matter of 15–30 minutes. A typical example is a baseball player who is struck on the temple by a thrown ball and is stunned or even briefly unconscious. He regains full alertness after several minutes and walks off the field. Within a matter of 15–30 minutes, he develops an excruciatingly severe headache above and beyond that experienced from the initial blow. The headache is accompanied by a progressive deterioration in state of consciousness from fully alert, to stupor, to coma over 15–20 minutes. During this time, the dura is being stripped away from the inner table of the skull by the rapidly expanding epidural blood clot, and unless extremely prompt neurosurgical intervention is afforded, death will result. What is particularly tragic about death from an epidural hematoma is that the brain itself is usually not significantly injured. If the hematoma can be recognized and treated, a completely normal neurologic outcome is to be anticipated.

Subdural Hematoma

A subdural hematoma continues to carry a 30–40% mortality rate even at the finest of neurosurgical centers. This is not because the lesion cannot be successfully removed, but because this lesion is commonly associated with extreme degrees of brain disruption. The severe associated brain injury causes death in a significant percentage of these cases. In most instances of subdural hematoma, the need for neurosurgical attention is obvious, because the patient is usually rendered unconscious at the time of the injury and remains unconscious. Occasionally, however, a football player or boxer may regain consciousness after the initial concussion, walk off the playing field or out of the ring only to collapse shortly thereafter from a rapidly evolving subdural hematoma and associated brain swelling. It is for this reason that all athletes should be observed closely for at least 24 hours after having been rendered unconscious and, if headache persists, more definitive neurologic observation with a CT scan or MRI is appropriate.

Intracerebral Hematoma

An intracerebral hematoma usually occurs deep within the brain and is associated with an extremely severe acceleration injury to the head. More commonly than not, consciousness is not regained unless the lesion is small. If conscious, the patient will have a severe attendant headache, and the need for neurosurgical and neuroradiographic evaluation with CT scan or MRI is obvious.

Subarachnoid Hemorrhage

Subarachnoid hemorrhage may result from a ruptured congenital vascular lesion such as an aneurysm, an arteriovenous malformation, or a cryptic arteriovenous malformation. There may or may not be a lucid period, and neurologic deterioration even to the point of death may be extremely rapid. When death occurs, fellow athletes, family, students, and even the community at large often become swept up in an intense grief reaction. It is imperative to obtain a complete autopsy in order to determine whether the cause of death was other than the presumed and ultimately unavoidable congenital anomaly. Only by such a full, factual investigation and elucidation will inappropriate feelings of guilt in fellow athletes, friends, and family be assuaged.

Malignant Brain Edema Syndrome

This condition occurs in the adolescent or pediatric athlete and consists of a rapid neurologic deterioration from an alert conscious state to coma and often death within minutes to several hours after in incident of head trauma.[29,37] While such a sequence would be much more typical of an epidural hematoma in an adult, in children and adolescents the pathologic injury is diffuse brain swelling with little or no brain tissue disruption.[1] Langfitt et al.[20,21] have shown that diffuse cerebral swelling is actually a result of a true hyperemia or vascular engorgement. Prompt recognition is extremely important because there is little initial brain injury and the serious or fatal neurologic outcome is secondary to increased intracranial pressure with brain herniation. Treatment includes prompt intubation, hyperventilation, and osmotic diuretics. These measures have helped to reduce mortality, which still remains high.

MINOR HEAD INJURIES

It is stated by some neurologists and neurosurgeons that there is no such thing as minor head injury. Evidence is surfacing that the ability to process new information may be reduced after a minor head injury,[11] and the severity and duration of functional impairment may be greater with repeated head injuries.[11-15] Although these findings have not been universally confirmed or accepted, studies definitely suggest that the effects of minor head injuries such as concussion may be cumulative. A cerebral concussion may produce shearing injury to nerve fibers and neurons in proportion to the degree the brain is accelerated.[8-12,27,31,35,38] Furthermore, it has been shown that after a player has suffered an initial cerebral concussion, the chances of incurring a second concussion may be as great as four times higher than for the individual who has never incurred a cerebral concussion. Another cause for concern is the so-called **second impact syndrome**, reported by Saunders and Harbaugh[31] and by Schneider in his classic book.[35] In this condition, which is limited to adults, fatal brain swelling occurs following minor head trauma in individuals who still have symptoms from a prior head injury. It is thought that auto-regulation of the brain is lost, resulting in catastrophic cerebral edema. The neurotransmitter substances within the brain have not yet returned to normal following a prior head injury. Despite hyperventilation and osmotic diuretics, this condition carries a 50% mortality rate. With these sobering facts in mind, it is clear that no head injury can truly be regarded as minor and all require prompt evaluation and decision making before return to competition is allowed.

Cerebral Concussion

There is no universal agreement on the definition of a concussion or on the various grades or severity of concussion. This fact renders evaluation of epidemiologic data in the literature extremely difficult. One working definition of concussion that has gained a degree of acceptance is the one proposed by the Committee of Head Injury Nomenclature of the Congress of Neurological Surgeons.[18] Concussion is defined by this body as "a clinical syndrome characterized by immediate and transient post-traumatic impairment of neural functions, such as alteration of consciousness, disturbance of vision, equilibrium, etc. due to brain stem involvement."[8] Others have defined concussion on the basis of duration of unconsciousness, whereas others have used the duration of post-traumatic amnesia in the grading of concussion.

TABLE 1.   Severity of Concussion

Grade	Loss of Consciousness		Duration of Post-traumatic Amnesia
I (mild)	None		Less than 30 minutes
II (moderate)	Less than 5 minutes	or	30 minutes or greater but less than 24 hours
III (severe)	5 minutes or greater	or	24 hours or more

Based on my many years as a team physician and neurosurgeon, caring for many athletes who have suffered cerebral concussions, in 1986 I developed a practical scheme for grading the severity of a cerebral concussion using both the duration of unconsciousness and/or retrograde of post-traumatic amnesia (Table 1). These definitions are quite readily applied to the playing field environment.

In Grade 1 cerebral concussion, which is certainly the most common (more than 90% of concussions), there is no loss of consciousness and the period of post-traumatic amnesia lasts less than 30 minutes. It is often difficult for the physician on the sideline to recognize that the player has sustained a concussion. The word "ding" is commonly applied to this concussion, in which an athlete seems to lose orientation but does not lose consciousness. For example, a football player may lose the snap count or lose track of what play is called. It is often a fellow athlete who senses the problem and brings the player to medical attention.

A Grade 2 or moderate cerebral concussion is usually associated with loss of consciousness for less than 5 minutes or a period of post-traumatic amnesia that lasts more than 30 minutes but less than 24 hours. Such a cerebral concussion, especially when it involves the loss of consciousness, is not difficult for the physician to recognize.

A Grade 3 or severe concussion is one in which the period of unconsciousness is greater than 5 minutes or in which the patient's post-traumatic amnesia lasts greater than 24 hours. This concussion is obviously not difficult to recognize. The initial treatment should be the same as for an individual in whom a cervical spine fracture is suspected: the neck should be immobilized either until the athlete regains consciousness and clearly indicates he does not have a neck injury or until cervical spine x-rays eliminate the possibility of a cervical fracture. Until a severe concussion has been ruled out, the athlete should be transported on a fracture board, with the head and neck immobilized, to a hospital where neurosurgical facilities are available. All athletes with severe concussions should be admitted for neurologic observation and neuroradiographic evaluation for possible intracranial bleeding.

Incidence.   In football, concussions most often occur while the player is making a tackle (43%), being tackled (23%), blocking (20%), or being blocked (10%).[10] In football, head injuries are twice as frequent as neck injuries, with nearly 9 of 10 being a cerebral concussion.[1] One of five high-school varsity football athletes can anticipate receiving a cerebral concussion each season.[10] This reported incidence of cerebral concussion may be low, as many athletes do not associate a brief loss of awareness or a few minutes of amnesia with a cerebral concussion. A comment from a player that "the coach took me out of the game to see if I had a concussion, but I did not" is not unique. In addition, the athlete, in his desire to play, may minimize symptoms. He often will not bring the symptoms of minor concussions to medical attention. Because a "second impact catastrophic brain injury" may follow a concussion, accurate documentation and treatment are of paramount importance.[31,35,36]

Recognition and Management. A Grade 3 cerebral concussion (profound loss of consciousness lasting over 5 minutes) is certainly obvious. It is mandatory that initial treatment be the same as for a suspected cervical spine fracture. Once one is certain that the airway is adequate, the athlete should be transported on a fracture board with the head and neck immobilized to a hospital with neurosurgery coverage.

In sports in which the athlete is wearing a helmet, as long as the airway is adequate, the helmet should not be removed. When there is any question about the adequacy of an airway, the athlete should be log-rolled to the face-up position with the head and neck immobilized on the spine board and the face mask removed with a bolt cutter or knife, depending on how it is affixed to the helmet (Fig. 1). If there is still concern that the airway is inadequate or that breathing is impaired, the helmet should be removed with the neck in a neutral position (neither flexed nor extended) (Fig. 2). The **jaw-thrust technique** is the safest first approach to opening the airway of a victim who is unconscious and suspected of having had a neck injury. This technique usually can be accomplished by grasping the angles of the victim's lower jaw and lifting with both hands, one on each side, displacing the mandible forward

FIGURE 1. The log roll. (From Halpern BC: Injuries and emergencies on the field. In Mellion MB, Walsh WM, Shelton GL (eds): The Team Physician's Handbook. Philadelphia, Hanley & Belfus, 1990, p 129, with permission.)

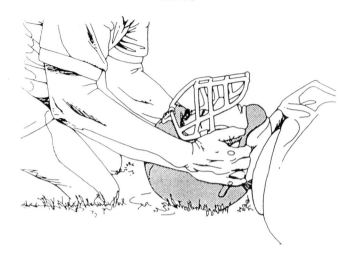

FIGURE 2. In-line traction to maintain the head and neck in neutral position. (From Halpern BC: Injuries and emergencies on the field. In Mellion MB, Walsh WM, Shelton GL (eds): The Team Physician's Handbook. Philadelphia, Hanley & Belfus, 1990, p 129, with permission.)

while tilting the head slightly backward. The rescuer's elbow should rest on the surface upon which the victim is lying.

If the jaw-thrust technique is not adequate to establish the airway, the head tilt–jaw lift should be substituted and care taken not to overextend the neck. The fingers of one hand are placed under the lower jaw on the bony part near the chin and lifted to bring the chin forward, supporting the jaw and helping to tilt the head back. The fingers must not compress the soft tissue under the chin, which might obstruct the airway. The other hand presses on the victim's forehead to tilt the head slightly in extension.

For a Grade 3 cerebral concussion, once at the medical facility, x-rays should be taken of the cervical spine in initially the lateral view with flexion and extension if necessary to determine if there is a cervical spine fracture. Also, a CT scan of the head should be done in most situations and repeated if neurologic symptoms of headache, nausea, vomiting, visual impairment, or disequilibrium have not abated within the first 12–24 hours. It is not unusual for microscopic hemorrhages to coalesce, forming a brain contusion that is readily apparent on follow-up CT scan but not visible on the initial admitting head CT scan. Such lesions are more readily apparent early on with MRI scans of the brain. It is recommended that all patients with severe cerebral concussions be admitted for neurologic observation for possible intracranial bleeding.[17,22]

With a Grade 2 or moderate concussion (period of unconsciousness less than 5 minutes and/or a period of retrograde amnesia longer than 30 minutes but less than 24 hours), the initial management is as for a Grade 3 concussion. Here, though, clinical judgment may dictate that if the period of unconsciousness is brief and if the now-conscious athlete has no neck complaints, removal on a fracture board may not be necessary. It is recommended that the athlete be removed from the game and undergo a thorough neurologic evaluation at a neurosurgery-staffed medical facility. If indicated, skull and cervical spine x-rays should be performed, and head CT done if neurologic symptoms warrant. Head CT or MRI scans should certainly be obtained if there is significant headache or any suggestion of obtundation.

Grade 1 or mild concussion is the most difficult to recognize and requires the greatest clinical judgment. There is no lapse of consciousness but rather impairment of cortical function, especially for recent memory, and in assimilating and interpreting new information, which leads to the syndrome of retrograde or post-traumatic amnesia. Retrograde amnesia is defined as a period in which these symptoms are less than 30 minutes in duration and often only a fleeting few minutes. This most frequent grade of concussion not infrequently escapes medical recognition.[9] It is not uncommon for a player to be "dinged" or have his "bell rung" and continue playing. Dave Meggyesy, a professional football player turned author, described this condition as "your memory is affected, although you can still walk around and sometimes continue playing. If you do not feel pain, the only way other players and the coaches know you have been 'dinged' is when they realize you cannot remember the plays."[26]

The initial treatment involves removing the player from the athletic contest and observing him on the bench. When the athlete has no headache, dizziness, or impaired concentration after a brief period of time, and has full recall of events without any persistent retrograde amnesia, then in selected instances return to the contest may be considered.[23,40] If any neurologic symptoms persist, either at rest or on exertion, including retrograde amnesia, then return to the contest is not appropriate. Prior to return to play, in those few instances when it is considered, the athlete should not only be asymptomatic at rest but also should demonstrate that he can move with his usual dexterity and speed. If the athlete has any neurologic symptoms or signs on exertion, he should not be allowed back into the contest. With a Grade 1 concussion, close neurologic observation is necessary for several hours. Often it is not necessary to admit the individual to a medical facility when all symptoms cease within a span of minutes to an hour.

Return to Competition After a Concussion

As for the definition of concussion, there are no universally accepted criteria for when to allow the athlete to return to competition. In 1986, in *The Physician and Sportsmedicine,* I addressed this issue, and those recommendations are summarized in Table 2. I want to make it perfectly clear that these are guidelines for return to competition in contact sports after a cerebral concussion based on both the world's literature and on my experience of more than 25 years as a neurosurgeon and football team physician. The final decision in every instance is a clinical judgment. This chapter is meant to serve only as a guideline. Deviation based on the clinical judgment of the treating physician may be entirely appropriate. When dealing with the scholar athlete,

TABLE 2.   Guidelines for Return to Play after Concussion

	First Concussion	Second Concussion	Third Concussion
Grade 1 (mild)	May return to play if asymptomatic* for 1 week	Return to play in 2 weeks if asymptomatic at that time for 1 week	Terminate season; may return to play next season if asymptomatic
Grade 2 (moderate)	Return to play after asymptomatic for 1 week	Minimum of 1 month; may return to play then if asymptomatic for 1 week; consider terminating season	Terminate season; may return to play next season if asymptomatic
Grade 3 (severe)	Minimum of 1 month; may then return to play if asymptomatic for 1 week	Terminate season; may return to play next season if asymptomatic	

* Asymptomatic means no headache, dizziness, or impaired orientation, concentration, or memory during rest or exertion.

one can never be faulted for being too conservative, especially when the results of a mistake can be so catastrophic (i.e., the "second impact syndrome").

A sobering influence is the realization that the ability to process new information may be reduced after a cerebral concussion, and the severity and duration of functional impairment may be greater with repeated concussions.[11,12,39] There are clearly studies that suggest that the damaging effects of the shearing injury to nerve fibers and neurons is proportional to the degree the head is accelerated, and that these changes[9,27,38] are cumulative. Studies[10] also suggest that once a player has incurred an initial cerebral concussion, his chances of incurring a second one are four times greater than the athlete who has never sustained a concussion.

The following recommendations for return to competition following a cerebral concussion are based on the grade of concussion and prior incidence of concussion. While from a medical standpoint the same standards should apply to both the high-school and college athlete, with professional athletes the implementation may not be as strict for obvious reasons.

Return After a Grade 3 Concussion.   Following a Grade 3 concussion, the athlete is held out of competition for at least 1 month and may return to play then only if asymptomatic at rest and upon exertion for the prior 7 days. Two Grade 3 concussions should terminate a player's season. Three Grade 3 concussions should raise considerable deliberations as to whether the individual should be allowed to return to any contact or collision sport. An athlete who has intracranial surgery for removal of a blood clot or has developed post-traumatic hydrocephalus should not be allowed to return to contact or collision sports. A working scheme for the number and severity of concussions and disposition is provided in Table 3.

TABLE 3.   Number and Severity of Concussions in Single Season that Preclude Future Participation That Season

Grade 1	Grade 2	Grade 3
3	2 or 3	1 or 2

Return to Competition After a Grade 2 Cerebral Concussion.
Following an initial Grade 2 cerebral concussion, the athlete may return to competition within 2 weeks if asymptomatic at rest and upon exertion for the prior 7 days. After a second Grade 2 concussion in the same season, return should be deferred for at least 1 month and termination of future participation for that season at least considered. A third Grade 2 concussion would terminate the season. An athlete with a history of three Grade 2 concussions in 1 year or over several seasons should have serious deliberations as to whether to continue in a contact or collision sport. CT or MRI abnormalities caused by trauma should preclude future participation in contact or collision sports, although they would not preclude competition in a non-collision sport such as golf or track.

Return to Competition After a Grade 1 Concussion. Following an initial Grade 1 concussion, if the athlete, after a suitable period of observation on the bench, is asymptomatic both at rest and exertion and has no evidence of retrograde amnesia, in a small number of select situations return to the contest may be permissible. For most Grade 1 concussions, though, removal from the contest is recommended, and it is definitely recommended in all instances in which retrograde amnesia persists and/or in which there are cerebral symptoms of headache, lightheadedness, or difficulty with disequilibrium. Return following an initial Grade 1 concussion may be as soon as 1 week if the individual has remained asymptomatic both at rest and upon exertion during that week. If a second Grade 1 concussion occurs during the same season, the individual is withheld from competition for at least 2 weeks and then may return only if asymptomatic both at rest and upon exertion for the immediately preceding 7 days. If headache or other associated neurologic symptoms occur or worsen in the first 24 hours or persist longer than 24 hours, a head CT is recommended. Magnetic resonance scanning is even more sensitive than the head CT and, if available, may be preferable, especially in detecting inferior frontal lobe and temporal lobe contusion or edema. The EEG has not been found to be a sensitive indicator of minor neuronal dysfunction following minor head injury. After a second concussion, a thorough review of the circumstances resulting in the concussion should be analyzed, if not already done after the first concussion. If available, video tapes or game films should be reviewed by the player, coach, and trainer. It should be determined if the player was using his head unwisely, illegally, or both. This review should also include assessment of the player's equipment in terms of whether he was wearing it correctly and whether it fit and was correctly maintained. This is especially true of the air pressure in air helmets in the sport of football. Finally, neck strength and development should be assessed. A player with three Grade 1 concussions in one season should not be allowed to continue for that season and should not be allowed to play a contact or collision sport in the season immediately following. Two seasons (not two years) removed, that individual could return to contact or collision sports if he remains asymptomatic. For instance, an individual who has been caused to refrain from football because of three Grade 1 concussions in the fall could return to a spring collision sport such as lacrosse if asymptomatic during the winter.

Post-concussion Syndrome

This syndrome consists of headache, especially upon exertion, dizziness, fatigue, irritability, and especially impaired memory and concentration. In this author's experience, the syndrome is not uncommon. Persistence of symptoms reflects altered neurotransmitter function[17] and usually correlates with the period of post-traumatic amnesia.[16] When symptoms persist, the athlete should be evaluated with CT scan and/or MRI and neuropsychiatric tests. Return to competition must be deferred until all symptoms have abated lest the athlete be put at risk for the "second impact syndrome." Return to competition should also be deferred until all neurologic symptoms have abated and all diagnostic studies are normal.

PREVENTION OF HEAD INJURIES

Unlike the musculoskeletal system, the brain cannot be conditioned to accept trauma. In fact, the reverse is true: once injured, the brain may be more susceptible to future injury.[10] Nonetheless, there are five main areas where we can work to effect a reduction in head injuries.

The first is in the area of improved medical care, especially in on-the-field recognition and treatment of head injuries. Also, by understanding when it is safe to return to competition following a head injury, the risk of catastrophic head injury is lessened.

A second area is the need for improved conditioning, especially of the neck. Although there are no absolute guarantees against head injury, as discussed under the mechanisms section, the best prevention is a strong neck and wise use of the head.

Equipment is a third area, as improved protective head gear, properly fitted and maintained, can reduce the incidence of head injury. This includes the need periodically to discard worn equipment.

Changes in rules and coaching techniques are the last two areas, and football is the classic example. When it was clearly understood that the use of the head as a battering ram in tackling was the cause of most serious head and neck injuries, the tactic was made illegal in the 1976 rules changes. Since then, responsible coaches have stopped teaching this tactic and have even warned against its use. As a result, the incidence of serious head and neck injury has significantly (approximately 50%) dropped since the mid-1970s.[6]

CONCLUSION

1. Additional data on concussion are needed. The adoption of a uniform definition is also desirable to allow interpretation of the data from multiple reports in the literature.

2. A continued aggressive educational effort directed at athletic trainers, coaches, and team physicians is needed. These individuals often lack special training in the recognition of injuries, especially minor head injuries and their associated symptoms.

3. After a cerebral concussion, the rapid processing and recall of new information may be impaired. For athletes who play positions in which such functioning is of highest importance (such as quarterbacks), return to competition may be delayed longer than the guidelines expressed in this chapter. This characteristic of concussion also explains why the delay in returning the athlete to certain noncontact but high-risk pursuits such as hang-gliding or automobile racing may also be longer than for contact sports.

4. More research on the cumulative effects of concussion is needed. In practicing neurosurgery for more than 25 years, most of it as a team physician, I have noted that once an athlete has fully recovered from a cerebral concussion, a subsequent concussion usually does not occur or is not necessarily more severe. I have found that the improper use of the head is most commonly associated with repeated concussions, not that an individual's brain is inherently more susceptible to concussion.

5. The guidelines expressed in this chapter should be regarded as minimums for return to competition. Many athletes, especially those who are slow, of limited dexterity, or slight of build, should consider terminating a season or dropping a contact sport in favor of a noncontact pursuit after only a single concussion. In my experience these athletes are most prone to injury in contact sports, and if they have little chance for success in the future, the risk of injury may be unwarranted. Obviously if these athletes grow and mature and the above characteristics no longer apply, then return to a contact sport at a later date is not precluded. In every instance when making such decisions with the athlete-patient, I attempt to have both parents present during the discussion of these issues, as the motivation for participation in the first place may not have entirely originated with the athlete.

References

1. Adams H, Graham DI: Pathology of blunt head injuries. In Critchley M, O'Leary JL, Jennet B (eds): Scientific Foundations of Neurology. Philadelphia, F.A. Davis, 1972, pp 478–491.
2. Albright JP, McAuley E, Martin RK, et al: Head and neck injuries in college football: An eight year analysis. Am J Sports Med 13:147–152, 1985.
3. Barber HM: Horse-play: Survey of accidents with horses. Br Med J 3:532–534, 1973.
4. Barclay WR: Equestrian sports. JAMA 240:1892–1893, 1978.
5. Bodnar LM: Sports medicine with reference to back and neck injuries. Curr Pract Orthop Surg 7:116–153, 1977.
6. Cantu RC, Mueller F: Catastrophic spine injury in football 1977–1989. J Spinal Dis Sept 1990.
7. Clarke K, Braslow A: Football fatalities: Actuarial perspective. Med Sci Sports Exerc 10:94, 1979.
8. Committee on Head Injury Nomenclature of the Congress of Neurological Surgeons: Glossary of head injury, including some definitions of injury to the cervical spine. Clin Neurosurg 12:386–394, 1966.
9. Gennarelli TA, Segawa H, Wald U, et al: Physiological response to angular acceleration of the head. In Grossman RG, Gildenberg PL (eds): Head Injury: Basic and Clinical Aspects. New York, Raven Press, 1982, pp 129–140.

10. Gerberich SG, Priest JD, Boen JR, et al: Concussion incidences and severity in secondary school varsity football playes. Am J Public Health 73:1370–1375, 1983.
11. Gronwall D, Wrightson P: Delayed recovery of intellectual function after minor head injury. Lancet 2:605–609, 1974.
12. Gronwall D, Wrightson P: Cumulative effect of concussion. Lancet 2:995–997, 1975.
13. Gronwall D: Paced auditory serial addition task: A measure of recovery from concussion. Perpet Mot Skills 4:367–373, 1977.
14. Gronwall D, Wrightson P: Duration of post-traumatic amnesia after mild head injury. J Clin Neuropsychol 2:51–60, 1985.
15. Gronwall D, Wrightson P: Memory and information processing capacity after closed head injury. J Neurol Neurosurg Psychiatry 44:889–895, 1981.
16. Guthkelch AN: Post-traumatic amnesia, post-concussional symptoms and accident neurosis. Eur Neurol 19:91–102, 1980.
17. Hugen Holtz H, Richard MT: Return to athletic competition following concussion. Can Med Assoc J 127:827–829, 1982.
18. Jennet B: Late effects of head injuries. In Critchley M, O'Leary JL, Jennet B (eds): Scientific Foundations of Neurology. Philadelphia, F.A. Davis, 1971, pp 441–451.
19. Krel FW: Parachuting for sport—study of 100 deaths. JAMA 194:264–268, 1965.
20. Langfitt TW, Kassell NF: Cerebral vasodilations produced by brainstem stimulation: Neurogenic control vs. autoregulation. Am J Physiol 215:90–97, 1978.
21. Langfitt TW, Tannenbaum HM, Kassell NF: The etiology of acute brain swelling following experimental head injury. J Neurosurg 24:47–56, 1966.
22. Lindsay KW, McLatchie G, Jennett B: Serious head injuries in sports. Br Med J 281:789–791, 1980.
23. Maroon JC, Steele PB, Berlin R: Football head and neck injuries: An update. Clin Neurosurg 27:414–429, 1980.
24. McCoy GF, Piggot J, Macafee AL, et al: Injuries of the cervical spine in schoolboy rugby football. J Bone Joint Surg 66B:500–503, 1984.
25. McLatchie GR, Davies JE, Caulley JH: Injuries in karate, a case for medical control. J Trauma 2:956–958, 1980.
26. Meggyesy D: Out of Their League. Berkeley, CA, Ramparts, 1970, p 125.
27. Peerless SJ, Rewcastle NB: Shear injuries of the brain. Can Med Assoc J 96:577–582, 1967.
28. Petras AF, Hoffman EP: Roentgenographic skeletal injury patterns in parachute jumping. Am J Sports Med 11:325–328, 1983.
29. Pickles W: Acute general edema of the brain in children with head injuries. N Engl J Med 241:607–611, 1950.
30. Putnam P: Going-going-gone. Sports Illustrated, June 6, 1983, pp 23–46.
31. Saunders RL, Harbaugh RE: The second impact in catastrophic contact-sports head trauma. JAMA 252:538–539, 1984.
32. Schneider RC, Reifel E, Crislor HO, Osterban B: Serious and fatal football injuries involving the head and spinal cord. JAMA 177:106–367, 1961.
33. Schneider RC, Charie G, Pantek H: The syndrome of acute central cervical spinal cord injury. J Neurosurg 11:546–577, 1954.
34. Schneider RC, Gosch HH, Norrell H: Vascular insufficiency and differential distortion of brain and cord caused by cervicomedullary football injuries. J Neurosurg 33:363–374, 1970.
35. Schneider RC: Head and Neck Injuries in Football. Baltimore, Williams & Wilkins, 1973.
36. Schneider RC, Kennedy JC, Plant ML: Sports Injuries. Baltimore, Williams & Wilkins, 1985.
37. Schnitker MT: A syndrome of cerebral concussion in children. J Pediatr 35:557–560, 1949.
38. Strick SJ: Shearing of nerve fibers as a cause of brain damage due to head injury. Lancet 2:443–448, 1961.
39. Symonds C: Concussion and its sequelae. Lancet 1:1–5, 1962.
40. Yarnell PR, Lynch S: The "ding" amnestic states in football trauma. Neurology 23:196–197, 1973.

Catastrophic Head and Neck Injuries

JOSEPH S. TORG, M.D.
THOMAS A. GENNARELLI, M.D.

Joseph S. Torg, M.D.
Professor of Orthopedic Surgery
Director, Sports Medicine Center
University of Pennsylvania School
of Medicine
Philadelphia, Pennsylvania

Thomas A. Gennarelli, M.D.
Professor of Neurosurgery
University of Pennsylvania School
of Medicine
Philadelphia, Pennsylvania

Reprint requests to:
Joseph S. Torg, M.D.
Sports Medicine Center
235 South 33rd Street
Philadelphia, PA 19104-6397

The purpose of this chapter is to present clear, concise guidelines for classification, evaluation, and emergency management of catastrophic injuries that occur to the head and neck as a result of participation in competitive and recreational activities.

Although all athletic injuries require careful attention, the evaluation and management of injuries to the head and neck should proceed with particular consideration. The actual or potential involvement of the nervous system creates a high-risk situation in which the margin for error is low. A proper diagnosis is imperative, but the clinical picture is not always representative of the seriousness of the injury at hand. An intracranial hemorrhage may initially present with minimal symptoms, yet follow a precipitous downhill course, whereas a less severe injury, such as neurapraxia of the brachial plexus that is associated with alarming paresthesias and paralysis, will resolve swiftly and allow for quick return to activity. Although the more severe injuries are rather infrequent, this low incidence coincidentally results in little, if any, management experience for the on-site medical staff.

Several principles should be considered by individuals responsible for athletes who may sustain injuries to the head and neck.[14]

1. The team physician or trainer should be designated as the person responsible for

ADOLESCENT MEDICINE: State of the Art Reviews—Vol. 2, No. 1, February 1991
Philadelphia, Hanley & Belfus, Inc.

155

supervising on-the-field management of the potentially serious injury. This person is the "captain" of the medical team.

2. Prior planning must ensure the availability of all necessary emergency equipment at the site of potential injury. At a minimum, this should include a spineboard, stretcher, and equipment necessary for the initiation and maintenance of cardiopulmonary resuscitation (CPR).

3. Prior planning must ensure the availability of a properly equipped ambulance, as well as a hospital equipped and staffed to handle emergency neurologic problems.

4. Prior planning must ensure immediate availability of a telephone for communicating with the hospital emergency room, ambulance, and other responsible individuals in case of an emergency.

Managing the unconscious or spine-injured athlete is a process that should not be done hastily or haphazardly. Being prepared to handle this situation is the best way to prevent actions that could convert a repairable injury into a catastrophe. Be sure that all the necessary equipment is readily accessible and in good operating condition, and that all assisting personnel have been trained to use it properly. On-the-job training in an emergency situation is inefficient at the least. Everyone should know what must be done beforehand, so that on a signal the game plan can be put into effect.

A means of transporting the athlete must be immediately available in a high-risk sport such as football and "on-call" in other sports. The medical facility must be alerted to the athlete's condition and estimated time of arrival so that adequate preparation can be made.

Having the proper equipment is an absolute must. A spineboard is essential (Fig. 1) and is the best means of supporting the body in a rigid position. It is somewhat like a full body splint. By splinting the body, the risk of aggravating a spinal cord injury, which must always be suspected in the unconscious athlete, is reduced. In football, bolt cutters and a sharp knife or scalpel are also essential in the event it becomes necessary to remove the face

FIGURE 1. A standard full-length spineboard made of ¾ inch plywood. Body straps are not shown. (From Torg JS (ed): Athletic Injuries to the Head, Neck and Face. Philadelphia, Lea & Febiger, 1982, with permission.)

mask. A telephone must be available to call for assistance and to notify the medical facility. Oxygen should be available and is usually carried by ambulance and rescue squads, although it is rarely required in an athletic setting. Rigid cervical collars and other external immobilization devices can be helpful if properly used. However, manual stabilization of the head and neck is recommended even if other means are available.

Properly trained personnel must know, first of all, who is in charge. Everyone should know how to perform CPR and how to move and transport the athlete. They should know where emergency equipment is located and how to use it, and the procedure for activating the emergency support system. Individuals should be assigned specific tasks beforehand, if possible, so that duplication of effort is eliminated. Being well prepared helps to alleviate indecisiveness and second-guessing.

Prevention of further injury is the single most important objective. Do not take any action that could possibly cause further damage. The first step should be to immobilize the head and neck by supporting them in a stable position (Fig. 2). Then, in the following order, check for breathing, pulse, and level of consciousness.

FIGURE 2. *A*, Athlete with suspected cervical spine injury may or may not be unconscious. However, all who are unconscious should be managed as though they had a significant neck injury. *B*, Immediate manual immobilization of the head and neck unit. First, check for breathing. (From Torg JS (ed): Athletic Injuries to the Head, Neck and Face. Philadelphia, Lea & Febiger, 1982, with permission.)

If the victim is breathing, simply remove the mouth guard, if present, and maintain the airway. It is necessary to remove the face mask only if the respiratory situation is threatened or unstable, or if the athlete remains unconscious for a prolonged period. Leave the chin strap on.

Once it is established that the athlete is breathing and has a pulse, evaluate the neurologic status. The level of consciousness, response to pain, pupillary response, and unusual posturing, flaccidity, rigidity, or weakness should be noted.

At this point, simply maintain the situation until transportation is available or until the athlete regains consciousness. If the athlete is face down when the ambulance arrives, change his position to face up by logrolling him onto a spineboard. Make no attempt to move him except to transport him or to perform CPR if it becomes necessary.

If the athlete is not breathing or stops breathing, the airway must be established. If he is face down, he must be brought to a face-up position. The safest and easiest way to accomplish this is to logroll the athlete into a face-up position. In an ideal situation the medical-support team is made up of five members: the leader, who controls the head and gives the commands only; three members to roll; and another member to help lift and carry when it becomes necessary. If time permits and the spineboard is on the scene, the athlete should be rolled directly onto it. However, breathing and circulation are much more important at this point.

With all medical-support team members in position, the athlete is rolled toward the assistants—one at the shoulders, one at the hips, and one at the knees. They must maintain the body in line with the head and spine during the roll. The leader maintains immobilization of the head by applying slight traction and by using the crossed-arm technique. This technique allows the arms to unwind during the roll (Fig. 3).

The face mask must be removed from the helmet before rescue breathing can be initiated. The type of mask that is attached to the helmet determines the method of removal. Bolt cutters are used with the older single- and double-bar masks. The newer masks that are attached with plastic loops should be removed by cutting the loops with a sharp knife or scalpel. Remove the entire mask so that it does not interfere with further rescue efforts (Fig. 4).

Once the mask has been removed, initiate rescue breathing following the current standards of the American Heart Association.

Once the athlete has been moved to a face-up position, quickly evaluate breathing and pulse. If there is still no breathing or if breathing has stopped, the airway must be established. The jaw-thrust technique is the safest first approach to opening the airway of a victim who has a suspected neck injury, because in most cases it can be accomplished by the rescuer grasping the angles of the victim's lower jaw and lifting with both hands, one on each side, displacing the mandible forward while tilting the head backward. The rescuer's elbows should rest on the surface on which the victim is lying (Fig. 5).

If the jaw thrust is not adequate, the head tilt–jaw lift should be substituted. Care must be exercised not to overextend the neck. The fingers of

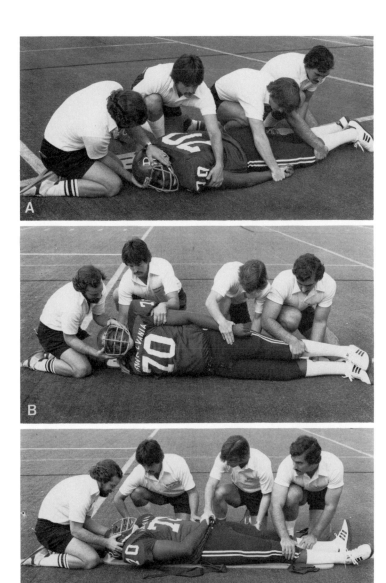

FIGURE 3. *A,* Logroll to a spineboard. This maneuver requires four individuals: the leader to immobilize the head and neck and to command the medical-support team; the remaining three individuals are positioned at the shoulders, hips, and lower legs. *B,* Logroll. The leader uses the cross-arm technique to immobilize the head. This technique allows the leader's arms to "unwind" as the three assistants roll the athlete onto the spineboard. *C,* Logroll. The three assistants maintain body alignment during the roll. (From Torg JS (ed): Athletic Injuries to the Head, Neck and Face. Philadelphia, Lea & Febiger, 1982, with permission.)

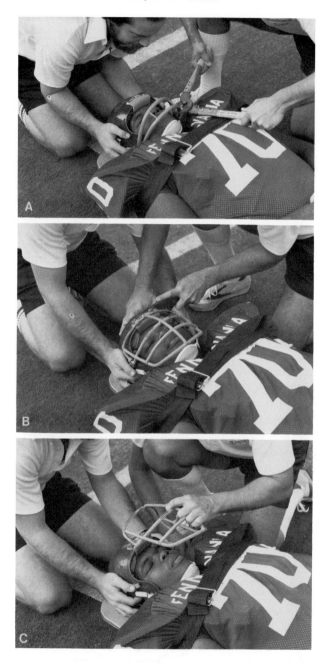

FIGURE 4. *A,* Remove double and single masks with bolt cutters. Head and helmet must be securely immobilized. *B,* Remove "cage"-type masks by cutting the plastic loops with a utility knife. Make the cut on the side of the loop away from the face. *C,* Remove the entire mask from the helmet so it does not interfere with further resuscitation efforts. (From Torg JS (ed): Athletic Injuries to the Head, Neck and Face. Philadelphia, Lea & Febiger, 1982, with permission.)

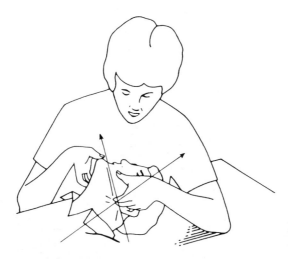

FIGURE 5. Jaw-thrust maneuver for opening the airway of a victim in whom cervical spine injury is suspected. (From Torg JS (ed): Athletic Injuries to the Head, Neck and Face. Philadelphia, Lea & Febiger, 1982, with permission.)

one hand are placed under the lower jaw on the bony part near the chin and lifted to bring the chin forward, supporting the jaw and helping to tilt the head back. The fingers must not compress the soft tissue under the chin, which might obstruct the airway. The other hand presses on the victim's forehead to tilt the head back (Fig. 6).

The transportation team should be familiar with handling a victim with a cervical spine injury and they should be receptive to taking orders from the

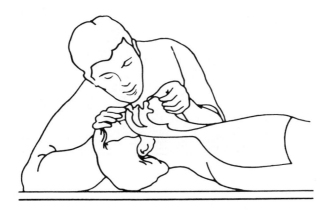

FIGURE 6. Head tilt–jaw lift maneuver for opening the airway. Used if jaw thrust is inadequate or if a helmet is being worn. (From Torg JS (ed): Athletic Injuries to the Head, Neck and Face. Philadelphia, Lea & Febiger, 1982, with permission.)

team physician or trainer. It is extremely important not to lose control of the care of the athlete; therefore, be familiar with the transportation crew that is used. In an athletic situation, prior arrangements with an ambulance service should be made.

Lifting and carrying the athlete require five individuals: four to lift, and the leader to maintain immobilization of the head. The leader initiates all actions with clear, loud, verbal commands (Fig. 7).

The same guidelines apply to the choice of a medical facility as to the choice of an ambulance: Be sure it is equipped and staffed to handle an emergency head or neck injury. There should be a neurosurgeon and an

FIGURE 7. *A*, Four members of the medical support team lift the athlete on the command of the leader. *B*, The leader maintains the manual immobilization of the head. The spineboard is not recommended as a stretcher. An additional stretcher should be used for trasporting over long distances. (From Torg JS (ed): Athletic Injuries to the Head, Neck and Face. Philadelphia, Lea & Febiger, 1982, with permission.)

orthopedic surgeon to meet the athlete upon arrival. Roentgenographic facilities should be alerted.

Once the athlete is in a medical facility and permanent immobilization measures have been instituted, the helmet is removed. The chin strap may now be unfastened and discarded. The athlete's head is supported at the occiput by one person while the leader spreads the earflaps and pulls the helmet off in a straight line with the spine (Fig. 8).

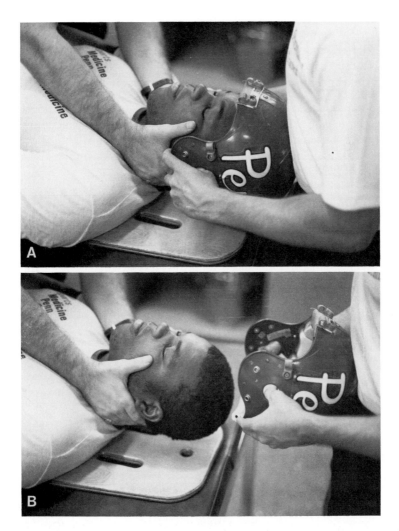

FIGURE 8. *A,* The helmet should be removed only whenever permanent immobilization can be instituted. The helmet may be removed by detaching the chinstrap, spreading the earflaps, and gently pulling off the helmet in a straight line with the cervical spine. *B,* The head must be supported under the occiput during and after removing the helmet. (From Torg JS (ed): Athletic Injuries to the Head, Neck and Face. Philadelphia, Lea & Febiger, 1982, with permission.)

HEAD INJURIES

The athlete who receives a blow to the head or a sudden jolt to the body that results in a sudden acceleration-deceleration force to the head should be carefully evaluated. If the individual is ambulatory and conscious, the entire spectrum of intracranial damage, ranging from a grade I concussion to a more severe intracranial condition, must be considered. Initial on-field examination should include an evaluation of:

1. Facial expression
2. Orientation to time, place, and person
3. The presence of post-traumatic amnesia
4. The presence of retrograde amnesia
5. Abnormal gait

Traumatic injuries to the brain can be classified as diffuse or focal.

The immediate and definitive management of athletically induced trauma to the brain depends on the nature and severity of the injury. Those responsible for managing such injuries must understand the problems from the standpoint of basic pathomechanics.

Diffuse Brain Injuries

Diffuse brain injuries are associated with widespread or global disruption of neurologic function and are not usually associated with macroscopically visible brain lesions. Diffuse brain injuries result from shaking of the brain within the skull, and thus are lesions caused by the inertial or acceleration effects of a mechanical input to the head. Both theoretical and experimental evidence points to rotational acceleration as the primary mechanism of injury in diffuse brain injuries.

Because diffuse brain injuries, for the most part, are not associated with visible macroscopic lesions, they have historically been lumped together to include all injuries not associated with focal lesions. More recently, however, diagnostic information has been gained from computed tomographic (CT) and magnetic resonance (MR) scanning, as well as from neurophysiologic studies, which make it possible to define more clearly several categories within this broad group of diffuse brain injuries.

Three categories of diffuse brain injury are recognized:

1. **Mild concussion.** Several specific concussion syndromes involve temporary disturbances of neurologic function without loss of consciousness.

2. **Classic cerebral concussion.** This is a temporary, reversible neurologic deficiency caused by trauma that results in temporary loss of consciousness.

3. **Diffuse axonal injury.** This takes the form of prolonged traumatic brain coma with loss of consciousness lasting more than 6 hours. Residual neurologic, psychologic, or personality deficits often result because of structural disruption of numerous axons in the white matter of the cerebral hemispheres and brain stem.

Focal Brain Syndromes

In discussing the occurrence of intracranial hematoma resulting from athletic injury, two major points must be emphasized. First, owing to recent developments in the clinical evaluation of patients and correlated animal research, there is a satisfactory understanding of the mechanism of occurrence of focal intracranial hematoma, which is somewhat different from older concepts of patients with head injuries. Second, management of such patients has advanced rapidly and changed dramatically over the last decade from what was accepted medical practice in the past.

The entire spectrum of traumatic intracranial hematomas occurs in sports injuries: cerebral contusions, intracerebral hematomas, epidural hematomas, and acute subdural hematomas. The presentation of athletes with head injuries who have had serious trauma is similar in most instances. Management depends on definitive diagnosis, and varies according to the underlying pathologic process.

INTRACEREBRAL HEMATOMA AND CONTUSION

These injuries occur in patients with a significant intracerebral pathologic condition who have not suffered loss of consciousness or focal neurologic deficit, but who do have persistent headache or periods of confusion after head injury and post-traumatic amnesia. As with any patients who have suffered head injuries, athletes with such symptoms should undergo a CT scan to permit early differentiation between solid intracerebral hematoma and hemorrhagic contusion with surrounding edema.

EPIDURAL HEMATOMA[3]

Epidural hematoma results when the middle meningeal artery, which is imbedded in a bony groove in the skull, tears as a result of a skull fracture, crossing this groove. Because the bleeding in this instance is arterial, accumulation of clot continues under high pressure and, as a result, serious brain injury can occur.

The classic description of an epidural hematoma is that of loss of consciousness at the time of injury, followed by recovery of consciousness in a variable period, after which the patient is lucid. This is followed by the onset of increasingly severe headache, decreased level of consciousness, dilation of one pupil, usually on the same side as the clot, and decerebrate posturing and weakness, usually on the side opposite the hematoma. In our experience, however, only one-third of the patients with epidural hematoma have this classic presentation. Another one-third of patients do not become unconscious until late in their course, and the remaining one-third are unconscious from the time of injury and remain unconscious throughout their course.

The absence of a classic clinical picture of epidural hematoma cannot be relied on to rule out this diagnosis, and the best diagnostic test for evaluating these patients is a CT scan.

ACUTE SUBDURAL HEMATOMA[3]

Athletic head injuries result from inertial loading that is lower than that of serious head injuries caused by vehicular accidents or falling from heights.

Also, acute subdural hematomas occur much more frequently than epidural hematomas in athletes. In patients with head injuries in general, approximately three times as many acute subdural hematomas occur as do epidural hematomas.

Two main types of acute subdural hematomas have been clearly identified: (1) those with a collection of blood in the subdural space apparently not associated with underlying cerebral contusion or edema; and (2) those with collections of blood in the subdural space, but associated with an obvious contusion on the surface of the brain and hemispheric brain injury with swelling. The mortality rate for simple subdural hematomas is approximately 20%, but this increases to more than 50% for subdural hematomas with an underlying brain injury.

Patients with an acute subdural hematoma typically are unconscious, may or may not have a history of deterioration, and frequently display focal neurologic findings. Patients with simple subdural hematomas are more likely to have a lucid interval following their injury and are less likely to be unconscious at admission than patients with hemispheric injury and brain swelling. It is necessary to obtain a CT or MR scan to diagnose an acute subdural hematoma. The size of the subdural clot relative to the size of the midline shift of the brain structures can be evaluated best by CT scan. Of patients with acute subdural hematoma, 84% also have an associated hemorrhagic contusion or intracerebral hematoma with associated brain swelling.

The term "acute subdural hematoma" raises the image of a large collection of clotted blood in the intracranial cavity, compressing the brain substance and causing compromise due to the space occupied by the hematoma. This is not an infrequent consequence of closed-head trauma, but this type of subdural hematoma is more common in adults who have a degree of cortical atrophy.

Young athletes, and especially children, frequently develop only minimal subdural hematomas with underlying cerebral hemispheric swelling. This type of brain injury is not the result of a space-occupying mass from clotted blood causing brain compression, but rather of swollen brain tissue causing consequent rises in intracranial pressure. CT and MR scanning permit accurate differential diagnosis of these two conditions, which frequently cause similar clinical pictures. The modalities of treatment for these two distinct types of acute subdural hematomas are quite different.

BRAIN SWELLING[3]

Brain swelling is a poorly understood phenomenon that can accompany any type of head injury. Swelling is not synonymous with cerebral edema, which refers to a specific increase in brain water. Such an increase in water content may not occur in brain swelling, and current evidence favors the concept that brain swelling results in part from increased intravascular blood within the brain. This is caused by a vascular reaction to head injury that leads to vasodilation and increased cerebral blood volume. If this increased cerebral blood volume continues long enough, vascular permeability may increase and true edema may result.

Although brain swelling may occur in any type of head injury, the magnitude of the swelling does not correlate well with the severity of the injury. Thus both severe and minor head injuries may be complicated by brain swelling. The effects of brain swelling are additive to those of primary brain injury, and may in certain instances be more severe than the primary injury itself.

Despite the lack of knowledge of the precise mechanism that causes brain swelling, it can be conceptualized in two general forms. It should be remembered that many different types of brain swelling exist and that acute and delayed brain swelling represent phenomenologic rather than mechanistic entities.

Acute brain swelling occurs in several circumstances. Swelling that accompanies focal brain lesions tends to be localized, whereas diffuse brain injuries are associated with generalized swelling. Focal swelling is usually present beneath contusions but does not often contribute additional deleterious effects. On the other hand, the swelling that occurs with acute subdural hematomas, although principally hemispheric in distribution, may cause more mass effect than the hematoma itself. In such circumstances, the small amount of blood in the subdural space may not be the entire reason for the patient's neurologic state. If the hematoma is removed, the acute brain swelling may progress so rapidly that the brain protrudes through the craniotomy opening. Every neurosurgeon is all too familiar with external herniation of the brain, which, when it occurs, is difficult to treat.

The more serious types of diffuse brain injuries are associated with generalized, rather than focal, acute brain swelling. Although not all patients with diffuse axonal injury have brain swelling, the incidence of swelling is higher than in patients with either classic cerebral concussion or one of the mild concussion syndromes. Because of the serious nature of the underlying injury, it is difficult to determine the extent of swelling in these patients. The swelling, although widespread throughout the brain, may not cause a rise in intracranial pressure for several days. This late rise in pressure probably reflects the formation of true cerebral edema, and it may be that diffuse swelling associated with severe diffuse brain injuries is harmful because it produces edema. In any event, this type of swelling is different from the type of swelling associated with acute subdural hematomas.

Delayed brain swelling may occur minutes to hours after head injury. It is usually diffuse and is often associated with the milder forms of diffuse brain injuries. Whether delayed swelling is the same as, or a phenomenon different from, the acute swelling of the more serious diffuse injuries is unknown. However, in less severe diffuse injuries there is a distinct time interval before delayed swelling becomes manifest, thus confirming that the primary insult to the brain was not serious. Considering the high frequency of the mild concussion, the incidence of delayed swelling must be low. However, when it occurs, delayed swelling can cause profound neurologic changes or even death.

In its most severe form, severe delayed swelling can cause deep coma. The usual history is that of an injury associated with a mild concussion or a classic cerebral concussion from which the patient recovers. Minutes or hours later the patient becomes lethargic, then stuporous, and finally lapses into a coma. The coma may be either a light coma with appropriate motor responses to painful stimuli, or a deep coma associated with decorticate or decerebrate posturing.

The key differences between these patients and those with diffuse axonal injury is that in the latter the coma and abnormal motor signs are present from the moment of injury, whereas with delayed cerebral swelling there is a time interval without these signs. This distinction is significant, however, because with diffuse axonal injury a certain amount of primary structural damage has occurred at the moment of impact, but this is not present in cases of pure delayed swelling. Therefore the deleterious effects of delayed swelling should be potentially reversible, and if these effects are controlled, the outcome should be good. However, such control may be difficult. Vigorous monitoring of and attention to intracranial pressure is necessary, and prompt and vigorous treatment of raised intracranial pressure is required in order to control brain swelling. If this is successfully accomplished, the mortality rate from increased intracranial pressure associated with diffuse brain swelling should be low.

Principles of Management[3]

As knowledge of physiology and pathophysiology has increased, so has the ability to resuscitate seriously ill or severely injured people successfully. The 1950s saw the start of successful treatment of acute respiratory and postoperative problems, followed by satisfactory cardiac resuscitation and emergency cardiac care in the 1960s. Innovations in critical care medicine were extended in the form of brain resuscitation in the 1970s. Such care is based on the concept that the degree of permanent neurologic, intellectual, and psychologic deficit after brain trauma with coma is only partly the result of the initial injury, and is certainly in part due to secondary changes, which can be worsened or improved by the quality of supportive care received. Head injuries, by their very nature, require resuscitation, i.e., therapy initiated after the insult. The proper care of patients with head injuries, athletic or otherwise, depends on the full appreciation and use of brain resuscitation measures in an intensive care setting.

First aid should consist of getting the patient safely into a supine position and determining vital signs and the significance of any associated injuries. Initial treatment should be to establish an adequate and useful airway and begin hyperventilation maneuvers. This can be accomplished by using a manual resuscitation bag with supplemental oxygen, if available. The patient should then be transferred as quickly as possible to a medical facility where diagnosis and treatment of brain injury can begin. Although these measures are important for all patients who have suffered concussion, they are vital for patients who remain comatose after trauma. Once the patient arrives in the emergency room and it is determined that the cardiorespiratory status is stable, endotracheal intubation is immediately performed on a comatose patient. A CT or MR scan is obtained as soon as possible to provide an immediate diagnosis of the intracranial condition. The patient is then categorized as either a surgical or nonsurgical candidate, depending on the size of the intracranial hematoma.

CERVICAL SPINE

Athletic injuries to the cervical spine may involve the bony vertebrae, intervertebral discs, ligamentous supporting structures, the spinal cord, roots, and peripheral nerves, or any combination of these structures. The panorama of injuries runs the spectrum from "cervical sprain syndrome" to fracture-dislocations with permanent quadriplegia. Fortunately, severe injuries with neural involvement occur infrequently. However, persons responsible for the emergency and subsequent care of the athlete with a cervical spine injury should possess a basic understanding of the variety of problems that can occur.[11]

The various athletic injuries to the cervical spine and related structures are:

1. nerve root–brachial plexus neurapraxia
2. stable cervical sprain
3. muscular strain
4. nerve root–brachial plexus axonotmesis
5. intervertebral disc injury (narrowing-herniation) without neurologic deficit
6. stable cervical fractures without neurologic deficit
7. subluxations without neurologic deficit
8. unstable fractures without neurologic deficit
9. dislocations without neurologic deficit
10. intervertebral disc herniation with neurologic deficit
11. unstable fracture with neurologic deficit
12. dislocation with neurologic deficit
13. quadriplegia
14. death

Acute Cervical Sprain Syndrome

An acute cervical sprain is a collision injury frequently seen in contact sports. The patient complains of having "jammed" his neck with subsequent pain localized to the cervical area. Characteristically, the patient presents with limitation of cervical spine motion, but without radiation of pain or paresthesia. Neurologic examination is negative and roentgenograms are normal.

Stable cervical sprains and strains eventually resolve with or without treatment. Initially, the presence of a serious injury should be ruled out by a thorough neurologic examination and determination of the range of cervical motion. Range of motion is evaluated by having the athlete actually nod his head, touch his chin to his chest, touch his left ear to his left shoulder, and touch his right ear to his right shoulder. If the patient is unwilling or unable to perform these maneuvers actively while standing erect, proceed no further. The athlete with less than a full, pain-free range of cervical motion, persistent paresthesia, or weakness should be protected and excluded from activity. Subsequent evaluation should include appropriate roentgenographic studies, including flexion and extension views to demonstrate fractures or instability. If the patient has pain and muscle spasm of the cervical spine, hospitalization and head-halter traction may be indicated.

In general, treatment of athletes with "cervical sprains" should be tailored to the degree of severity. Immobilizing the neck in a soft collar and using analgesics and anti-inflammatory agents until there is a full, spasm-free range of neck motion are appropriate. It should be emphasized that individuals with a history of collision injury, pain, and limited cervical motion should have routine cervical spine x-rays. Also, lateral flexion and extension roentgenograms are indicated after the acute symptoms subside.

Cervical Vertebral Subluxation Without Fracture

Axial compression-flexion injuries incurred by striking an object with the top of the helmet can result in disruption of the posterior soft-tissue supporting elements with angulation and anterior translation of the superior cervical vertebrae. Fractures of the bony elements are not demonstrated on roentgenograms, and the patient has no neurologic deficit. Flexion-extension roentgenograms demonstrate instability of the cervical spine at the involved level manifested by motion, anterior intervertebral disc-space narrowing, anterior angulation and displacement of the vertebral body, and fanning of the spinous processes (Fig. 9). Demonstrable instability on lateral flexion-extension roentgenograms in young, vigorous individuals may require surgical

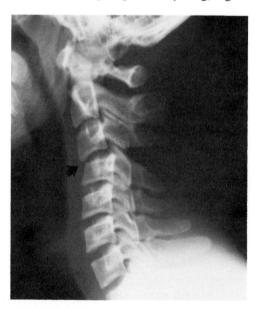

FIGURE 9. Roentgenograph demonstrates C3–C4 subluxation as manifested by anterior intervertebral disc space narrowing, anterior angulation and displacement of the superior vertebral body, and fanning of the spinous processes. (From Torg JS (ed): Athletic Injuries to the Head, Neck and Face. Philadelphia, Lea & Febiger, 1982, with permission.)

treatment. When soft-tissue disruption occurs without an associated fracture, it is likely that instability will result despite conservative treatment. When anterior subluxation greater than 20% of the vertebral body is due to disruption of the posterior supporting structures, a posterior cervical fusion is recommended.

Cervical Fractures and/or Dislocations: General Principles

Fractures and/or dislocations of the cervical spine may be stable or unstable, and may or may not be associated with neurologic deficit. When fracture or disruption of the soft-tissue supporting structure immediately violates or threatens to violate the integrity of the spinal cord, implementation of certain management and treatment principles is imperative.

The first goal is to protect the spinal cord and nerve roots from injury through mismanagement. It has been estimated that many neurologic deficits occur after the initial injury—that is, if a patient with an unstable lesion is carelessly manipulated when being transported to a medical facility or subsequently inappropriately managed, further encroachment on the spinal cord can occur.

Second, the malaligned cervical spine should be reduced as quickly and gently as possible. This will effectively decompress the spinal cord. When dislocation or anterior angulation and translation are demonstrated roentgenographically, immediate reduction is attempted with skull traction utilizing Gardner-Wells tongs. These tongs can be easily and rapidly applied under local anesthesia, without shaving the head, in the emergency room or in the patient's bed. Because these tongs are spring-loaded, it is not necessary to drill the outer table of the skull for their application. The tongs are attached to a cervical-traction pulley and weight is added at a rate of 5 lbs/disc space or 25–40 lbs for lower cervical injury. Reduction is attempted by adding 5 lbs every 15–20 minutes and is monitored by lateral roentgenograms.

Unilateral facet dislocations, particularly at the C3–C4 level, are not always reducible using skeletal traction. In such instances, closed skeletal or manipulative reduction under nasotracheal anesthesia may be necessary. The expediency of early reduction of cervical dislocations must be emphasized.

The generous use of parenteral corticosteroids to decrease the inflammatory reactions of the injured cord and surrounding soft-tissue structures are indicated in the management of cervical spine fractures and dislocations.

The results of the Second National Acute Spinal Cord Injury Study[2] indicate that patients with acute spinal cord injury treated with methylprednisolone have improved neurologic recovery when the medication is given in the first 8 hours. The regimen consists of an initial bolus of methylprednisolone, 30 mg/kg body weight, intravenously followed by an infusion of 5.4 mg/kg/hr for 23 hours.

The third goal in managing fractures and dislocations of the cervical spine is to effect rapid and secure stability in order to prevent residual deformity and instability with associated pain, and the possibility of further trauma to the neural elements. The method of immobilization depends on the post-reduction status of the injury. Thompson et al.[10] have concisely delineated indications for nonsurgical and surgical methods for achieving stability. These concepts for managing cervical spine fractures and dislocations may be summarized as follows:

1. Patients with stable compression fractures of the lamina or lateral masses, or soft-tissue injuries without detectable neurologic deficit can be adequately treated with traction and subsequent protection with a cervical brace until healing occurs.

2. Stable, reduced facet dislocation without neurologic deficit can also be treated conservatively by application of a halo jacket brace until healing has been demonstrated by negative lateral flexion-extension roentgenograms.

3. Unstable cervical spine fractures or fracture-dislocations without neurologic deficit may require either surgical or nonsurgical methods to ensure stability.

4. Aboslute indications for surgical stabilization of an unstable injury without neurologic deficit are late instability following closed treatment, and flexion-rotation injuries with unreduced locked facets.

5. Relative indications for surgical stabilization in unstable injuries without neurologic deficit are anterior subluxation greater than 20%, certain atlantoaxial fractures or dislocations, and unreduced vertical compression injuries with neck flexion.

6. Cervical spine fractures with complete cord lesions require reduction followed by stabilization by closed or open means, as indicated.

7. Cervical spine fractures with incomplete cord lesions require reduction followed by careful evaluation for surgical intervention.

The fourth and final goal of treatment is rapid and effective rehabilitation started early in the treatment process.

A more specific categorization of athletic injuries to the cervical spine can be made. Specifically, these injuries can be divided into those that occur in the upper cervical spine, the midcervical spine, and the lower cervical spine.

Cervical Spine Stenosis with Cord Neurapraxia and Transient Quadriplegia[12]

Characteristically, the clinical picture of cervical spinal cord neurapraxia with transient quadriplegia involves an athlete who sustains an acute transient neurologic episode of cervical cord origin with sensory changes that may be associated with motor paresis involving both arms, both legs, or all four extremities after forced hyperextension, hyperflexion, or axial loading of the cervical spine.

Sensory changes include burning pain, numbness, tingling, or loss of sensation; motor changes consist of weakness or complete paralysis. The episodes are transient and complete recovery usually occurs in 10–15 minutes, although in some cases gradual resolution does not occur for 36–48 hours. Except for burning paresthesia, neck pain is not present at the time of injury. There is complete return of motor function and full, pain-free cervical motion. Routine x-ray films of the cervical spine show no evidence of fracture or dislocation; however, a demonstrable degree of cervical spine stenosis is present.

THE STANDARD METHOD OF MEASUREMENT

In order to identify cervical stenosis, a method of measurement is needed. The standard method, the one most commonly employed for determining the sagittal diameter of the spinal canal, involves measuring the distance between the middle of the posterior surface of the vertebral body and the nearest point on the spinolaminar line. Using this technique, Boijsen[1] reported that the average sagittal diameter of the spinal canal from the fourth to the sixth cervical vertebra in 200 healthy individuals was 18.5 mm (range, 14.2 to 23 mm). The target distance he used was 1.4 mm. Kessler[5] noted that values of less than 14 mm are uncommon and fall below the standard deviation for any cervical segment. Other measurements reported in the literature vary greatly. It is the variations in the landmarks and the methods used to determine the sagittal distance, as well as the use of different target distances for roentgenography, that have resulted in inconsistencies in the so-called normal values. Therefore the standard method of measurement for spinal stenosis is a questionable one.

THE RATIO METHOD OF MEASUREMENT

An alternative way to determine the sagittal diameter of the spinal canal was devised by Pavlov[12] and is called the ratio method. It compares the standard method of measurement of the canal with the anteroposterior width of the vertebral body at the midpoint of the corresponding vertebral body (Fig. 10).

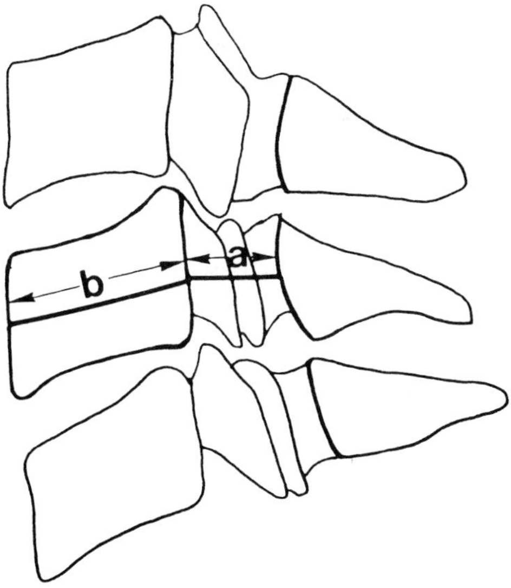

FIGURE 10. The ratio of the spinal canal to the vertebral body is the distance from the mid-point of the posterior aspect of the vertebral body to the nearest point on the corresponding spinolaminar line (a) divided by the anteroposterior width of the vertebral body (b). (From Torg JS, et al: Neurapraxia of the cervical spinal cord with transient quadriplegia. J Bone Joint Surg 68A: 1354–1370, 1986, with permission.)

$$\text{ratio} = \frac{a}{b}$$

The actual measurement of the sagittal diameter in millimeters, as determined by the conventional method, is misleading both as reported in the literature and in actual practice; this is because of variations in the target distances used for roentgenography and in the landmarks used for obtaining the measurement. Using the standard method, the actual measurement of the canal in our observations has occasionally been within the acceptable normal range. The ratio method compensates for variations in roentgenographic technique because the sagittal diameter of both the canal and the vertebral body is affected similarly by magnification factors. The ratio method is independent of variations in technique, and the results are statistically significant. Using the ratio method of determining the dimension of the canal, a ratio of the spinal canal to the vertebral body of less than 0.80 is indicative of significant cervical stenosis. We believe that the ratio of the anteroposterior diameter of the spinal canal to that of the vertebral body is a more reliable way to determine cervical stenosis (Fig. 11).

On the basis of these observations, it may be concluded that the factor identified that explains the described neurologic picture of cervical spinal cord neurapraxia is diminution of the anteroposterior diameter of the spinal canal, either as an isolated observation or in association with intervertebral disc

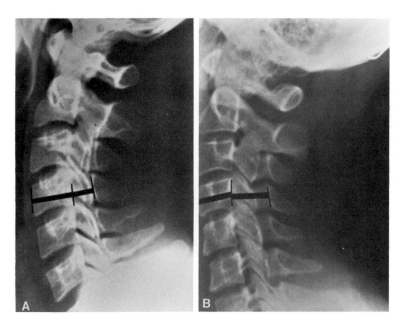

FIGURE 11. A comparison between the ratio of the spinal canal to the vetebral body of a stenotic patient versus that of a control subject is demonstrated on lateral roentgenograms of the cervical spine. The ratio is approximately 1:2 (0.50) in the stenotic patient compared with 1:1 (1.00) in the control subject. (From Torg JS, et al: Neurapraxia of the cervical spinal cord with transient quadriplegia. J Bone Joint Surg 68A:1354–1370, 1986, with permission.)

FIGURE 12. The pincers mechanism, as described by Penning,[6] occurs between the posterior inferior aspect of the vertebral body and the anterior superior aspect of the spinolaminar line of the subjacent vertebra. With extreme hyperextension or hyperflexion, there can be a decrease in the AP diameter of the spinal canal with a pinching of the spinal cord and a transient aberration of function.

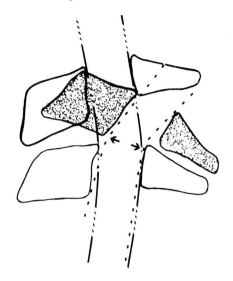

herniation, degenerative changes, posttraumatic instability, or congenital anomalies. In instances of developmental cervical stenosis, forced hyperflexion, or hyperextension of the cervical spine, a further decrease in the caliber of an already stenotic canal occurs, as explained by the pincers mechanism of Penning (Fig. 12).[6] In patients whose stenosis is associated with osteophytes or a herniated disc, direct pressure can occur, again with the spine forced in the extremes of flexion and extension. It is further postulated that with an abrupt but brief decrease in the anteroposterior diameter of the spinal canal, the cervical cord is mechanically compressed, causing transient interruption of either its motor or its sensory function, or both, distal to the lesion. The neurologic aberration that results is transient and completely reversible.

INCIDENCE

A review of the literature revealed that few reported cases of transient quadriplegia occurred in athletes. Attempts to establish the incidence indicate that the problem is more prevalent than expected. Specifically, in the population of 39,377 exposed participants, the reported incidence of transient paresthesia in all four extremities was 6 per 10,000, whereas the reported incidence of paresthesia associated with transient quadriplegia was 1.3 per 10,000 in the one football season surveyed. From these data it may be concluded that the prevalence of this problem is relatively high and that an awareness of the etiology, manifestations, and appropriate principles of management is warranted.

RESTRICTION OF ACTIVITY

Characteristically, after an episode of cervical spinal cord neurapraxia with or without transient quadriplegia, the first question raised concerns the advisability of restricting activity. In an attempt to address this problem, 117 young athletes have been interviewed who sustained cervical spine injuries associated with complete permanent quadriplegia while playing football between the years of 1971 and 1984. None of these patients recalled a prodromal experience of transient motor paresis. Conversely, none of the patients in this series who had experienced transient neurologic episodes subsequently sustained an injury that resulted in permanent neurologic injury. On the basis of these data, it is concluded that a young patient who has had an episode of cervical spinal cord neurapraxia with or without quadriplegia is not predisposed to permanent neurologic injury because of it.

With regard to restrictions in activity, no definite recurrence patterns have been identified to establish firm principles in this area. However, athletes who have this syndrome associated with demonstrable cervical spinal instability or acute or chronic degenerative changes should not be allowed further participation in contact sports. Athletes with developmental spinal stenosis or spinal stenosis associated with congenital abnormalities should be treated on an individual basis. Of the six youngsters with obvious cervical stenosis who returned to football, three had a second episode and withdrew from the activity, and three returned without any problems at 2-year follow-up. The data clearly indicate that individuals with developmental spinal stenosis are not predisposed to more severe injuries with associated permanent neurologic sequelae.

PREVENTION

Data on cervical spine injuries resulting from participation in football have been compiled by a national registry since 1971.[13] Analysis of the epidemiologic data and cinematographic documentation clearly demonstrate that the majority of cervical fractures and dislocations were due to axial loading. On the basis of this observation, rule changes banning both deliberate "spearing" and the use of the top of the helmet as the initial point of contact in making a tackle were implemented at the high-school and college levels. Subsequently, a marked decrease in cervical spine injury rates has occurred. The occurrence of permanent cervical quadriplegia decreased from 34 in 1976 to five in the 1984 season (Fig. 13).

Identifying the cause and prevention of cervical quadriplegia resulting from football involves four areas: (1) the role of the helmet–face mask protective system; (2) the concept of the axial loading mechanism of injury; (3) the effect of the 1976 rule changes banning spearing and the use of the top of the helmet as the initial point of contact in tackling; and (4) the necessity for continued research, education, and rules enforcement.

The protective capabilities provided by the modern football helmet have resulted in the implementation of playing techniques that have placed the cervical spine at risk of injury with associated catastrophic neurological sequelae. Available cinematographic and epidemiologic data clearly indicate that cervical spine injuries associated with quadriplegia occurring as a result of football are not hyperflexion accidents.[13] Instead, these injuries are caused by purposeful axial loading of the cervical spine as a result of spearing and head-first playing techniques. As an etiologic factor, the present-day helmet–face

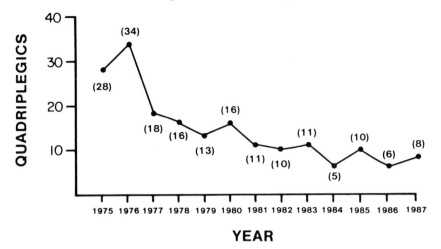

FIGURE 13. Permanent cervical quadriplegia, 1975–1987. Yearly incidence of permanent cervical quadriplegia for all levels of participation demonstrates significant decrease in 1977, the first year after rules change. Total quadriplegia has continued to decline to a low of five in 1984. (From Torg JS, et al: The National Football Head and Neck Injury Registry: 14-year report on cervical quadriplegia, 1971–1984. JAMA 254:3439–3443, 1985, with permission.)

mask system is secondary, contributing to these injuries because its protective capabilities have permitted the head to be used as a battering ram, thus exposing the cervical spine to injury.

Classically, the role of hyperflexion has been emphasized in cervical spine trauma whether the injury was incurred while diving or trampolining or playing rugby or American football. Epidemiologic and cinematographic analyses have established that most cases of cervical spine quadriplegia that occur in football have resulted from axial loading. Rather than an accident— an untoward event—techniques are deliberately used that place the cervical spine at risk of catastrophic injury. Recent laboratory observations also indicate that athletically induced cervical spine trauma results from axial loading.

In the course of a collision activity, such as tackle football, most energy inputs to the cervical spine are effectively dissipated by the energy-absorbing capabilities of the cervical musculature through controlled lateral bending, flexion, or extension. However, the bones, discs, and ligamentous structures can be injured when contact occurs on the top of the helmet with the head, neck, and trunk positioned in such a way that forces are transmitted along the longitudinal axis of the cervical spine.[43]

With the neck in the anatomic position, the cervical spine is extended owing to normal cervical lordosis (Fig. 14). When the neck is flexed to 30 degrees, the cervical spine straightens (Fig. 15). In axial loading injuries, the neck is slightly flexed and normal cervical lordosis is eliminated, thereby converting the spine into a straight, segmented column. Assuming the head, neck, and trunk components to be in motion, rapid deceleration of the head occurs when it strikes another object, such as another player, trampoline bed,

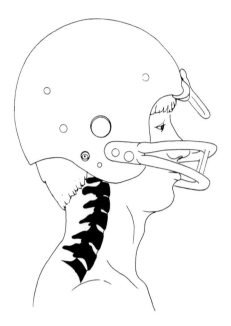

FIGURE 14. When the neck is in a normal, upright, anatomical position, the cervical spine is slightly extended because of the natural cervical lordosis.

or lake bottom. This results in the compression of the cervical spine between the rapidly decelerated head and the force of the oncoming trunk. When the maximal vertical compression is reached, the straightened cervical spine fails in a flexion mode, and fracture, subluxation, or unilateral or bilateral facet dislocation can occur (Fig. 16).

Refutation of the "freak accident" concept with the more logical principle of cause and effect has been most rewarding in dealing with problems of football-induced cervical quadriplegia. Definition of the axial-loading mechanism—in which a football player, usually a defensive back, makes a tackle by

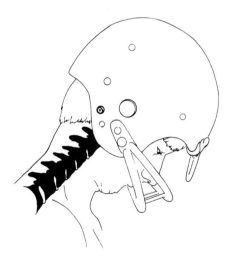

FIGURE 15. When the neck is flexed slightly, to approximately 30°, the cervical spine is straightened and converted into a segmented column.

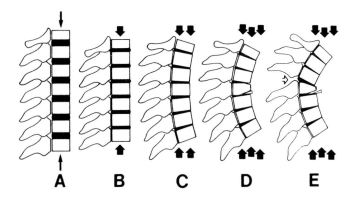

FIGURE 16. Axial loading of the cervical spine first results in compressive deformation of the intervertebral discs (*A* and *B*), followed by maximum compressive deformation, and then angular deformation and buckling occur. The spine fails in a flexion mode *(C)* with resulting fracture, subluxation, or dislocation. *D* and *E,* Compressive deformation to failure with a resultant fracture, dislocation, or subluxation occurs in as little as 8.4 msec.

striking an opponent with the top of his helmet—was key in this process. Implementation of rules changes and coaching techniques eliminating the use of the head as a battering ram have resulted in a dramatic reduction in the incidence of quadriplegia since 1976. We believe that the majority of athletic injuries to the cervical spine associated with quadriplegia also occur as a result of axial loading.

Tator et al.[8] identified 38 acute spinal cord injuries caused by diving accidents and observed that, "In most cases the cervical spine was fractured and the spinal cord crushed. The top of the head struck the bottom of the lake or pool." Sher,[7] reporting on vertex impact and cervical dislocation in rugby players, observed that, "When the neck is slightly flexed, the spine is straight. If significant force is applied to the vertex when the spine is straight, the force is transmitted down the long axis of the spine. When the force exceeds the energy-absorbing capacity of the structures involved, cervical spine flexion and dislocation will result." Tator and Edmonds[9] have reported the results of a national questionnaire survey by the Canadian Committee on the Prevention of Spinal Injuries Due to Hockey, which recorded 28 injuries involving the spinal cord, 17 of which resulted in complete paralysis. They noted that in this series, the most common mechanism involved was a check, with the injured players striking the boards "with the top of their heads, while their necks were slightly flexed."[9]

These reports in the recent literature that deal with the mechanism of injury in cervical spine injuries resulting from water sports (diving), gymnastics, rugby, and ice hockey support our thesis.

References

1. Boijsen E: The cervical spinal cord in intraspinal expansive processes. Acta Radiol 42:101–115, 1954.
2. Brachen MB, Shepard MJ, Collins WF, et al: A randomized, controlled trial of methylprednisolone or naloxone in the treatment of acute, spinal cord injury. N Engl J Med 322:1405–1411, 1990.
3. Bruno LA: Focal intracranial hematoma. In Torg JS (ed): Athletic Injuries to the Head, Neck and Face. Philadelphia, Lea & Febiger, 1982.
4. Gennarelli TA: Cerebral concussion in diffuse brain injuries. In Torg JS (ed): Athletic Injuries to the Head, Neck and Face, Philadelphia, Lea & Febiger, 1982.
5. Kessler JT: Congenital narrowing of the cervical spinal canal. J Neurol Neurosurg Psychiat 38:1218–1224, 1975.
6. Penning L: Some aspects of plain radiography of the cervical spine in chronic myelopathy. Neurology 12:513–519, 1962.
7. Scher AT: Vertex impact and cervical dislocation in rugby players. S Afr Med J 59:227–228, 1981.
8. Tator CH, Edmonds VE, New ML: Diving: Frequent and potentially preventable cause of spinal cord injury. Can Med Assoc J 124:1323–1324, 1981.
9. Tator CH, Edmonds VE: National survey of spinal injury to hockey players. Can Med Assoc J 130:875–880, 1984.
10. Thompson R, et al: Current concepts in management of cervical spine fractures and dislocations. Am J Sports Med 3:159, 1975.
11. Torg JS, Weisel SW, Rothman RH: Diagnosis and management of cervical spine injuries. In Torg JS (ed): Athletic Injuries to the Head, Neck and Face. Philadelphia, Lea & Febiger, 1982.
12. Torg JS, Pavlov H, et al: Neurapraxia of the cervical spinal cord with transient quadriplegia. J Bone Joint Surg 68A:1354–1370, 1986.
13. Torg JS, Vegso JJ, O'Neill M, Sennett B: The epidemiologic, pathologic, biomechanical, and cinematographic analysis of football-induced cervical spine trauma. Am J Sports Med 18:50–57, 1990.
14. Vegso JJ, Bryant MH, Torg JS: Field evaluation of head and neck injuries. In Torg JS (ed): Athletic Injuries to the Head, Neck and Face. Philadelphia, Lea & Febiger, 1982.

Overuse Syndromes of the Shoulder and Arm

ARTHUR M. PAPPAS, M.D.

Professor and Chairman
Department of Orthopedics and
   Physical Rehabilitation
University of Massachusetts
   Medical Center
Worcester, Massachusetts

Reprint requests to:
Arthur M. Pappas, M.D.
Department of Orthopedics and
   Physical Rehabilitation
University of Massachusetts
   Medical Center
55 Lake Avenue North
Worcester, MA 01655

While overuse syndromes are generally defined as the result of repetitive microtrauma, they are more likely the end-products of a variety of etiologic factors. These include congenital anatomic variations, the increased vulnerability of tissues during musculoskeletal development, the variable effects of repetitive stress (microtrauma) on different tissues, improper biomechanics of performance, muscle imbalance (which may result from inappropriate conditioning programs), and the residual effects of previous injury (macrotrauma). It is likely that more than one factor contributes to the development of an overuse syndrome.

The presenting complaints of overuse syndromes range from mild discomfort associated with function to incapacitating pain and inability to perform specific functions. The findings on physical examination range from mild discomfort secondary to deep palpation to obvious visual physical alterations or joint malfunction (or both). The radiographic findings range from no abnormality noted on two-plane radiographs to obvious changes on radiographs or supplemental diagnostic imaging techniques.

The physician or other health care provider must understand the normal anatomy and function of the upper extremity, the functional demands of the sport, and the various possible etiologies of overuse syndromes in order to interpret correctly the presenting complaint, physical findings, and radiographic

ADOLESCENT MEDICINE: State of the Art Reviews—Vol. 2, No. 1, February 1991
Philadelphia, Hanley & Belfus, Inc.

and imaging results. Once the overuse syndrome has been diagnosed, a rational treatment program and a realistic prognosis regarding long-term expectations can be provided.

ANATOMY

Shoulder

Total or global shoulder motion includes movement at the glenohumeral, scapulothoracic, acromioclavicular, and sternoclavicular articulations. This motion is coordinated through the glenohumeral and scapulothoracic musculature. The glenohumeral component contributes about two-thirds of total shoulder motion, and the scapulothoracic component about one-third.

The glenohumeral joint (Fig. 1), between the humeral head and glenoid fossa, can be compared to a golf ball on a tee (Fig. 2). The articular area of the humeral head is more than three times greater than that of the shallow glenoid fossa. Thus, the joint has little intrinsic bony stability. Much of the stability comes from the soft tissues surrounding the joint, e.g., the glenoid labrum, capsule, glenohumeral ligaments, and rotator cuff (the subscapularis, supraspinatus, infraspinatus, and teres minor) (Fig. 3). The labrum increases

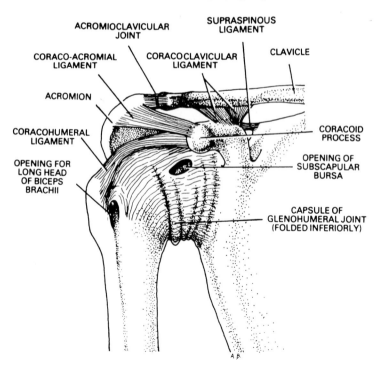

FIGURE 1. Right glenohumeral and acromioclavicular joints. (From Joseph J: A Textbook of Regional Anatomy. Baltimore, University Park Press, 1982, p 359, with permission.)

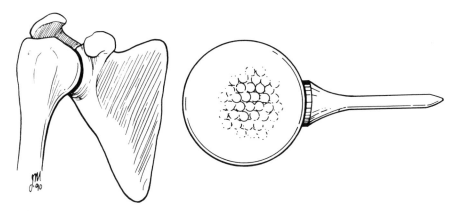

FIGURE 2.   The relationship between the humeral head and the glenoid is comparable to that of a golf ball on a tee.

the contact area of the glenoid with the humeral head by approximately 65% in the transverse plane and 75% in the vertical plane.

Abduction of the humerus (Fig. 4) is effected primarily by the deltoid and supraspinatus muscles. Adduction is effected primarily by the pectoralis major, latissimus dorsi, subscapularis, and teres major muscles. The shoulder is flexed by the action of the anterior deltoid, coracobrachialis, and biceps, and extended by the posterior deltoid and teres major. Internal rotation of the humerus is effected by the pectoralis major, anterior deltoid, subscapularis, latissimus dorsi, and teres major, and external rotation by the infraspinatus, posterior deltoid, and teres minor.

Scapular motion contributes to the global range of motion of the upper extremity and directs the glenoid to accommodate changing humeral head positions. Stabilization of the scapula is necessary to allow forces on the arm to act from a fixed point, e.g., in the acceleration phase of pitching. The different positions of the scapular glenoid are the result of specific muscle actions. Elevation of the scapula is effected by the trapezius and levator scapulae, and depression by the trapezius, pectoralis minor, latissimus dorsi, and teres major. The scapula is protracted by the serratus anterior, teres major, and latissimus dorsi, and retracted by the trapezius and rhomboids.

The acromioclavicular joint (Fig. 1) is a plane-type synovial joint with a fibrocartilaginous disc between the articular surfaces. The joint allows the acromion (scapula) to swing in an arc around the clavicle. The fibrous capsule surrounding the joint is reinforced superiorly by the acromioclavicular ligament and inferiorly by the coracoclavicular ligaments (the conoid and trapezoid ligaments), which guide and retain the clavicle in contact with the acromion during rotation of the clavicle on its longitudinal axis. The coraco-acromial ligament separates the subacromial bursa from the acromioclavicular

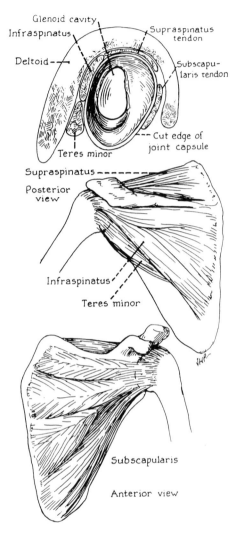

FIGURE 3. Muscles of the rotator cuff. The upper figure shows a lateral view of the socket of the shoulder joint after the humerus with its muscles has been removed. The posterior and anterior aspects of the cuff are also shown with the humerus in position. Note the lack of similar reinforcement inferiorly. (From Rosse C, Clawson DK: Introduction to the Musculoskeletal System. New York, Harper and Row, 1970, p 66, with permission.)

joint and, with the superior capsule, forms a protective arch above the shoulder joint, the superior component of the impingement interval. The anatomic region defined as the impingement interval is between the undersurface of the anterior acromion and the superior surface of the proximal humerus. Soft tissues contained within the interval include the supraspinatus muscle, the tendon of the biceps, and the subacromial bursa.

The sternoclavicular joint is a saddle-shaped synovial joint. The capsule is reinforced by the sternoclavicular ligament. The costoclavicular ligament provides additional stability, assisted by the subclavius muscle.

The brachial plexus and axillary vessels lie within the axilla medial to the glenohumeral joint. The axillary artery is directly anterior to the glenohumeral joint in the position of abduction/extension/external rotation, as in throwing,

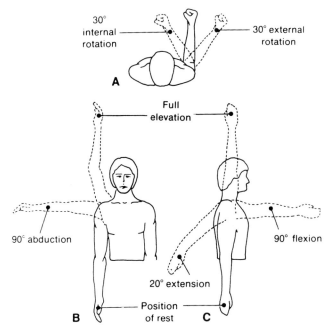

FIGURE 4.   Motions of the glenohumeral joint. *A*, Rotation. *B*, Abduction. *C*, Flexion and extension. (From Ramamurti CP, Tinker RV (eds): Orthopaedics in Primary Care. Baltimore, Williams and Wilkins, 1979, p 22, with permission.)

and thus is subject to potential compression and contusion. The suprascapular nerve originates from the brachial plexus distal to the junction of the roots of C-5 and C-6. It passes posteriorly through the suprascapular notch to innervate the supraspinatus muscle, then through the spinoglenoid notch to innervate the infraspinatus muscle.

Elbow

The elbow (Fig. 5) is a complex joint composed of three articulations, the humeroulnar, humeroradial, and radioulnar. It allows motion in flexion, extension, pronation, and supination. The trochlea of the distal humerus articulates with the sigmoid notch of the proximal ulna to form the humeroulnar joint on the medial side of the arm. The sigmoid notch is bordered by the olecranon posteriorly and the coronoid process anteriorly. On the distal humerus, the coronoid fossa accommodates the coronoid process in full flexion, and the olecranon fossa accommodates the olecranon in full extension.

The ulnar (medial) collateral ligament (Fig. 5) is an important stabilizing structure of the elbow. It is a triangular structure composed of anterior, posterior, and transverse bands. The anterior and posterior bands extend from the medial epicondyle to the medial aspect of the ulna. The transverse band extends between the olecranon and coronoid process. The ulnar nerve courses behind the medial epicondyle and runs distally into the forearm.

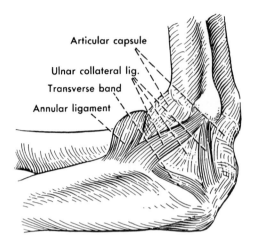

Articular capsule
Ulnar collateral lig.
Transverse band
Annular ligament

FIGURE 5. Medial view of the elbow joint. (From Hollinshead WH, Jenkins DB: Functional Anatomy of the Limbs and Back, 5th ed. Philadelphia, W.B. Saunders Co., 1981, p 117, with permission.)

On the lateral side of the arm, the capitellum of the distal humerus articulates with the head of the radius to form the humeroradial joint. The proximal radioulnar joint is formed by the circumference of the radial head and the lesser sigmoid notch of the ulna. The annular ligament contains the radial head in contact with the ulna.

Elbow flexion is effected by the brachialis, biceps, and brachioradialis muscles, and extension by the triceps. Forearm pronation is effected by the pronator teres and quadratus, and supination by the supinator and biceps muscles.

BIOMECHANICAL DEMANDS

Analysis of the baseball pitch will be used as a model for discussion of the forces generated through the shoulder and arm in overhead activities. The act of throwing requires total body coordination with the ultimate force being directed through the shoulder complex and along the upper extremity. Throwing is customarily divided into the phases of cocking, acceleration, and follow-through (Fig. 6).

Cocking directs the shoulder complex into a position of abduction, hyperextension, and extreme external rotation. The elbow is in 90° of flexion. This position places great stress at the acromion, at the impingement interval, and across all of the supportive structures of the anterior capsule of the glenohumeral joint. The elbow is subjected to valgus stress across the medial supportive structures and compression at the humeroradial joint (Fig. 7). The valgus stress causes stretch of the medial structures, especially the ulnar nerve and ulnar (medial) collateral ligament.

In the next phase of pitching, **acceleration**, the shoulder complex is brought forward and the glenohumeral joint derotates, while the elbow rapidly extends to approximately 25° of flexion at ball release. The forearm pronates to 90° at ball release. To achieve this motion there is a sudden contraction of all

FIGURE 6. Phases of a baseball pitch. *A,* Cocking phase. *B,* Acceleration phase. *C,* Follow-through phase. (Reproduced with permission from Pappas AM, et al: Biomechanics of baseball pitching: A preliminary report. Am J Sports Med 13:216–222, 1985.)

the muscles across the anterior glenohumeral joint. The scapula is stabilized so internal rotation of the humerus occurs about a fixed point. Compressive force on the humeroradial joint continues through the acceleration phase (Fig. 7).

The **follow-through** phase begins at ball release and continues through completion of motion. Its primary purpose is to decelerate the throwing limb. The deceleration forces act phasically. Eccentric contractions of the vertebral scapulothoracic musculature, i.e., trapezius, rhomboids, serratus anterior; the scapulohumeral musculature, including the rotator cuff; and the other posterior shoulder musculature actively decelerate the arm. This active deceleration is followed by a less active phase of the body's catching up with the arm.

The elbow undergoes rapid deceleration during follow-through (Fig. 7). Forces are exerted on the elbow by the triceps contraction through its insertion on the olecranon. The joint undergoes a rebound effect and flexes to approximately 45°, and the forearm pronates rapidly. This rapid rotational pronation of the forearm is associated with a combined compressive and shearing force of the radial head on the capitellum.

HISTORY AND EXAMINATION

The athlete's perceptions of pain and alteration of function are important clues in diagnosing overuse injuries of the upper extremity. In addition to the

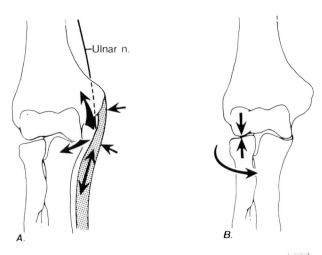

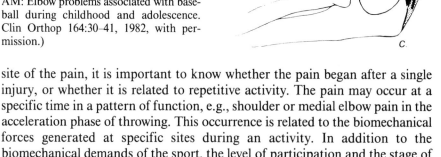

FIGURE 7. Elbow forces in throwing. *A,* Cocking and early acceleration phases. *B,* Acceleration phase. *C,* Deceleration and follow-through phase. (From Pappas AM: Elbow problems associated with baseball during childhood and adolescence. Clin Orthop 164:30–41, 1982, with permission.)

site of the pain, it is important to know whether the pain began after a single injury, or whether it is related to repetitive activity. The pain may occur at a specific time in a pattern of function, e.g., shoulder or medial elbow pain in the acceleration phase of throwing. This occurrence is related to the biomechanical forces generated at specific sites during an activity. In addition to the biomechanical demands of the sport, the level of participation and the stage of development of the athlete are important factors. For example, it is important to know the number of pitches per game and per week thrown by an adolescent baseball pitcher.

Physical Examination

The usual sequence recommended for physical examination includes visual inspection, palpation, passive motion, active motion, specific muscle evaluation, and a review of other anatomic areas that may contribute to alteration of performance. Both sides are examined and any differences noted.

VISUAL INSPECTION

The visual inspection of an athlete's shoulder is done from the front and from the back to review known anatomic landmarks and compare topographic anatomy of both shoulders. Obvious atrophy of the supraspinatus and/or infraspinatus is frequently evident in individuals who present with chronic or attritional shoulder discomfort and dysfunction. Deltoid atrophy results in an abnormal shoulder contour and may be associated with specific brachial plexus injury or residual axillary nerve injury following shoulder dislocation.

The clavicle and the sternoclavicular joint may reveal variations that are consistent with previous injury and repetitive trauma, and that contribute to an overuse syndrome. Persistent abnormality of the clavicle contour may be associated with a fracture that has incompletely healed.

Visual inspection of the elbow includes assessing the carrying angle between the humerus and the forearm for angular deformities associated with previous injury, malunion of a fracture, or alteration of epiphyseal growth. Visual inspection may also reveal appreciable alteration in muscular anatomy, such as focal swelling adjacent to the medial epicondyle, within the pronator teres, or within the flexor mass distal to the medial epicondyle. On the lateral side, swelling may be observed over the brachioradialis or the extensors arising from the lateral epicondyle, or along the lateral olecranon–humeral or radiohumeral areas, reflecting joint effusion. Swelling or enlargement directly over the posterior portion of the olecranon is most likely associated with a reactive olecranon bursitis (Fig. 8).

PALPATION

Palpation of the shoulder area may locate areas of tendon or articular sensitivity, changes in comparative muscle volume, and nodules or fibrous areas within the muscles. Sensitivity to palpation on the medial side of the elbow may be due to irritation of the ulnar nerve as it passes through the ulnar groove, avulsion of the medial epicondyle (in adolescents), disruption of the ulnar (medial) collateral ligament, or concentric and eccentric stresses in the pronator and flexor muscle groups. Lateral elbow sensitivity may be caused by tears of the brachioradialis or extensor muscles. Avulsions may cause sensitivity

FIGURE 8. Elbow bursa.

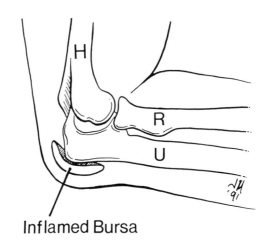

Inflamed Bursa

at the lateral epicondyle or olecranon. Palpation may also reveal skeletal irregularities, such as osteophytes or heterotopic bone, on the medial or lateral side of the elbow.

PASSIVE MOTION

Shoulder passive motion (movement performed by the examiner) provides evidence of instability or loss of flexibility, which may be secondary to muscle imbalance or tendon, capsule, and ligament contractures and fibrosis. Although normal mobility may be slightly increased during adolescence, hypermobility of the glenohumeral, acromioclavicular, sternoclavicular, and scapulothoracic articulations may be indicative of joint instability. The apprehension test for anterior dislocation of the glenohumeral joint is performed by abducting and externally rotating the patient's arm (Fig. 9). The arm is positioned in adduction and forward flexion to test for posterior dislocation. A look of apprehension will be evident on the patient's face if the shoulder is about to sublux or dislocate. An audible or palpable click may indicate a torn glenoid labrum. Young patients, however, may voluntarily sublux the shoulder anteriorly or posteriorly and show no apprehension.[3] This may be primary joint instability or a "trick" to acquire secondary gain.

Loss of glenohumeral joint flexibility is usually in the capsular tissues, and is best demonstrated by two distinct maneuvers: horizontal flexion and combined abduction (Fig. 10). It is important to evaluate these motions in two phases, with and without scapular stabilization. Without stabilization these motions may appear complete; however, observation of the scapular axillary

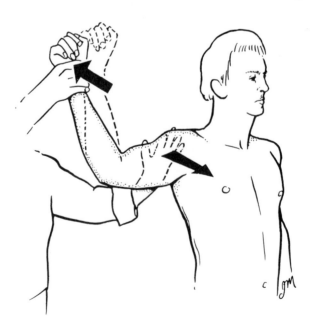

FIGURE 9. Apprehension test for anterior dislocation of the shoulder.

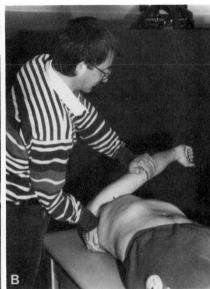

FIGURE 10.   Glenohumeral flexibility is evaluated using two maneuvers: *A,* horizontal flexion and *B,* combined abduction.

outline is significant. If there is contracture of the glenohumeral capsule, the scapula appears more prominent along the posterior axillary line in both of these maneuvers. With scapular stabilization, passive horizontal flexion of less than 45° indicates decreased flexibility. The consequence of this tightness is increased demand on the scapulohumeral musculature, altered humeral head-glenoid relationship, and ultimately abnormal shoulder complex motion.

Examination of elbow passive motion includes flexion-extension, forearm pronation and supination, and valgus stability. Flexion and extension are controlled primarily by the humeroulnar and humeroradial joints. Full extension is the first movement to be lost and the last to be regained. Valgus instability is evaluated by gently stressing the medial side of the joint with the elbow in full extension and in 25° of flexion. Instability indicates attenuation or rupture of the ulnar (medial) collateral ligament.[4] Forearm rotation (pronation and supination) is evaluated in two positions: with the humerus in a vertical position and the elbow at 90°, and with the elbow in maximum extension. This allows evaluation of intra-articular and extra-articular factors.

ACTIVE MOTION

Active motion is movement performed by the athlete without assistance. In the shoulder complex, it is important to observe the synchrony of scapulothoracic and glenohumeral motion, and compare with contralateral shoulder motion. These motions are best investigated by standing in front of and then behind the athlete, and observing the motions as the arms are sequentially abducted to maximum abduction and gradually returned to 90° of abduction. At that stage the shoulders are horizontally extended and externally rotated, and the scapulae adducted (retracted). This allows for inspection of any changes in synchrony, such as an early deviation in either the elevation or winging of the scapula, muscle fasciculations indicating abnormal muscle function, and other irregular or asymmetric movements of the scapula. Irregular movements are evidence of inability to stabilize the scapula, indicating muscle weakness, imbalance, or both. Excessive elevation or rotation of the scapula during external rotation is consistent with abnormal capsular tightness and secondary muscle imbalance. A resisted isometric examination may be performed after the observation of active motion to localize a painful site of a specific muscle.

For the elbow, the ranges of flexion/extension and pronation/supination are documented. Pronation/supination should be evaluated with the elbow in 90° of flexion and then in maximum extension. If there is limitation of any of these ranges, the examiner should attempt to detect the cause of the limitation, i.e., whether it is associated with an intra-articular osteocartilaginous fragment, bony block, soft tissue contracture, severe muscle injury, or spasm of the various individual muscle groups in the medial, anterior, lateral, and posterior areas.

MUSCLE STRENGTH

After completing the passive and active motion evaluation, it is important to document strength of each of the muscle components contributing to shoulder and elbow function. Shoulder evaluation includes observations of strength during the complete range of motion without gravity, with gravity, and with grades of hand or mechanical resistance. Elbow evaluation is conducted with the forearm in neutral rotation and full extension, and with the elbow at 90° of flexion. Measurements include grip strength and grades of resistance in pronation and supination. The information is then graded by either numerical or descriptive grades. The complete physical examination should evaluate the cervical spine, lower back, hips, and legs.

Supplemental Evaluation

Additional tests may provide supplemental information to establish a diagnosis or locate the site of pathology.

Electrodiagnosis is commonly used for evaluating neuromuscular activity. In the shoulder, a nerve conduction study is particularly informative in revealing damage to the suprascapular nerve, which may be responsible for weakness and atrophy of the supraspinatus and infraspinatus muscles. If the nerve conduction study indicates greater weakness in the infraspinatus, damage is to the more distal portion of the anatomic course of the nerve, probably near the spinoglenoid notch. In the elbow, the ulnar nerve may be damaged by repetitive stretching that causes secondary inflammatory changes. Persistent neurologic complaints and abnormal findings in the nerve conduction study may indicate the need for surgical relocation of the ulnar nerve. Neurologic symptoms may also be present when the median nerve is compressed due to anterior elbow pathology.

Needle electromyography is a valuable diagnostic tool in evaluating neuromuscular dysfunction of individual and portions of muscles.

If it is necessary to further evaluate the intra-articular aspects of a joint for a specific diagnosis, arthrography, computed contrast arthrotomography, magnetic resonance imaging (MRI), and diagnostic arthroscopy should be considered.

It is my current experience that the **standard shoulder arthrogram** is only of value in determining complete tears of the rotator cuff. When it is important to achieve better definition of the glenoid labrum, the rim of the glenoid, or the capsular ligaments, **computed contrast arthrotomography** or **MRI** have proven of maximum benefit. In many athletes with subclinical anatomic instability, computed arthrotomography and MRI have revealed a variety of tears of the labrum, damage to the glenoid, disruption of the labral-ligamentous conjoined architecture, and posterior joint pathology (Fig. 11). These individuals have presented frequently with vague, nonspecific complaints and have an associated deteriorating athletic performance that has not responded to conventional rehabilitative measures. MRI is useful in evaluating structures in the superior portion of the glenohumeral joint (the superior glenohumeral ligament, coracoclavicular ligament, coracohumeral ligament, superior anterior labrum, and rotator cuff) (Fig. 12). If uncertainty persists, **diagnostic arthroscopy** may reveal unidentified or unrecognized variations that may be amenable to arthroscopic surgery.

Elbow arthrography is most commonly used to detect loose osteocartilaginous fragments that have minimal ossification and are not evident on conventional radiographs. **CT arthrogram** is particularly helpful in identifying osteochondrotic lesions or intra-articular spurs, and the extravasation of dye provides information regarding capsular injuries, particularly ulnar (medial)

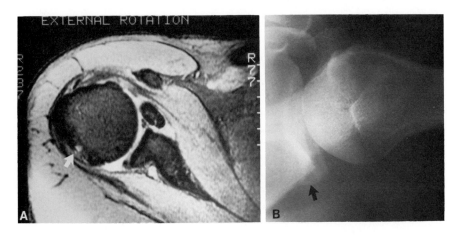

FIGURE 11.   Shoulder arthrograms. *A*, Loose body (arrow). *B*, New bone growth.

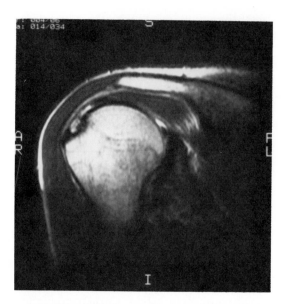

FIGURE 12. Magnetic resonance (anteroposterior) image of right shoulder with incomplete tear of the rotator cuff (supraspinatus tendon).

collateral ligament disruptions (Fig. 13). **MRI** is particularly helpful in detecting soft tissue injuries in the extra-articular area and evidence of avascular necrosis (osteonecrosis) as part of an osteochondrotic process. **Diagnostic arthroscopy** of the elbow provides a more direct evaluation for all of the aforementioned intra-articular abnormalities as well as the opportunity to detect

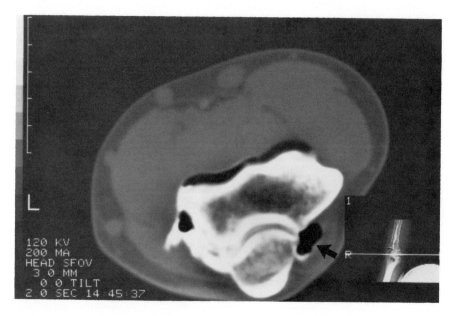

FIGURE 13. Arthrogram of right elbow. Extrusion of dye (arrow) indicates disruption of the ulnar (medial) collateral ligament.

and remove loose cartilaginous fragments and irregular areas of fibrous tissue, either reactive or congenital bands akin to those of the plica of the knee.

CLINICAL CONCERNS

Multiple factors may be implicated in the etiology of overuse syndromes of the shoulder and arm (Table 1). It is important to encourage the health professional to approach the ultimate diagnosis on the basis of probable cause.

Congenital Disorders

It is common for some anomalies of the musculoskeletal system to remain undiagnosed until the stressful demands of athletic activity focus attention to them. The anomalies may present as a source of discomfort limiting performance, or possibly of sufficient severity to preclude some aspects of motions required for performance.

ANOMALIES OF SKELETAL DEVELOPMENT

A failure of the acromion physis to fuse or an aberrant acromion physis that results in an incomplete acromion or excessive mobility within the acromion may be the source of superior shoulder discomfort secondary to any stressful upper extremity activity (Fig. 14).[7,8] Normally, the humeral head is in 30° of retroversion relative to the shaft of the humerus. Increased relative anteversion or true anteversion causes excessive stress on the anterior capsular structures of the glenohumeral joint with resultant discomfort, subluxation, or dislocation.[2] Any athlete who experiences anterior shoulder discomfort with minimal provocation or recurrent subluxation or dislocation with minimal trauma should be evaluated for such an anatomical variance. A youngster with Sprengel's deformity (Fig. 15), a congenital abnormality in the development of the scapula, is unable to achieve normal scapulothoracic motion. This places increased stress on the glenohumeral joint, with resultant limited total motion, stretching of the shoulder ligaments and capsule and, frequently, secondary

TABLE 1.   Etiologic Considerations for Overuse Syndromes

Congenital Disorders
    Anomalies of skeletal development
    Soft tissue abnormalities

Musculoskeletal Development
    Overdemand syndromes
    Epiphyseal stress syndromes
    Adaptive skeletal changes

Patterns of Function
    Excessive and repetitive microtrauma
    Improper biomechanics of function
    Muscle imbalance
    Neurovascular injury

Macrotrauma Effects
    Incomplete rehabilitation
    Joint instability
    Ligamentous disruption

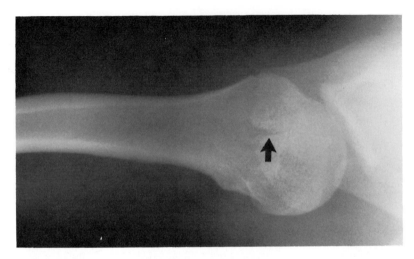

FIGURE 14. Axillary view of left shoulder of a baseball player with nonunion of the acromion physis.

discomfort, subluxation, or dislocation. A congenital synostosis of the proximal radius and ulna results in an inability to achieve normal pronation and supination (Fig. 16). When a child is learning to throw, an abnormal pattern of function is immediately evident, and persistence in attempting such activities results in unusual throwing mechanics and elbow pain. A congenital

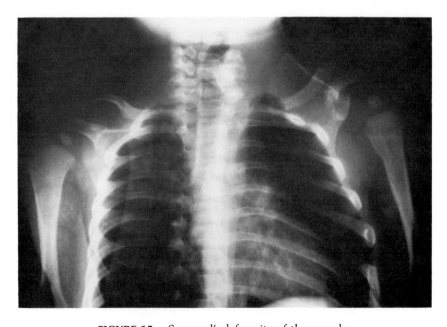

FIGURE 15. Sprengel's deformity of the scapula.

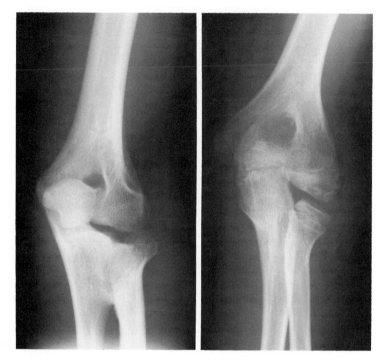

FIGURE 16 *(left).*   Congenital synostosis of the radius and ulna.

FIGURE 17 *(right).*   Congenital angular deformity of the proximal radius.

angular deformity of the proximal radius causes abnormal intra-articular forces on the head of the radius and the capitellum, resulting in progressive discomfort and radiographic changes during late childhood and early adolescence, which ultimately result in degenerative joint disease and progressive limitation of all motions (Fig. 17).

SOFT TISSUE ABNORMALITIES

Soft tissue abnormalities may also present as overuse syndromes. The extreme example of the soft tissue laxity syndromes is the Ehlers-Danlos syndrome. This is a collagen abnormality resulting in intrinsic laxity and subluxation and dislocation, frequently of the glenohumeral joint.

In many individuals, a slight increase in ligamentous laxity is evident during childhood and early adolescence. Minor subluxations are not uncommon in these age groups. The subluxation noted most often in early childhood is a "pulled elbow" or "nursemaid's elbow." With increasing muscle strength during adolescence, a moderate laxity may become the source of mild discomfort associated with repetitive action. On some occasions this laxity in an apparently normal individual is developed to excess and the individual is able voluntarily to sublux shoulders and elbows. If this voluntary hypermobility is not limited, a continuing pattern of abnormal joint mechanics ensues, probably leading to early degenerative joint disease.

Some children present with an abnormal contracture of the superior posterior shoulder musculature that is highlighted by a skin dimple overlying the superior posterior aspect of the glenohumeral joint. This persistent tightness results in abnormal scapulohumeral synchrony, and anterior subluxation and discomfort of the shoulder joint.

Musculoskeletal Development

Many young athletes frequently perform the same motion on a repetitive basis while practicing and attempting to perfect a specific skill. As a result of this approach, overuse problems may develop from excessive force on tissues transforming from cartilage to bone and extraordinary stress on growing bone, causing pain and possible deformity.

OVERDEMAND SYNDROMES

During adolescence, the secondary centers of ossification are enlarging and fusing to their respective bones. Repetitive stress during the transitional development of an apophysis or epiphysis from cartilage to bone may result in significant injury, which may cause permanent damage and possibly end an athletic career.

Proximal humeral apophysitis is a form of osteochondrosis that is characterized by shoulder pain, focal tenderness about the greater tuberosity, and a positive impingement sign (shoulder pain when the patient abducts the arm to 90° while the examiner stabilizes the scapula with one hand). The condition is common in swimmers, tennis players, and overhead throwers. Comparative x-rays of the two shoulders may demonstrate changes consistent with variations in development or a true bone reaction to injury.

The most frequently observed overdemand syndrome in the upper extremity is the **Little League elbow**, which is most often noted in the medial epicondyle of the humerus where the wrist and hand flexors and pronator teres originate. Repetitive actions such as throwing may result in avulsion injuries and secondary osteochondrial changes in the medial epicondyle, accompanied by exquisite discomfort on compression of the medial epicondyle (Fig. 18). Without treatment a more significant avulsion may develop, involving a larger portion of bone and possibly the entire medial epicondyle (Fig. 19).[11]

Complaints of vague elbow discomfort may be related to development of the trochlea. The history is usually of a talented child urged to improve by excessive throwing or tennis practice. During progressive ossification of the trochlea, a classical form of osteochondrosis may develop (Fig. 20). The presenting complaint is usually discomfort with a significant flexion contracture. This self-limiting problem requires reduction in stressful activity during the phases of repair and final trochlea ossification.

During the development of the secondary ossification center of the olecranon, overuse may cause irregular patterns of ossification and secondary pain (Fig. 21) which may be classified as osteochondrosis.

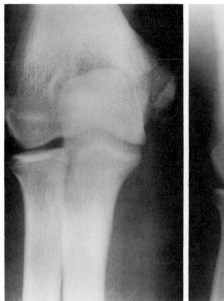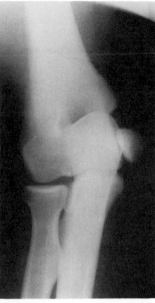

FIGURE 18 *(left).*   Radiograph of elbow of a 13-year-old boy with classic changes of the medial epicondyle consistent with osteochondrosis or overdemand syndrome. (From Pappas AM: Elbow problems associated with baseball during childhood and adolescence. Clin Orthop 164:30–41, 1982, with permission.)

FIGURE 19 *(right).*   A previously undiagnosed avulsion of the medial epicondyle in a 17-year-old athlete. He recalled having had severe elbow discomfort at approximately age 14 years after pitching on 3 successive days. He never pitched afterward. (From Pappas AM: Elbow problems associated with baseball during childhood and adolescence. Clin Orthop 164:30–41, 1982, with permission.)

During the phase of rapid growth and final development of the capitellum and radial head, a local avascular necrosis and secondary osteonecrosis or osteochondrosis may develop (Fig. 22). Compression of the lateral side of the elbow is a normal force in pitching and in weight-bearing activities performed with the arm in valgus, as in gymnastics. Repetitive forces at this time may result in deformation of the capitellum (Fig. 23), which, in turn, causes an alteration in the normal mechanics of the humeroradial joint with subsequent articular cartilage fibrillation and loose-body formation (Fig. 24).

EPIPHYSEAL STRESS SYNDROMES

During adolescence multiple biochemical and physical changes about the physes are associated with the rapid changes of skeletal maturation. The biochemical changes are noted in hydroxyproline levels[12] and in various hormones. In addition there is a known decrease in strength at the physeal-metaphyseal junction.[1,6] Repetitive stress at the time of these biochemical and physical changes may cause focal discomfort at an epiphysis or apophysis, or may cause disabling discomfort, i.e., epiphyseal stress syndrome. This epiphyseal

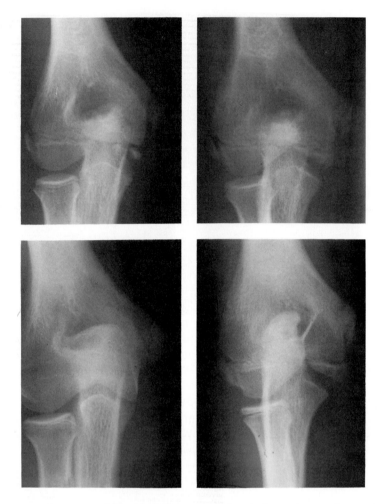

FIGURE 20.   A 10-year-old boy initially presented with the earliest evidence of elbow discomfort and flexion contracture. Classical osteochondrotic changes of the trochlea are evident in these radiographs obtained on four annual visits, beginning in the upper left and proceeding in a clockwise sequence. (From Pappas AM: Elbow problems associated with baseball during childhood and adolescence. Clin Orthop 164:30–41, 1982, with permission.)

stress reaction may occur at the base of the coracoid (Fig. 25) and be a source of disabling pain, or appear as a delayed fusion of the tip of the coracoid (Fig. 26). Some athletes may develop sufficient chronic stress to the medial epicondyle to prevent fusion to the humerus (Fig. 27). In a similar way, the olecranon physis may fail to unite (Fig. 28).

ADAPTIVE SKELETAL CHANGES

The repetitive motion of a specific athletic maneuver may result in adaptive changes in skeletal development. This is best exemplified by the

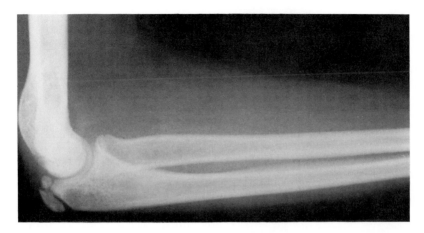

FIGURE 21. Radiograph of the olecranon of a 13-year-old boy who presented with persistent pain in the elbow after pitching, demonstrating the classic osteochondrotic pattern of the ossification center. (From Pappas AM: Elbow problems associated with baseball during childhood and adolescence. Clin Orthop 164:30–41, 1982, with permission.)

repetitive internal rotation–adduction force across the anterior shoulder in swimming and the progressive remodelling of the coracoid to a more anterolateral position, resulting in a coracohumeral impingement that presents as anterior shoulder pain (Fig. 29).

Patterns of Function

As more growing athletes limit themselves to a single major sport, specific patterns of physical performance are necessarily repeated in the quest for

FIGURE 22. The earliest presentation of avascular necrosis of the capitellum in a 12-year-old boy, causing general elbow discomfort following periods of pitching. He demonstrated bilateral evidence of the process but was not ambidextrous. (From Pappas AM: Elbow problems associated with baseball during childhood and adolescence. Clin Orthop 164:30–41, 1982, with permission.)

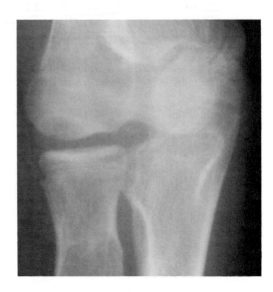

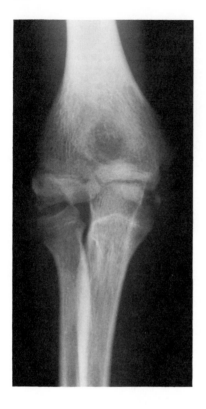

FIGURE 23. Roentgenogram of the elbow of an 11-year-old boy with osteochondrosis of both capitellum and trochlea causing progressive elbow discomfort and flexion deformity following periods of baseball pitching. (From Pappas AM: Elbow problems associated with baseball during childhood and adolescence. Clin Orthop 164:30–41, 1982, with permission.)

perfection. These year-round, single-sport athletes frequently exceed the biological tolerance of some tissues bearing the majority of the stress. This may occur in skilled performers, resulting in focal microtrauma and tissue disruptions. In some instances, a deviation from recommended biomechanics alters the usual forces and causes a physical problem and an abnormal performance. Some athletes are not properly directed to an appropriate weight conditioning program and create a muscle imbalance that ultimately influences their athletic performance.

EXCESSIVE AND REPETITIVE MICROTRAUMA

Repetitive activities, such as pitching, swimming, and gymnastics, that place the arm in extreme positions result in stretching, compression, and possible irritation of soft tissues in the shoulder. Microtears of tendons may cause tendinitis, or overdemand of an apophysis may present as impingement syndrome. This syndrome also results from squeezing of the anterior structures between the humeral head and the acromion.

Repetitive microtrauma may influence the development of some osteochondroses of certain apophyses and epiphyses during the period of transition from cartilage to bone. As discussed in the section on "Overdemand Syndromes," changes in the medial epicondyle frequently associated with Little

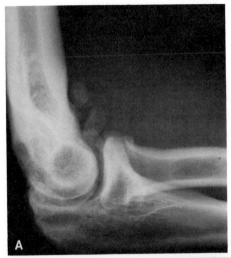

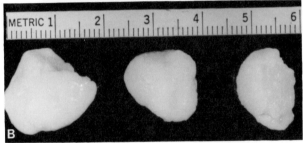

FIGURE 24. *A*, Lateral view of the elbow of a baseball player demonstrating multiple osteocartilaginous fragments. *B*, Osteocartilaginous fragments removed from the elbow. (From Pappas AM: Injuries of the upper extremities. In Vinger PV and Hoerner EF (eds): Sports Injuries: The Unthwarted Epidemic. Littleton, MA, PSG Publishing Co., Inc., 1981, p 226, with permission.)

League elbow occur during a specific period of musculoskeletal development. In the skeletally mature athlete, similar forces on the medial side of the elbow cause a different spectrum of injuries: microavulsion tears of the wrist and finger flexors, eccentric injuries of the pronator teres, ulnar nerve symptomatology, or partial or total disruption of the ulnar (medial) collateral ligament complex. The biomechanics of the throwing motion causes excessive valgus stress to the elbow and, when performed on a repetitive basis, are implicated in this spectrum of injuries.

"Tennis elbow" is a common problem in older athletes but rare in children. The characteristic source of discomfort is in the region of the extensor muscle origin from the lateral epicondyle. Most observers agree that the basic pathologic process is inflammation of the aponeurosis overlying the extensor carpi radialis and the extensor communis.[9]

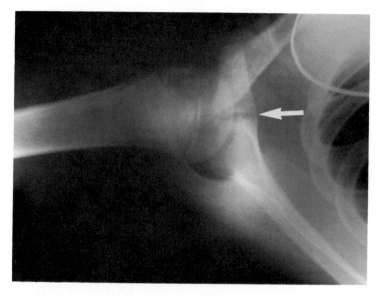

FIGURE 25. Axillary view of shoulder of a 12-year-old baseball player demonstrating epiphyseal stress reaction at the base of the coracoid (arrow).

IMPROPER BIOMECHANICS OF FUNCTION

In the throwing athlete, lack of total body coordination may result in shoulder pain. For example, a baseball pitcher with symptomatic low back pain will not be able to forward-flex sufficiently to pitch effectively. His pitches will usually be too high in the strike zone. A baseball pitcher who does not properly synchronize scapulothoracic and glenohumeral motion develops an irregular pitching pattern that produces extraordinary stress on the anterior shoulder ligament-muscle complex. This is demonstrated by computer analysis as an irregular pattern of pitch (Fig. 30). The pitcher complains of shoulder discomfort and ineffective pitching performance. In the later stages, it may be manifested as shoulder subluxation and inability to pitch.

In figure skaters, the stress of repetitive lifting and overhead activity or poor biomechanics may cause injury to the acromioclavicular joint (Fig. 31).

The best methods for evaluating functional biomechanics are observation by an experienced coach, movie or video review, and computer analysis.

MUSCLE IMBALANCE

Weakness of the scapulothoracic musculature, i.e, the trapezius-rhomboid-serratus stabilizer group, results in a disproportionate force being directed to the glenohumeral muscles and soft tissues. This results in impingement with discomfort in the glenohumeral joint, and muscle fatigue with secondary nodules and spasm in the trapezius-rhomboid-serratus complex. It is not uncommon for excessive stretch or even internal muscle disruption to be associated with excessive eccentric contraction of the posterior shoulder girdle muscles in the deceleration phase of throwing. This results in weakness in the

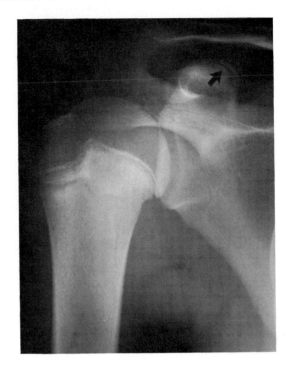

FIGURE 26. Anteroposterior view of shoulder of a 15-year-old pitcher showing separation of the coracoid tip (arrow).

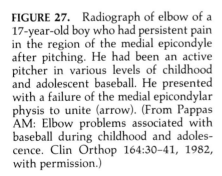

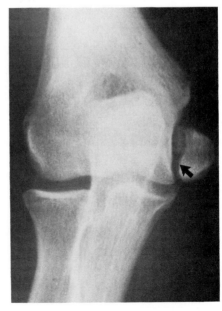

FIGURE 27. Radiograph of elbow of a 17-year-old boy who had persistent pain in the region of the medial epicondyle after pitching. He had been an active pitcher in various levels of childhood and adolescent baseball. He presented with a failure of the medial epicondylar physis to unite (arrow). (From Pappas AM: Elbow problems associated with baseball during childhood and adolescence. Clin Orthop 164:30–41, 1982, with permission.)

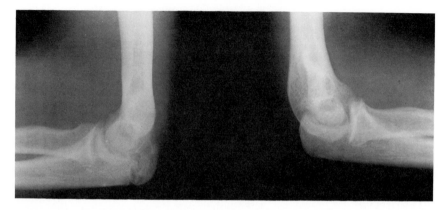

FIGURE 28. Comparative lateral view of both elbows of an adolescent baseball pitcher who presented with persistent elbow pain secondary to failure of normal closure of the olecranon epiphysis. (From Pappas AM: Injuries of the upper extremities. In Vinger PV and Hoerner EF (eds): Sports Injuries: The Unthwarted Epidemic. Littleton, MA, PSG Publishing Co., Inc., 1981, p 227, with permission.)

posterior scapulothoracic muscles, and presents clinically as weakness on examination as well as lateral positioning of the scapula in relationship to the vertebral spines.

NEUROVASCULAR INJURY

It is not uncommon in throwing athletes to identify weakness and atrophy with secondary dysfunction in the supraspinatus-infraspinatus-teres minor

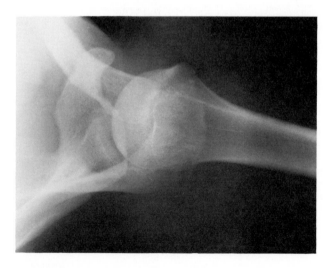

FIGURE 29. Axillary view of left shoulder demonstrating remodelling of the coracoid. This competitive swimmer complained of shoulder pain, which was caused by the hypertrophic coracoid impinging on the humerus.

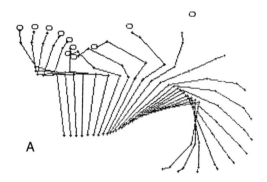

A

FIGURE 30. Computer analysis
of a pitch. *A*, Normal pattern. *B*,
Abnormal, irregular pattern.

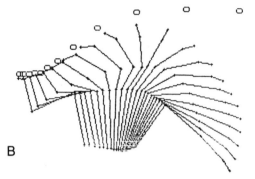

B

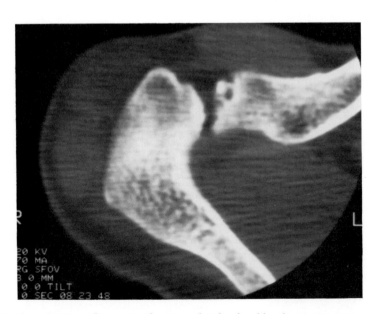

FIGURE 31. Computed tomography scan of right shoulder demonstrating cystic and
articular degeneration of the acromioclavicular joint.

complex. The cause may range from entrapment of the suprascapular nerve as it passes through the suprascapular notch, to a traction injury in the spinoglenoid area, to impairment of blood supply to the vasa vasorum of the nerve caused by a repetitive traction injury.

The repetitive mechanical trauma of the throwing motion can cause intermittent compression and intimal contusion of the axillary artery by the humeral head. This changes the physics of blood flow and increases the likelihood of axillary artery thrombosis. Anterior instability or subluxation produces more impingement on the artery and increases the potential for axillary artery thrombosis.[13]

Repetitive valgus stress on the medial side of the elbow, as in throwing, may cause ulnar neurapraxia and secondary inflammatory changes with resultant pain, distal symptoms, and physical findings of ulnar neuropathy.

Macrotrauma Effects

Macrotrauma may result in residual weaknesses that, with repetitive function, may cause discomfort, recurrent instability, or abnormal patterns of function. This effect may be due to any of the following: residual healing deficiency, incomplete rehabilitation, joint instability, ligamentous disruption, and intra-articular derangement. Secondary healing follows major injury, and a coordinated rehabilitation process must be pursued to ensure maximum recovery. If the healing process is not understood and respected, residual problems are likely to ensue. If comprehensive rehabilitation of all associated anatomic structures is not completed, residual imbalance and contracture may result. With repeated function, discomfort and dysfunction become evident as an overuse syndrome.

INCOMPLETE REHABILITATION

All major injuries cause sufficient tissue damage to demand a prescribed rehabilitation program. If the primary injury is a ligamentous disruption, grade I, II, or III, there is a likely period of protection for control of pain, swelling, and initial stages of healing. The more severe the injury, the longer this period for the development of muscle atrophy, ligamentous catabolism, and relative bone atrophy. These factors must be considered in the prescribed rehabilitation program.

Without this respect for healing, reinjury or another local injury is more likely. For example, a rotator cuff tear may not be sufficiently severe to require surgery; it may only require 3 weeks to 3 months to undergo the necessary healing prior to return to sport participation. If the athlete has not been advised regarding specific exercises to achieve desired patterns of motion and muscle strength and endurance, there will be a progressive depreciation of skills, increasing discomfort, and probable inability to participate. This overuse syndrome is a medical/rehabilitative failure: an avoidable problem.

JOINT INSTABILITY

Physiologic or acquired laxity of the supportive structures of the gleno-humeral joint can result in altered function and instability. Excessive motion or decentralization of the humeral head–glenoid relationship increases shearing stress on the articular surface of the glenoid and the labrum, contributing to anterior pathology.

Overuse syndrome of the shoulder is a common secondary effect of anterior dislocation. After the initial reduction and rehabilitation of this injury, approximately 75% of young athletes either frankly redislocate or sublux. This is associated with residual effects of the primary injury, i.e., soft tissue laxity, imbalanced muscle strength, and probable injury to the glenoid labrum. Instability is most often evident when the arm is in the position of abduction/extension/external rotation, as in the arm tackle in football or when a ski pole gets caught and forces the arm into this position. The classic description provided by an athlete with recurrent subluxation of the glenohumeral joint is that the shoulder "slips," or the arm "goes dead" momentarily. The primary finding on physical examination is apprehension or slip of the humerus in relation to the glenoid when the arm is placed in abduction/ extension/external rotation. Additional rehabilitation, an external support (Fig. 32), or surgery may be advised in some cases.

LIGAMENTOUS DISRUPTION

If the middle and inferior glenohumeral ligaments are avulsed from the glenoid labrum complex, repetitive anterior instability is almost certain to result. Glenoid labrum tears may be symptomatic as solitary problems without associated major ligamentous instability. In heavily muscled individuals who have tight ligaments, forces that characteristically cause subluxation or dislocation may cause an isolated tear of the labrum. The symptoms, which are similar to those of a torn knee meniscus, include catching, clicking, momentary locking, and the feeling of losing strength and function of the shoulder for a brief time. A tear in the medial inferior portion of the labrum causes locking or giving way, i.e., functional instability of the shoulder,

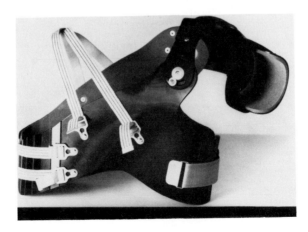

FIGURE 32. Shoulder Subluxation Inhibitor. (Courtesy of MSH Marketing Group, Inc., Keene, NH.)

whereas a tear in the superior glenohumeral–biceps area causes persistent discomfort with activity.

Weakening or disruption of the elbow ulnar (medial) collateral ligament complex, particularly the anterior band, causes the elbow joint to become painful and unstable. Stretch of the ulnar nerve may cause secondary inflammatory changes and pain. Pain and instability are frequently noted when the elbow is subjected to valgus stress, as in the acceleration phase of pitching (Fig. 7).

TREATMENT

Treatment of an overuse syndrome is determined by the underlying etiology. The initial treatment is generally rest. Rest in itself is inadequate, however, because the effect of injury or inflammation is not limited to the focal area of involvement. Instead, injury or inflammation may cause a sequence of biological events, including pain, disuse, atrophy, fibrosis, and contracture.

These apparent individual concerns should be considered as part of a related continuum, i.e., a pain-inflammation cycle (Fig. 33). Whenever there is soft tissue damage caused by an external force or internal focal inflammation, there is a period of pain and inhibitory disuse of the injured and adjacent areas. Continued pain and disuse result in clinical evidence of progressive weakness and atrophy. The biological response of repair to noninfectious inflammation is fibrogenesis. This results in fibrosis and a lack of flexibility, in addition to weakness and atrophy. If these consequences are not recognized and treated, contractures and muscle imbalance develop. The resultant limited excursion and existing weakness may cause altered function, usually a compensatory functional change observed as altered skill performance and a diminished quality of performance.

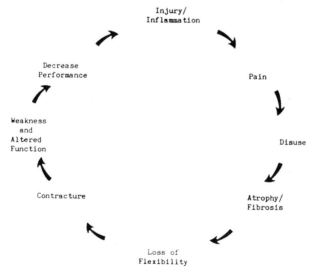

FIGURE 33.   The cyclical effects of injury or inflammation.

The most important goals of rehabilitation are to restore a full range of motion (flexibility and lack of deformity), strengthen weak muscles, and correct improper biomechanics. These goals must be accomplished sequentially. Strengthening muscles before a full range of motion is established reinforces abnormal patterns of motion and increases the chance of reinjury. Weak muscles must be strengthened to reestablish the dynamic muscle balance necessary for proper skill mechanics. Proper biomechanics must be emphasized to prevent the establishment of abnormal patterns that lead to reinjury. The need for external supportive devices must be carefully evaluated for potential effects on stability as well as performance. For example, an athlete with a subluxation of the shoulder would probably benefit from a motion-limiting external support (Fig. 32); however, it would be very difficult to throw or catch with that arm.

If there is evidence of inflammation, rather than a congenital anomaly or primary trauma, the use of anti-inflammatory medication is appropriate. The use of injectable steroids must be judiciously evaluated. They should be used infrequently and never on a repetitive, short-term basis.

If there are specific anatomic changes, further evaluation as to surgical intervention, open or arthroscopic, should be entertained. In instances in which anatomic changes cannot be resolved, recommendations must be made regarding a change of position on a team. For example, a pitcher with Little League elbow may become a first baseman; a swimmer must limit performing a stroke that causes the majority of the symptoms. In some instances, the changes may be severe enough to require a change of athletic events on a short-term or permanent basis.

PREVENTION AND CONDITIONING

While it is impossible to avoid all of the high-demand, repetitive stresses of throwing and other athletic activities, many overuse injuries can be prevented by a comprehensive preseason conditioning program, continued conditioning throughout the season, and limitation of performance at critical stages of growth. For example, the young baseball pitcher who continues to have open epiphyses should follow the restrictions for limited pitching defined by Little League Baseball regulations. The greater the number of innings pitched by a child with open epiphyses, the greater the likelihood of some anatomic impairment and, ultimately, restriction of the athletic career.[10] The conditioning program includes flexibility, cardiopulmonary endurance, and balanced strength of the muscles controlling the shoulder complex and elbow.

Shoulder

The primary goal of a shoulder conditioning program is to allow the shoulder to function in accordance with the normal biomechanics of shoulder complex integrated motion. To develop balanced shoulder function, upper body conditioning should focus on "conditioning" the larger muscles, rather than on power lifting. The larger muscles of the shoulder may be conditioned using any of the popular weight training machines; however, it is imperative to use less weight (8 pounds maximum) and more repetitions. The use of a heavy-weight exercise program to strengthen the shoulders, either through free weights or exercise equipment, generally results in greater strength in the larger muscles of the shoulder and imbalance in the smaller rotator cuff and scapula muscles.

The rotator cuff muscles (Fig. 3) and the scapula muscles are of paramount importance in providing the stability necessary for scapula fixation and glenohumeral movement.[5] Specific exercises are performed to strengthen the deltoid, supraspinatus, infraspinatus, teres minor, and lower trapezius muscles and the medial scapula musculature. Wall push-ups are used to strengthen the serratus anterior.

Elbow

The muscles controlling the elbow (biceps and triceps) and the forearm muscles controlling the wrist and hand are conditioned with conventional weight training techniques utilizing supplemental weights. Elbow curls in both directions (flexion and extension) should be performed. Wrist exercises should be done in six planes of motion, i.e., flexion, extension, radial and ulnar deviation, and pronation and supination. More repetitions with less weight are more effective than fewer repetitions with heavy weight for developing strength and endurance.

References

1. Bright RW, Burstein AH, Elmore SM: Epiphyseal-plate cartilage. A biomechanical and histological analysis of failure modes. J Bone Joint Surg 56A:668–703, 1974.
2. Debevoise NT, Hyatt GW, Townsend GB: Humeral torsion in recurrent shoulder dislocations. A technic of determination by x-ray. Clin Orthop 76:87–93, 1971.
3. Ireland ML, Andrews JR: Shoulder and elbow injuries in the young athlete. Clin Sports Med 7:473–494, 1988.
4. Jobe FW, Stark H, Lombardo SJ: Reconstruction of the ulnar collateral ligament in athletes. J Bone Joint Surg 68A:1158–1163, 1986.
5. Jobe FW, Tibone JE, Perry J, Moynes D: An EMG analysis of the shoulder in throwing and pitching: A preliminary report. Am J Sports Med 11:3–5, 1983.
6. Morscher E: Strength and morphology of growth cartilage under hormonal influence of puberty. Animal experiments and clinical study on the etiology of local growth disorders during puberty. Reconstr Surg Traumatol 10:3–104, 1968.
7. Mudge MK, et al: Rotator cuff stress tears associated with os acromiale. J Bone Joint Surg 66A:427–429, 1984.
8. Neer CS II: Impingement lesions. Clin Orthop 173:70–77, 1983.
9. Pappas AM: Injuries of the upper extremities. In Vinger PV and Hoerner EF (eds): Sports Injuries. The Unthwarted Epidemic. Littleton, MA, PSG Publishing Co., Inc., 1981, pp 215–233.
10. Pappas AM: Elbow problems associated with baseball during childhood and adolescence. Clin Orthop 164:30–41, 1982.
11. Pappas AM: Osteochondroses: Diseases of growth centers. Phys Sportsmed 17(6):551–62, 1989.
12. Pappas AM, Miller ME, Anderson M, Green WT: Relationship between maturity, growth, and urinary hydroxyproline. Clin Orthop 74:241–248, 1971.
13. Rohrer MJ, Cardullo PA, Pappas AM, et al: Axillary artery compression and thrombosis in throwing athletes. J Vasc Surg 11:761–769, 1990.

Overuse Syndromes of the Back and Legs in Adolescents

JACK T. ANDRISH, M.D.

Department of Orthopedics
The Cleveland Clinic Foundation
Cleveland, Ohio

Reprint requests to:
Jack T. Andrish, M.D.
Department of Orthopedics,
 Desk A-51
The Cleveland Clinic Foundation
9500 Euclid Avenue
Cleveland, OH 44106

Overuse syndromes are common in adolescents and youth participating in sports. The incidence appears to be directly related to the degree of organization.[1,27,44,55] In a review of athletic injuries in youth 15 years of age and younger seen in the Section of Sports Medicine at the Cleveland Clinic, 40% involved overuse. Seventy-two percent of these injuries affected the lower extremities and 9% affected the spine.[4]

Overuse syndromes usually result from repetitive microtrauma.[67] In soft tissues such as muscle and tendon, injury produced by repetitive microtrauma leads to an inflammatory response. On a positive note, inflammation is required to clear the region of injured tissue. On the other hand, inflammation causes a cellular response with proteolytic enzymes required for digestion of tissue debris. A vascular response and swelling also accompany the inflammatory phase of healing.[5,25]

Tissue breakdown and repair as a response to repetitive stress can result in remodeling of soft-tissue structures, ultimately resulting in increased strength.[12] As the strength of the structure improves, so does performance. If the body is given sufficient recovery time after repetitive stress to allow for healing and remodeling, complications from future tissue breakdown are minimized. In a sense, this represents one aspect of training. Failure to allow for sufficient recovery time will lead to clinically demonstrable overuse syndromes.

ADOLESCENT MEDICINE: State of the Art Reviews—Vol. 2, No. 1, February 1991
Philadelphia, Hanley & Belfus, Inc.

Bones can be injured by overuse. Normally, bone is in a constant state of remodeling with ongoing simultaneous resorption and formation.[38,66] In the face of repetitive mechanical stress, provided with sufficient recovery times, bone can hypertrophy. On the other hand, with repetitive mechanical overload, bone resorption occurs at a faster rate than bone formation, causing a weak osseous structure.[38,66] The end result of this type of overuse of bone is stress fracture.

Young people are inclined to avoid significant overuse syndromes if they are allowed sufficient time for recovery. Left to their own instincts, this is usually the case. However, in this age of earlier and earlier specialization within sports by young people, there is an increasing emphasis on organized training that often does not include sufficient opportunity for recovery. A philosophy of "let the kids play the game" would probably prevent most overuse syndromes.

GENERAL TREATMENT GUIDELINES

A common observation of adolescents and pre-adolescents presenting to our sports clinic with overuse syndromes is abnormal tightness of the affected region (Fig. 1). Garrett has recently demonstrated within the laboratory setting various properties of the muscle-tendon unit that make it more susceptible to injury when subjected to sudden or forceful strain.[14–16,49] Treatment options for youth with overuse syndromes emphasize the importance of obtaining and maintaining adequate flexibility. In addition to counseling about activity modification, this is probably the single most important treatment we can offer our young patients.

FIGURE 1. This flexibility pattern is typically found in our young patients with overuse syndromes of the lower extremities and back.

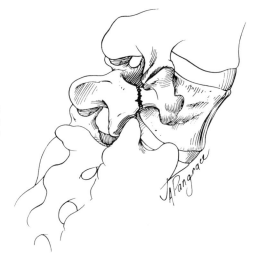

FIGURE 2. The break in the pars interarticularis represents a stress fracture often associated with low back pain.

OVERUSE INJURIES OF THE BACK

Spondylolysis

The term "spondylolysis" refers to a bony defect or fracture through the pars interarticularis. The pars interarticularis occupies the area of bone between the superior and inferior facets (Fig. 2). This discussion addresses patients with spondylolysis only and not spondylolisthesis. Instability of the spine in spondylolisthesis represents more than an overuse syndrome and engages principles of treatment used in the management of spinal deformity.

Spondylolysis has become a common cause of low back pain in young athletes.[37,40] Although approximately 5–7% of the population at large is affected by this condition, the incidence has been reported to be much higher in certain types of athletes.[13,46] Wiltse and others have described the anatomic and etiologic variants of spondylolysis.[45,70] The most common and the type with which we are concerned in young athletes is the isthmic variety. There may be a congenital predisposition to the development of this stress fracture; for example, congenital insufficiency of the posterior arches of the lumbar vertebrae may make them susceptible to stress fractures from repetitive load. Whether or not there is a congenital predisposition, spondylolysis in young athletes most often represents a stress fracture that is acquired rather than congenital.[65]

The etiology has been shown to include repetitive hyperextension of the lumbar spine.[13,37,40] Flexion of the spine produces compressive loads on the anterior structures, including the disc and vertebral bodies. Tensile stresses are placed across the posterior elements of the spine by the ligaments of the facet capsules, laminae, and spinous processes. With extension, direct loading occurs through the facet joints to the underlying bone. Biomechanical studies have produced estimates of forces across the pars interarticularis resulting from extension of the lumbar spine.[37] As noted, bone responds to repetitive loading by a remodeling process. The initial response is one of bone resorption, followed by bone deposition. If the load imposed upon the bone is great and insufficient time is allowed for remodeling, bone resorption outweighs bone formation, resulting in bone atrophy. Continuation of these loads will then produce stress fracture.

Although symptomatic spondylolysis occurs in individuals participating in virtually any sport, there appears to be an increased predilection in sports that emphasize repetitive hyperextension activities to the lumbar spine, such as gymnastics, and those that involve repetitive impact loading combined with sudden hyperextension, such as blocking and tackling in football (Fig. 3).[23]

RELEVANT HISTORY AND PHYSICAL EXAMINATION

The pain associated with spondylolysis is typically mechanical. Located in the lumbosacral region of the spine, pain is aggravated by activities and relieved by rest. Activities that aggravate the pain may include running, jumping, and heavy lifting, as well as prolonged standing, hiking, and even sitting.[57] True radicular symptoms are not typically associated with this condition, although pain may be referred down the buttock and posterior thigh.

The physical examination is varied. The patient may present with the typical back posture that seems to predispose to this condition; that is, hyperlumbar lordosis associated with forward tilt of the pelvis. The individual may have reasonable flexibility or apparent tight hip flexors and hamstrings. The posture may be characterized by a loss of normal lumbar lordosis, vertical orientation of the sacrum, and extremely tight hamstring muscles with marked limitation of forward bending (Fig. 4). Forward flexion and extension are limited by pain and spasm. In both instances, the neurologic examination is

FIGURE 3. The sudden shift from flexion to hyperextension of the lumbar spine found with blocking and tackling in football has been demonstrated to generate sufficient stress upon the posterior elements of the lumbar vertebrae to induce fatigue fracture.

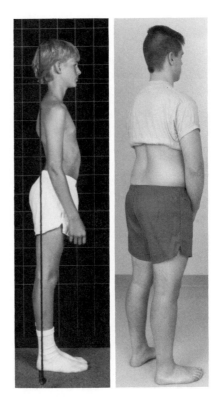

FIGURE 4. Hyperlumbar lordosis, found in many teenage and pre-teenage athletes, is a common presenting posture type associated with spondylolysis (left); as well as the young patient with lumbosacral spasm and a loss of normal lordosis (right).

normal and nerve root tension signs are absent. If hamstrings are exceedingly tight, stride length may be shortened. Hyperextension of the lumbar spine is associated with pain and apprehension. Pain produced by hyperextension of the lumbar spine is an extremely important finding.

RADIOGRAPHIC ASSESSMENT

Plain x-ray films of the lumbar spine usually reveal the bony defect of the pars interarticularis. This is frequently true with anteroposterior and lateral views, but the sensitivity is increased if oblique views of the lumbar spine are included. Oblique views demonstrate the "Scotty dog" outline formed by the pedicle, transverse process, and pars interarticularis (Fig. 5). The break is located in the neck of the Scotty dog.

Not uncommonly, this lesion produces clinical symptoms early in the course of development, before significant bone resorption has taken place. In this case, the lesion may not be detectable with plain x-ray films alone. A technetium bone scan as well as a CT scan will be helpful in depicting the pars defect (Fig. 6).

Occasionally, spondylolysis may be unilateral. Bony hypertrophy of the contralateral pedicle has been described in association with a unilateral pars defect.[62]

TREATMENT OPTIONS

As with most types of mechanical back pain, the mainstays of treatment for spondylolysis are activity modification and a physical therapy exercise

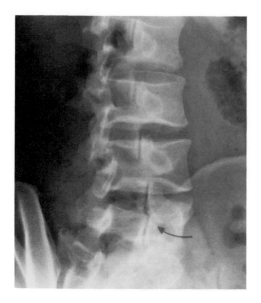

FIGURE 5. This oblique-view radiograph of the lumbar spine demonstrates a break in the neck of the "Scotty dog" of the fifth lumbar vertebrae as formed by the pedicle, transverse process, pars interarticularis, and facets.

program. Activity modification includes avoidance of activities that produce pain and avoidance of repetitive lumbar hyperextension. For some, this may not be so obvious. For example, the present emphasis on strength training has large numbers of young people performing progressive resistance exercises, all too often using improper technique. Machines or free weights that allow the individual to arch the back during the lift frequently exacerbate the pain associated with spondylolysis and should be avoided. Proper instruction in weight lifting technique is often the most important treatment rendered.

Physical therapy exercise programs are helpful. Because many young people present with poor posture, poor abdominal strength, and hyperlumbar

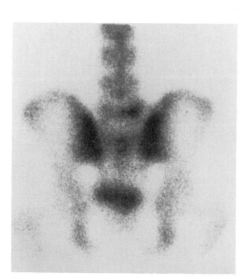

FIGURE 6. Bone scans can be extremely helpful in detecting the presence of a spondylolysis before it appears on plain radiographs.

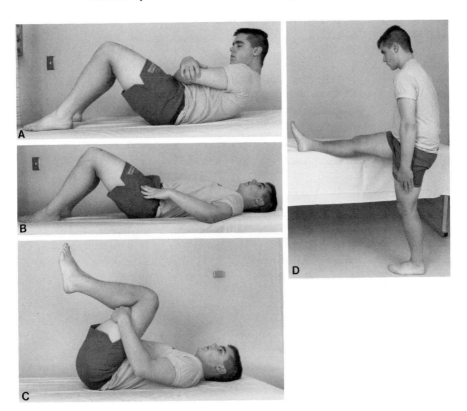

FIGURE 7.   A series of basic therapeutic exercises can be performed in the home or at school that emphasizes abdominal strengthening, anti-lumbar lordosis, and general flexibility training.

lordosis, significant clinical improvement and prevention of recurrence of symptoms can be accomplished by compliance with a proper exercise program. Quite naturally, these exercises emphasize abdominal strengthening (sit-ups with the knees bent), pelvic tilt (abdominal isometrics), Williams' flexion exercises, and general flexibility exercises for hamstrings and hip flexors (Fig. 7).

The role of bracing in the management of spondylolysis is controversial. There is no doubt that some patients feel better when placed in a lumbar support. Most effective is the Boston brace (Fig. 8). This bracing system can generate antilumbar lordotic posturing, thus relieving stress from the pars interarticularis. A simple lumbar corset may provide symptomatic relief as well. Either orthosis may be used in athletic participation, including contact/collision sports such as football.

The use of a Boston brace to promote healing of the pars interarticularis stress fracture is also controversial. It is reasonable to assume that because the majority of these lesions are stress fractures, the potential exists for healing to occur. A formal program described by Micheli uses the Boston brace worn full

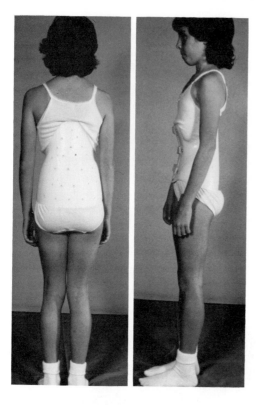

FIGURE 8. The Boston brace has been a useful orthotic aid in the management of spondylolysis.

time for 6 months, which has been reported to result in a healing rate of 25%.[68] The problem, however, is that the natural history of nondisplaced spondylolysis in the young is not well documented as a basis of comparison. Nevertheless, it is the author's feeling that it is reasonable to offer this treatment option for the adolescent or pre-adolescent patient with a nondisplaced pars interarticularis stress fracture. This treatment will probably have the highest success rate in lesions detectable only by bone scan.

Surgery is rarely indicated for the management of low back pain in adolescents with spondylolysis without spondylolisthesis. Indications for surgery include the presence of chronic back pain that produces significant disability and is unresponsive to adequate efforts with physical therapy and activity modification. Surgery consists of a posterior, lateral mass fusion. Implantable instrumentation is not required, nor is postoperative immobilization. The length of time for sufficient fusion to occur to allow full return to athletic participation is 6–12 months.

Lumbosacral Strain

This diagnosis is usually arrived at by the process of elimination. It is beyond the scope of this chapter to discuss in detail all entities that may present as low back pain in adolescents. However, it is important to remember that simply because a young person exacerbates back pain by participation in a sport does not necessarily mean that the sport is the cause of the problem. The differential diagnosis includes herniated lumbar disc, tumor, infection (discitis), Scheuermann's disease, spondylitis, and spondylolysis. For lumbosacral strain, mechanical stresses applied to the low back from participation in sports may create strain within the paraspinal tissues, resulting in soft tissue injury and inflammation.

Poor posture and poor athletic technique are common causative factors.[46] Poor posture consists of relatively weak abdominal muscles, forward pelvic tilt, and hyperlumbar lordosis. Hamstring tightness may also be prominent. Poor technique may consist of improper strength training (Fig. 9) or improper techniques in the sport itself. Simple mechanical overload may result from unrealistic training and conditioning programs.

RELEVANT HISTORY AND PHYSICAL EXAMINATION

The history is one of mechanical back pain; that is, pain located in the lumbosacral area of the back that is aggravated by activities and relieved by rest. The pain generally does not awaken the individual at night. No true radicular symptoms are present. Pain may radiate down the buttocks or

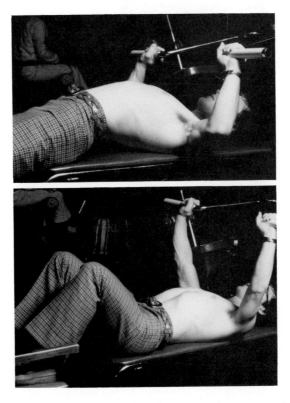

FIGURE 9. As demonstrated with the bench press, techniques can be modified to minimize lumbar stress.

posterior thighs but usually does not pass distal to this. Examination of the young patient may demonstrate a flattening of the normal lumbar lordosis secondary to muscle spasm. There is tenderness to palpation over the paraspinal soft tissues. Hamstring muscles are frequently tight and forward bending is limited. An important feature of the forward bend test is that there is no list. The presence of a list should arouse strong suspicion that an underlying neuropathic process, such as herniated disc or tumor, exists (Fig. 10). Lesser severity of lumbosacral strain is frequently associated with hyperlumbar lordosis. Straight leg raising demonstrates tight hamstrings but no evidence of nerve root tension signs or radicular pain. The neurologic examination is normal.

TREATMENT OPTIONS

As for spondylolysis, treatment of lumbosacral strain includes relative rest and activity modification. Ice compresses can be helpful to reduce muscle spasm, and nonsteroidal anti-inflammatory agents may help to relieve pain and minimize inflammation of soft tissues. If the initial presentation consists of severe pain and spasm, physical therapy exercises are withheld until a period of rest allows for some resolution, usually 7–14 days. Then, institution of a physical therapy exercise program that emphasizes abdominal strengthening activities and flexibility of hamstring and hip flexor muscles will help to promote resolution of symptoms and prevention of recurrence.

For some athletes, an elastic lumbar support or corset may help during athletic participation. This is certainly not the primary treatment and is no substitute for relative rest, activity modification, and physical therapy exercises.

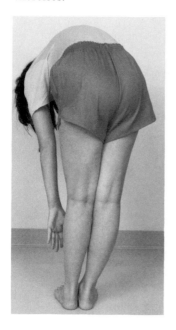

FIGURE 10. An atypical scoliosis or list in the young patient with back pain should signal the possibility of an underlying neuropathic process such as herniated disc or tumor.

Posterior Iliac Apophysitis

Commonly seen in adolescent cross-country runners, this true overuse syndrome of the low back is characterized by pain over the posterior iliac crest. As with other apophyseal overuse syndromes, there is a perception of muscle tightness, repetitive microtrauma at tendinous insertions into cartilaginous apophyses, and subsequent inflammation. The erector spinae as well as the quadratus lumborum may be involved.

The treatment is the same as for lumbosacral strain, but with an emphasis on stretching exercises. Attention to proper warm-up and stretching prior to workouts as well as repetition of stretching exercises after workouts is important. Continued participation is determined by the amount of pain reasonably tolerated.

OVERUSE SYNDROMES OF THE LOWER EXTREMITIES

Apophysitis/Tendinitis

In the skeletally immature athlete, numerous overuse syndromes are characterized by inflammation at tendon insertions into cartilaginous apophyses.[67] Physes are growth plates that contribute to longitudinal growth of extremities. Apophyses are growth plate–like structures that serve as sites of attachment for muscle-tendon units. Although muscles primarily originate from the periosteum about long bones, tendons insert into the perichondrium with fibers that continue directly into the apophysis.[71] This not only serves as a strong attachment for tendon insertions, but also provides a more gentle transition of force from the flexible muscle-tendon unit to the more rigid underlying bone.

Chronic, repetitive, submaximal tensile stress of muscle-tendon units in the skeletally immature athlete can lead to the repetitive microtrauma and soft-tissue injury seen at the tendon/apophyseal transition. The inflammatory phase of this injury is accompanied by a cellular and vascular response.[5,25] It is the increased vascular response that at times is sufficient to produce warmth, erythema, and even growth stimulation. Although entities referred to as apophysitis imply that there is inflammation within the apophysis, the inflammation actually occurs within the tendon itself, adjacent to the site of insertion.

Anterior Superior Iliac Spine

This apophysitis/tendinitis serves as the site of attachment for the sartorius muscle and the tensor fascia lata muscle. Tightness of hip flexor hamstring, and hip abductor muscles frequently accompany this condition.

RELEVANT HISTORY AND PHYSICAL EXAMINATION

The young athlete typically presents with hip pain that is exacerbated by running activities and relieved by rest. Initially, pain may occur only at the start of a running workout or afterward. As the condition worsens, pain may be experienced throughout the workout and become severe enough to prevent participation. The condition typically affects runners. Upon closer examination of the patient, the extremes of hip rotation and extension may produce pain. Tenderness is elicited by direct palpation at or just distal to the anterior superior iliac spine of the pelvis.

Plain x-ray films of the pelvis are usually interpreted as normal. Separation of the anterior superior iliac spine apophysis can occur but does not require operative reduction.

TREATMENT OPTIONS

Treatment includes activity modification, relative rest, ice compresses, and stretching exercises for hip flexor, abductor, and hamstring muscles. A brief course of nonsteroidal anti-inflammatory medication may be helpful as well. We have not found surgical exploration to be necessary in the skeletally immature athlete, but in the adult, surgical exploration with local debridement of chronically inflamed tissue can be helpful.

Rest and activity modification are "relative." Adequate time must be provided during initial interviews with patients to assess exactly what their training habits have been, what their expectations are, and what recent changes, if any, have occurred in their activity levels that may have led to the development of the overuse syndrome. After this discussion, a mutually agreed upon level of activity restriction can usually be arrived at. The simplest form of treatment is to stop all activities that may have produced the problem in the first place. Although effective, this is not always necessary. In apophysitis/tendinitis of the anterior superior iliac spine, for instance, it may be possible to alleviate symptoms by restricting activities that involve running on hilly terrain, climbing stairs, jumping, vaulting, or sprinting. This still allows for light participation at a pace that keeps the young person involved to some extent. When pain has subsided, a graduated return to full running activities is allowed. The amount of time required for treatment and rehabilitation is highly variable, ranging from a few days to 6 weeks.

We have not found it necessary in young patients to use physical therapy modalities such as ultrasound or phonophoresis, nor would we recommend cortisone injections.

Osgood-Schlatter's Disease

In a general sports medicine clinic, approximately 4–16% of overuse syndromes of the lower extremities in skeletally immature individuals will be given this diagnosis.[17,51] First described independently in 1903 by Osgood of Boston and Schlatter of Germany, this condition represents the classic example of "growing pains."[50,61] A great deal of apprehension may be expressed by the parents. The presence of a painful, tender swelling about the knee conjures up fears of a bone tumor (Fig. 11). Perhaps the most significant service that can be rendered includes the explanation that this is a benign, self-limited condition. Even without treatment, the condition will resolve and not lead to permanent damage within the knee joint. The bump remains, but pain and tenderness usually resolve.

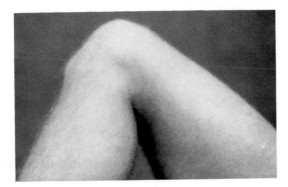

FIGURE 11. The typical Osgood-Schlatter bump.

The tibial tubercle serves as the apophyseal attachment for the distal portion of the patellar tendon. This apophysis may be in continuity with the proximal tibial growth plate, or it may be radiographically separate (Fig. 12). Henning has reported his findings in young patients with Osgood-Schlatter's disease and found abnormal tightness of the quadriceps, hamstring, and gastrocnemius/soleus muscles.[28] EMG analysis demonstrated relative over-activity of the quadriceps compared with the hamstring muscles. In other words, muscle imbalances combined with abnormal tightness of muscle-tendon units predispose to soft tissue overload and injury. Biopsy specimens from patients with Osgood-Schlatter's disease have demonstrated the typical histologic signs of inflammation and tendinitis.[47] Not infrequently, this inflammation within the patellar tendon may eventually lead to the formation of an ossicle (Fig. 13). Chronic inflammation can also stimulate overgrowth of the tibial tubercle resulting in the well-known bony prominence anteriorly.

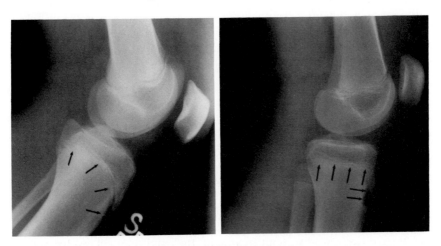

FIGURE 12. The radiographic appearance of the proximal tibial growth plate varies. At times, the physis is in continuity with the tibial tubercle (left), and at times it is separate (right). Fragmentation of the tubercle may be a normal variant as well.

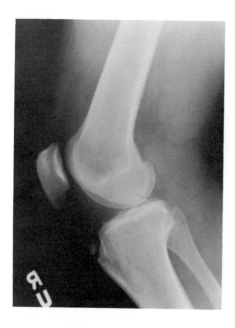

FIGURE 13. This large bony ossicle, a cause of persistent pain in this 19-year-old basketball player, required surgical removal.

RELEVANT HISTORY AND PHYSICAL EXAMINATION

The amount of pain experienced by the young patient with Osgood-Schlatter's disease is variable. In mild cases, pain is present at the start of running activities but resolves after an adequate period of warm-up. Jumping, in particular, may cause sharp pain over the tibial tubercle. Perhaps more dramatic is the degree of tenderness over the swollen and prominent tibial tubercle.

Fragmentation of the tibial tubercle on plain x-ray films is not diagnostic of Osgood-Schlatter's disease. In fact, radiographic fragmentation of this apophysis is a normal variant. However, true heterotopic bone formation within the distal patellar tendon itself is diagnostic.

TREATMENT OPTIONS

Immobilization has not been necessary in our experience. Occasionally, persistent pain over the tibial tubercle associated with a bony ossicle in the skeletally mature patient may accompany chronic patellar tendinitis. This can be relieved by surgical debridement of the ossicle and the inflamed, degenerated portions of the patellar tendon. There is no place for corticosteroid injection in the treatment of Osgood-Schlatter's disease.

For adolescent athletes, the author has been pleased with the treatment program described by Henning.[28] This treatment consists of hamstring, quadriceps, and heel cord stretching exercises combined with hamstring progressive resistance strength training. These exercises are performed daily. Relative rest is also recommended and usually does not entail cessation of running as long as the pain is mild and nonprogressive and does not affect performance. It has been suggested that this treatment program provides 85% satisfactory results within 3–12 weeks. The author's experience has been similar.

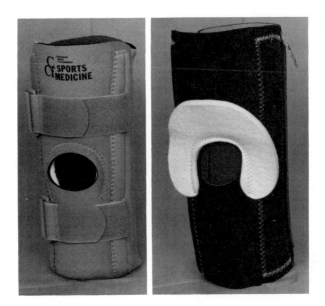

FIGURE 14.   The counterforce brace can be a handy adjunct in the athletically active patient with Osgood-Schlatter's disease.

Nonsteroidal anti-inflammatory agents may also be prescribed. The use of a counterforce brace can be helpful when worn for running and jumping activities (Fig. 14). These braces are not prescribed as a substitute for physical therapy, but serve as an adjunct that allows an increased level of participation until the exercise regimen achieves satisfactory results.

Jumper's Knee

Anterior knee pain associated with running and jumping activities associated with marked tenderness to palpation over the inferior pole of the patella characterizes the overuse syndrome called "jumper's knee."[10] Fibrinoid degeneration, a proximal patellar tendinitis, has been described within the central portion of the proximal patellar tendon.[10] Occasionally, in the skeletally immature individual, an ectopic calcification may be present adjacent to the inferior pole of the patella, suggesting chronic avulsion. In this instance, the condition may be referred to as Sinding-Larsen syndrome.[63]

RELEVANT HISTORY AND PHYSICAL EXAMINATION

Whereas Osgood-Schlatter's disease is a self-limited process, jumper's knee is not. The latter condition tends to be more indolent and chronic, ultimately leading to greater disability with regard to athletic participation. Whereas Osgood-Schlatter's disease responds consistently to various treatment regimens, jumper's knee does not. Anterior knee pain is aggravated by running and jumping activities. The condition occurs frequently in basketball players and high jumpers.

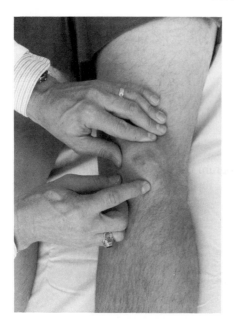

FIGURE 15. Point tenderness is typically found along the inferior pole of the patella in the patient with jumper's knee. Manual depression proximally will tilt the inferior pole of the patella forward, allowing greater sensitivity for the detection of tenderness.

The characteristic finding on physical examination is exquisite tenderness to direct palpation over the inferior pole of the patella. This may be missed if the patella is palpated when the knee is extended, but may be easily found if palpation to the distal pole is performed while tilting the patella and simultaneously applying downward pressure on the superior pole (Fig. 15).

Hamstring tightness is the predominant biomechanical abnormality found. Secondary muscle imbalances to compensate for tight muscle-tendon units have been suggested as an underlying cause, combined with chronic mechanical stress overload.

Plain x-ray films are typically normal, although a small linear fleck of bone may be apparent just 1–2 mm anterior and distal to the inferior pole of the patella.

TREATMENT OPTIONS

In the young athlete, our management of jumper's knee is similar to that for Osgood-Schlatter's disease. Emphasis is on hamstring stretching exercises and cryotherapy. Ice compresses are applied for 20–30 minutes after each workout or ice massage is performed for 5–10 minutes. Treatments may be repeated 3–4 times daily. The need for adequate warm-up, stretching, and warm-down (to include stretching) exercises is emphasized.

Running activities are allowed if the pain is present only at the beginning of or after activities. A counterforce brace may help to control mild symptoms during activities. If symptoms affect performance, restriction of running is necessary; running is restricted for 6 weeks and gradually returned to pre-treatment levels over the ensuing 6–12 weeks.

There is no place for local corticosteroid injection in this condition. If done, the weakening that occurs within the patellar tendon may predispose the knee to spontaneous rupture.[7,8,33,53,58,59]

Chronic resistant cases can be managed by surgical exploration. With the use of local anesthesia, the proximal patellar tendon is explored and debrided. Typically, the inflamed and diseased portion of tendon is not located superficially but rather is found deep within the central region of the proximal tendon. Postoperatively, running activities are restricted for 6 weeks, with gradual resumption over the following 6 weeks. Surgical management is not a substitute for a therapeutic exercise program but is viewed as an adjunct. The author's experience with additional physical therapy modalities such as ultrasound and phonophoresis has been inconsistent, generally they have not been helpful.

Sever's Disease

The skeletally immature adolescent with heel pain is often found to have a condition termed "Sever's disease." The Achilles tendon is formed by the distal tendons of the gastrocnemius and soleus muscles. This tendon inserts upon the calcaneal apophysis. Abnormal tightness of the heel cord is frequently present and is believed to contribute to increased stress across the tendo-apophyseal insertion.

RELEVANT HISTORY AND PHYSICAL EXAMINATION

The pain and tenderness associated with Sever's disease usually occur directly over the calcaneal apophysis posteriorly. Occasionally the tenderness is found diffusely about the calcaneal apophysis. The pain is made worse by running and may occur with everyday walking.

Plain lateral radiographs of the foot frequently demonstrate a fragmented and sclerotic calcaneal apophysis (Fig. 16), which is commonly believed to be

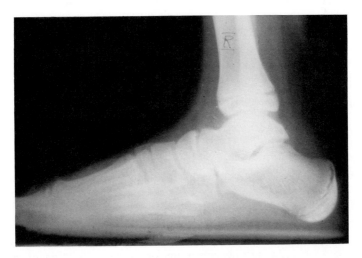

FIGURE 16. Although the sclerotic and fragmented posterior calcaneal apophysis has been associated with Sever's disease, in reality this is a normal finding in the skeletally immature foot.

diagnostic of Sever's disease. In reality, this finding is a normal variant and not diagnostic of the condition. Sever's disease is a clinical diagnosis, not a radiographic one.

TREATMENT OPTIONS

Traditionally, a heel pad was all that was necessary to treat Sever's disease, and, in fact, still may be best for most of the mild cases that present to our office. The heel pad may be formed from $3/8$ inch felt, or may be supplied as a commercially available Sorbithane or foam rubber heel pad. The newer viscoelastic heel pads have improved shock-absorbing characteristics and better patient acceptance (Fig. 17). These heel pads are worn not only in athletic footwear but in everyday shoes as well. Upon inspection of the young person's footwear, it is not unusual to find a preference for inadequate loafers with poor quality insole and heel cushion.

Heel cord stretching exercises and proper warm-up and warm-down techniques are prescribed. We have not had much success with physical therapy modalities other than exercise. Rarely, the pain may be severe enough to warrant the use of a non-weight-bearing short leg cast for 6 weeks. The subsequent rehabilitation is prolonged, restrictive, and protective. Rarely is such extensive protection required.

Again, there is no place in this condition for the use of corticosteroid injections. Surgery has not been required.

Patellofemoral Pain Syndrome

It is impossible to discuss overuse syndromes of the lower extremity without discussing patellofemoral pain. Over 30% of all knee injuries presenting to our Sports Medicine Clinic carry this label.[4] Traditionally referred to as chondromalacia of the patella, patellofemoral pain syndrome is a better descriptive term when applied to young athletes. Whereas chondromalacia refers to a degenerative process of articular cartilage often seen in middle-aged recreational athletes, articular cartilage changes are much less common in adolescents (Fig. 18).[32]

FIGURE 17. The newer, viscoelastic heel pads can often provide immediate relief from the painful heel of Sever's disease.

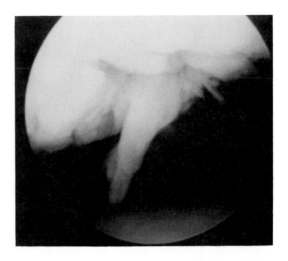

FIGURE 18. As seen in this arthroscopic view of the patella, chondromalacia is a degenerative process of articular cartilage. This presentation, common in the adult, is distinctly uncommon in the adolescent or preadolescent athlete.

The patella is the largest sesamoid bone in the body. It not only provides protection to the anterior aspect of the knee joint from direct blows, but it enhances the mechanical efficiency of the quadriceps extensor mechanism about the knee. It increases the lever arm through which the quadriceps muscles exert their force and thus improves effective strength and power.[21]

The quadriceps angle is formed by the intersection of a line drawn down the long axis of the femur to the central portion of the patella, with a line drawn from the tibial tubercle to the central portion of the patella. The angle so formed (the "Q" angle) illustrates the lateralizing forces exerted upon the patella with active muscle contraction (Fig. 19). The greater the "Q" angle, the greater the force exerted to produce lateral subluxation. Restraining forces consist of the medial parapatellar retinaculum and the vastus medialis obliquus musculature as well as the shape and congruence of the femoral trochlea and patella.[21] In patellofemoral pain syndrome in adolescent athletes, malalignment of the patella is a frequent predisposing anatomic variant. Incongruence between the patella and the femur associated with lateral subluxation produces uneven stresses, not only within the patella itself and its underlying articular cartilage, but within the musculotendinous and fascial insertions as well. Excessive pressure to the lateral patellar facet and the underlying lateral femoral condyle may result.[22]

There are many causes for patellar malalignment. Rotational malalignment of the femur or tibia is the most common (Fig. 20). Medial femoral torsion producing a "kneeing-in" posture is frequently seen; external tibial torsion may be associated with lateralization of the tibial tubercle. Both of these conditions, either separately or in combination, will increase the quadriceps angle. Flat feet secondary to excessive pronation may also be associated with excessive medial rotation of the leg, at times producing a valgus thrust about the knee. Mild proximal tibia vara can increase the quadriceps angle by its frequent association with lateralization of the tibial

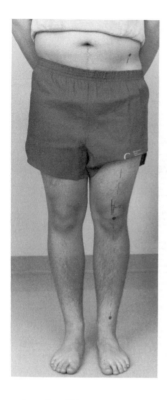

FIGURE 19. As the Q angle increases beyond 15 to 20 degrees, the likelihood of patellofemoral incongruity and instability increases.

tubercle. Finally, a high-riding patella (patella alta) may contribute to abnormal patellofemoral mechanics.[18,29,35,36,54]

RELEVANT HISTORY AND PHYSICAL EXAMINATION

Typically, the young person presents with anterior knee pain that is aggravated by activities such as running and jumping and relieved by rest. The pain may worsen after prolonged sitting (positive movie sign), kneeling, squatting, or stair-climbing. Occasionally, effusion within the knee may be present and the symptoms may be associated with signs of mechanical instability (giving way or catching sensations).

Physical findings are characterized by pain and apprehension when the patella is manually compressed against the femur while being subluxated alternatively medially and laterally. There may be tenderness to direct palpation beneath the medial facet and a painful arc of motion during active knee extension against resistance. Subpatellar crepitation may be present.

Although this condition certainly occurs in highly competitive male and female athletes, it is more often found in recreational athletes (often trying to rise above their recreational status by participating in an organized competitive sport).

TREATMENT OPTIONS

A wide variety of therapeutic approaches exist to the management of patellofemoral pain.[18,30,35,36,54] Our approach, however, has been to emphasize

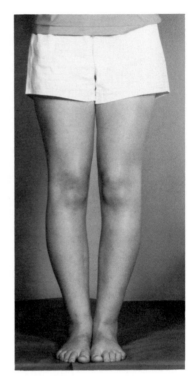

FIGURE 20.   Femoral anteversion and/or external tibial torsion produce the typical "kneeing in" posture frequently associated with the patellofemoral pain syndrome.

to patients and their parents that this is a manageable problem. Most often, the management is nonoperative and includes activity modification and the institution of a therapeutic exercise program.

The exercises consist of short arc quadriceps progressive resistance strength training (Fig. 21). In other words, leg extension exercises are performed from 30° of flexion to full extension with incremental increases in ankle weights. Our goal is to selectively improve the strength of the vastus medialis obliquus, although recent evidence suggests that these traditional exercises are really not as specific as once believed.[26] In order to maintain proper balance of musculature about the knee, hamstring strengthening exercises are employed and attention is given to flexibility. The literature suggests that satisfactory results are achieved in 76–93% of individuals.[18,29]

Activity modification is emphasized. The patient should avoid excessive kneeling, squatting, deep knee bends, stair climbing, and running hills (in particular, running down long grades). Patients are advised that if they can refrain from performing half of the activities that produce pain in the knee, plus comply with the exercise program, pursuit of those sporting activities they really care about can be done more comfortably. As with any exercise program, 6–12 weeks are required in order to obtain objective results.

Numerous orthotics have been used about the knee for this condition. The author prefers a simple elastic cartilage brace and expects at least 50% of

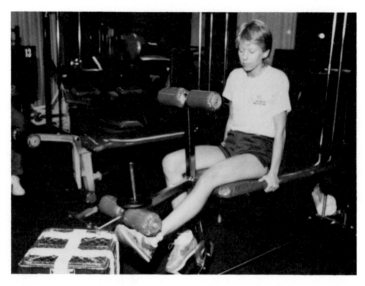

FIGURE 21. Strength training for the quadriceps muscles is carried out by performing "short arc" progressive resistance exercises from 0 to 30 degrees of flexion.

patients to "feel better" when this is used for athletic and recreational activities (Fig. 22). Occasionally, foot orthotics in the form of longitudinal arch supports to prevent excessive foot pronation can help. Attention to rotational alignment

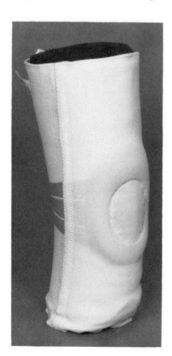

FIGURE 22. A simple elastic cartilage brace can provide symptomatic improvement in at least 50% of patients with patellofemoral pain.

and foot position during the stance phase can provide some objective criteria for this selection. Nonsteroidal anti-inflammatory medication may be a helpful adjunct in the short term. Ice compresses after activities help. There is no place for corticosteroid injections within the knee joint. Additional physical therapy modalities have not been beneficial in our experience.

For the relatively few patients who are compliant with physical therapy and activity modification but continue to be significantly disabled because of patellofemoral pain, an arthroscopic examination can be helpful. This is usually combined with a lateral retinacular release. Our experience is similar to that described in the literature.[9,24,30] Eighty percent of our patients receive a satisfactory result from this form of surgical treatment.

Shin Splint Syndrome

This term has been loosely applied to conditions producing pain in the leg as a result of repetitive impact loading such as occur with running, marching, or hiking.[2,64] Various injuries can produce this clinical syndrome. A more appropriate term is the medial tibial stress syndrome.[20,48]

The most common site of pain and tenderness is along the posteromedial border of the tibia at the mid and distal third levels (Fig. 23). Traditionally, shin splints have been believed to result from inflammation of the tibialis posterior muscle or from micro-tears of the muscle origin from the tibia (periostitis) of the flexor digitorum longus.[3] However, anatomic studies have demonstrated that the location of tenderness actually corresponds more often

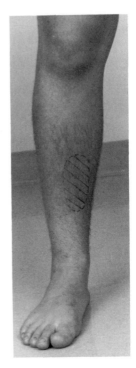

FIGURE 23.   Most frequently, the pain and tenderness of typical shin splints are located along the posteromedial border of the tibia about the junction of the middle and distal thirds.

to the bony origin of the soleus muscle.[43] With impact-loading activities such as walking and running, stress is propagated from the ground contact proximally up the foot and lower extremity. Although the leg musculature stabilizes foot and ankle motion and assists in propelling gait forward, this eccentric loading upon the musculature can result in repetitive microtrauma to the periosteal site of origin. The result is inflammation with swelling and tenderness as well as pain with weight bearing.

Pes planus has been described as a feature that predisposes to the development of medial tibial stress.[42,69] The increased pronation that occurs with a flat-foot deformity places greater stress upon the supporting musculature. Tight heel cord musculature is believed to contribute to the development of this syndrome for the reasons previously described.

RELEVANT HISTORY AND PHYSICAL EXAMINATION

Pain in the legs that is aggravated by running activities and relieved by rest is the classic presentation. The pain is most often located along the posteromedial border of the tibia. Almost invariably, the development of this syndrome is associated with a change in activity, usually one of increased intensity in the level of training. For example, the non-athlete may decide to begin a running program or a well-trained athlete may significantly increase the duration and intensity of training in preparation for a future event. However, the change may also relate to surface, terrain, or footwear.

Initially, the pain may be present only during the late stages of running. As the syndrome develops, pain can be present during the entire event of running and with everyday walking.

The physical examination is characterized by tenderness on direct palpation over the posteromedial border of the tibia. Usually located around the junction of the middle and distal thirds of the leg, slight swelling may be palpable in this area as well.

TREATMENT OPTIONS

A host of treatment options is available for the management of shin splints.[3,20,43,48] Although most will be effective, the common ingredient appears to be rest.[3] This rest is "relative rest," which means that it must be tailored to the individual patient according to symptoms. If pain is present with daily activities, then restriction from running should be prescribed. If pain occurs only during or after running, simply cutting back the pace and duration to approximately one-half of normal may help. Then, a gradual increase in intensity over a period of time within the limits of pain is allowed. We usually have young runners gradually increase their distance until they arrive at the amount necessary for the desired training level and then gradually increase their pace.

The addition of nonsteroidal anti-inflammatory agents, heel cord stretching exercises, casts, or heel pads to the treatment regimens appears to provide no additional advantage.[3] We do, however, have the young athlete apply ice to the affected area periodically throughout the day, especially after workouts. If this syndrome is associated with lower extremity malalignment and hyperpronation

FIGURE 24.   A wide assortment of orthotics are available to choose from in an effort to prevent hyperpronation of the foot with secondary valgus stress of the knee.

of the foot during weight bearing, the use of an orthotic to stabilize the longitudinal arch and prevent hyperpronation can be helpful (Fig. 24).

This condition is preventable. For one entering into a seasonal sport, the existence of an adequate training level prior to participation is associated with a reduced incidence of shin splints. Also, a training program that incorporates a graduated increase of running activities over 6 weeks, as opposed to a sudden increase, may lower the risk of development of a medial tibial stress syndrome.

We have not used surgical approaches to the management of this syndrome, although some have suggested that release of the soleus attachment along the posteromedial aspect of the tibia is effective for the treatment of chronic, resistant cases.[43]

Chronic Compartment Syndrome

In recent years it has become better recognized that exertional chronic compartment syndromes of the leg do occur.[20,56] Although the clinical presentation may be misleading and associated with a prolonged delay in the establishment of a diagnosis, the entity should be kept in mind when any athlete experiences pain in the leg that is aggravated by running and relieved by rest, particularly when an athlete has the condition only during the "in-season" and becomes asymptomatic out of season, year after year.

The lower extremity has four major myofascial compartments in the leg (Fig. 25).[11] Some authors have pointed out more recently that the tibialis posterior lies within its own individual fascial compartment as well.[11] The

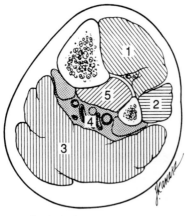

FIGURE 25. There are four well-defined myofascial compartments of the leg, and a fifth has been described about the tibialis posterior.

1 Anterior
2 Lateral
3 Superficial Posterior
4 Deep Posterior
5 Tibialis Posterior

existence of an unyielding circumferential fascia creates an environment in which muscle swelling can produce elevated intracompartmental tissue pressures to the point that microcirculation is disrupted. Repetitive activity produces enlargement of muscle mass and is directly proportional to the intensity and duration of effort.[19] Clearly, a 20% increase in muscle volume can occur with activity. Virtually any muscle compartment in the body can be associated with a compartment syndrome.

RELEVANT HISTORY AND PHYSICAL EXAMINATION

Pain is typically located within a compartment of the leg. The pain occurs with activity and is relieved by rest. Because nerves pass through these muscle compartments, paresthesias may be present. The location of paresthesias can be a significant aid in localizing which compartment is involved. For instance, the anterior compartment contains the deep peroneal nerve supplying sensation to the dorsum of the first web space. The superficial peroneal nerve travels through the lateral compartment and supplies sensation to the dorsum of the foot. The sural nerve travels through the superficial posterior compartment and will supply sensation to the lateral aspect of the foot and heel. The deep posterior compartment contains the posterior tibial nerve, which will supply sensation to the plantar and medial aspect of the foot.

Tenderness is located over the affected compartment during and immediately after running. Pedal pulses are always intact and normal. Capillary refill is also normal.

Confirmation of a compartment syndrome rests with the documentation of elevated intracompartmental tissue pressures (Fig. 26).[56] Several authors

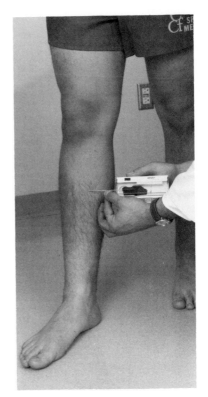

FIGURE 26. The Stryker intracompartmental pressure monitor system has been found to be a relatively simple and efficient technique.

have attempted to define limits of normality in measuring compartment pressures.[11,56] Mubarak considered the following criteria to be diagnostic of chronic compartment syndrome of the leg: (1) pre-exercise pressure of equal to or greater than 15 mm Hg; (2) a 1-minute post-exercise pressure of equal to or greater than 30 mm Hg; and (3) a 5-minute post-exercise pressure of equal to or greater than 20 mm Hg.

Many techniques have been developed to measure intracompartmental pressures.[6,41,60] Recently, an electronic digital monitor with a polyethylene slit catheter or needle as described by Awbrey has been found to be quick, reproducible, and convenient both for the patient and the doctor.[6] It is our preferred method of measurement of compartment pressures at the present time.

TREATMENT OPTIONS

The treatment of compartment syndrome is surgical. Fasciotomy is performed to allow for accommodation of the increased intracompartment volume that occurs with exercise. For the chronic exertional type of compartment syndrome, a subcutaneous fasciotomy of the involved compartment is carried out and can often be performed on an outpatient basis. This, of course, is different from the acute compartment syndrome, which requires open fasciotomy with delayed wound closure. If the diagnosis is correct and the correct compartment is released, the success of treatment is almost universal.

Stress Fractures

Significant axial stress and bending moments are applied to the long bones of the lower extremities with ambulation. As with soft tissues, bones are susceptible to repetitive microtrauma and tissue failure. In the case of bone, this is fracture. Bone is in a constant state of remodeling, with resorption being required to precede bone formation. As bone constantly adjusts to the stresses applied to it with the use of this remodeling process, overstress has been shown to increase the activity toward the bone resorption process.[38,66] This can actually weaken the bone and make it more susceptible to fracture. Virtually any bone in the lower extremity may be subject to stress fracture. In the adolescent athlete, the bones most often involved are the tibia, fibula, and metatarsals. On the other hand, stress fractures involving the tarsal navicular, calcaneus, and femur are not rare.[31,39,52]

RELEVANT HISTORY AND PHYSICAL EXAMINATION

Pain aggravated by activities and relieved by rest is the most common complaint. In the case of the tibia, palpation directly over the bone that elicits tenderness can suggest the diagnosis. Bones in the foot are also primarily subcutaneous in location and can be easily palpated. This is not the case for the femur, and stress fractures of this bone can be more difficult to detect clinically.

Plain x-rays are frequently normal. We should keep in mind that stress fractures are usually nondisplaced and it is usually only the radiographic evidence of fracture healing that confirms the diagnosis. Periosteal reaction or new bone formation may be found with diaphyseal stress fractures. Metaphyseal stress fractures may well be characterized by only a thin sclerotic line passing perpendicular to the trabecular stress pattern. Technetium bone scanning can be extremely helpful for the detection of a stress fracture before it becomes radiographically apparent (Fig. 27).[39] Typically, an intense localized uptake is seen. A CT scan of the area will usually reveal the extent of the lesion.

In the tibia, stress fractures in adolescents most commonly involve either the proximal or distal thirds. When the central third of the tibia is involved, it may be on the anterior cortex. These are a problem. As most stress fractures that occur on the compression side of the bone, stress fractures of the anterior cortex of the tibia involve the tensile portion of bone and are frequently associated with delayed healing. They are seen as incomplete linear striations or lucencies and may be single or multiple.

In the foot, the metatarsal stress fractures usually involve the diaphysis. The tarsal navicular stress fracture can be elusive. Frequently occurring in basketball players, it is characterized by nondescript pain in the arch of the foot, usually with tenderness over the dorsum and localized to the navicular region. Plain x-ray films are usually interpreted as normal, but the bone scan will be positive and a CT scan or a tomogram will reveal the fracture.

TREATMENT OPTIONS

For most stress fractures of the lower extremity, the treatment is merely to stop running. In stress fractures of the tibia, this usually requires 3–4 weeks,

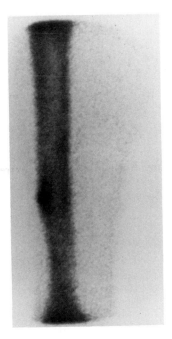

FIGURE 27. An intense, localized area of increased uptake as seen in this tibial anterior cortex stress fracture may well be apparent before plain radiographs are positive.

with a gradual return to activity over the ensuing 3–4 weeks. Metatarsal stress fractures may heal more quickly. Certain types of stress fractures, such as those that occur at the base of the fifth metatarsal (Jones type), the tarsal navicular stress fracture, calcaneal stress fracture, or femoral stress fracture may require special treatment. Such treatment usually includes a period of non-weight-bearing protection with crutches and cast. In some cases, the treatment may be operative, including bone grafting and internal fixation.[34]

In order to prevent recurrence, several factors are important. A graduated return to pre-injury training is important. Attention to abnormal biomechanics of the lower extremity may be helpful. As discussed, excessive foot pronation associated with a lower extremity malalignment can be an underlying etiologic factor. Orthotics for prevention of hyperpronation may prevent stress fractures of the foot and tibia. Heel cord stretching exercises are an important part of the general rehabilitation regimen. Footwear with proper impact-absorbing capabilities is helpful.

CONCLUSION

Adolescent athletes are susceptible to a wide variety of overuse syndromes of the back and lower extremities. Although diverse in presentation and underlying pathoanatomy, they share a common etiologic factor of stress-induced tissue failure resulting from repetitive microtrauma that may involve the soft tissues of the body or bone. These overuse syndromes are most often associated with a significant change or increase in normal training habits, or

ANDRISH

they may involve repetitive stresses to structures abnormally loaded, as in the case of the low back.

Young tissues have a great capacity for healing if given the opportunity. The treatment for most overuse syndromes involves a period of rest followed by a gradual return to pre-injury training levels. Attention to the biomechanics of the lower extremity or the low back can provide direction for additional therapies to prevent recurrence. We should remember that for children and youth, if we let the kids play the game at their own pace, overuse injuries will occur infrequently. As the organization and intensity of the sport increase, so does the incidence of stress-related injury.[1,27,44,55]

References

1. Adams JE: A study of traumatic changes in the elbow joints of boy baseball players. Calif Med 102:127–132, 1965.
2. American Medical Association Subcommittees on Classification of Sports Injuries: Standard nomenclature of athletic injuries. Chicago, American Medical Association, 1966, pp 122–126.
3. Andrish JT, Bergfeld JA, Walheim J: A prospective study on the management of shin splints. J Bone Joint Surg 56A:1697–1700, 1974.
4. Andrish JT: Overuse syndromes of the lower extremity in youth sports. In Boileau RA (ed): Advances in Pediatric Sport Sciences, Vol. 1. Biological Issues. Champaign, IL, Human Kinetics Publishers, Inc., 1984, pp 189–202.
5. Andriacchi T, Sabiston P, DeHaven P, et al: Ligament: Injury and repair. In Woo S L-Y, Buckwalter JA (eds): Injury and Repair of the Musculoskeletal Soft Tissues. Park Ridge, IL, American Academy of Orthopaedic Surgeons, 1988, pp 103–128.
6. Awbrey BJ, Sienkiewicz PS, Mankin HJ: Chronic exercise-induced compartment pressure elevation measured with a miniaturized fluid pressure monitor: A laboratory and clinical study. Am J Sports Med 16:610–615, 1988.
7. Balasubramaniam P, Prathap K, Lumpur K: The effect of injection of hydrocortisone into rabbit calcaneal tendons. J Bone Joint Surg 54B:729–734, 1972.
8. Bedi SS, Ellis W: Spontaneous rupture of the calcaneal tendon in rheumatoid arthritis after local steroid injection. Ann Rheum Dis 29:494–495, 1970.
9. Betz RR, Magill JT, Lonergan RP: The percutaneous lateral retinacular release. Am J Sports Med 15:477–482, 1987.
10. Blazina ME, Kerlan RK, Jobe FW: Jumper's knee. Orthop Clin North Am 4:665–678, 1973.
11. Bourne RB, Rorabeck CH: Compartment syndromes of the lower leg. Clin Orthop Rel Res 240:97–104, 1989.
12. Caplan A, Carlson B, Faulkner J, et al: Skeletal muscle. In Woo S L-Y, Buckwalker JA (eds): Injury and Repair of the Musculoskeletal Soft Tissues. Park Ridge, IL, American Academy of Orthopaedic Surgeons, 1988, pp 213–291.
13. Ciullo JV, Jackson DW: Pars interarticularis stress reaction, spondylolysis, and spondylolisthesis in gymnastics. Clin Sports Med 4:95–110, 1983.
14. Chow GH, LeCroy CM, Seaber AV: The effect of fatigue on muscle strain injury. Transactions of the 36th Annual Meeting, Orthopaedic Research Society, Vol. 15, February 5–8, 1990, p 148.
15. Dalton JD, Glisson RR, Seaber AV, Garrett WE: Stretch rate dependency of passively stretched muscle: Viscoelasticity vs. reflex effects. Transactions of the 36th Annual Meeting, Orthopaedic Research Society, Vol. 15, February 5–8, 1990, p 548.
16. Dalton JD, Seaber AV, Garrett WE: The biomechanical effects of passive stretch on muscle-tendon units pulled to failure. Transactions of the 36th Annual Meeting, Orthopaedic Research Society, Vol. 15, February 5–8, 1990, p 531.
17. DeHaven KE: Athletic injuries in adolescents. Pediatr Ann 7:96–119, 1978.
18. DeHaven KE, Dolan WA, Mayer PJ: Chondromalacia patellae in athletes. Am J Sports Med 7:5–11, 1979.
19. Detmer DE: Chronic leg pain. Am J Sports Med 8:141–144, 1980.
20. Detmer DE: Chronic shin splints: Classification and management of medial tibial stress syndrome. Clin Sports Med 4:436–446, 1986.

21. Ficat RP, Hungerford DS: Biomechanics. In Disorders of the Patellofemoral Joint. Baltimore, Williams & Wilkins, 1977, pp 22–35.
22. Ficat RP, Hungerford DS: The excessive lateral pressure syndrome. In Disorders of the Patellofemoral Joint. Baltimore, Williams & Wilkins, 1977, pp 123–148.
23. Ferguson RJ, McMaster JH, Stanitski CL: Low back pain in college football linemen. Am J Sports Med 2:63–69, 1974.
24. Fulkerson JP: Awareness of the retinaculum in evaluating patellofemoral pain. Am J Sports Med 10:147–149, 1982.
25. Gelberman R, Goldberg V, An Kai-Nan, Banes A: Tendon. In Woo S L-Y, Buckwalter JA (eds): Injury and Repair of the Musculoskeletal Soft Tissues. Park Ridge, IL, American Academy of Orthopaedic Surgeons, 1988, pp 5–40.
26. Grabiner MD, Miller GF, Koh TJ: Fatigue rates of vastus medialis obliquus and vastus lateralis during statis and dynamic knee extension. J Orthop Res, in press.
27. Gugenheim JJ, Stanley RF, Woods GW, Tullos HS: Little League survey: The Houston study. Am J Sports Med 4:189–200, 1976.
28. Henning CE: Personal communication, 1990.
29. Henry JH, Crosland JW: Conservative treatment of patellofemoral subluxation. Am J Sports Med 7:12–14, 1979.
30. Henry JH, Goletz TH, Williamson B: Lateral retinacular release in patellofemoral subluxation: Indications, results, and comparison to open patellofemoral reconstruction. Am J Sports Med 14:121–129, 1986.
31. Hulkko A, Orava S: Stress fractures in athletes. Int J Sports Med 8:221–226, 1987.
32. Insall J: Current concepts review. J Bone Joint Surg 64A:147–151, 1982.
33. Ismail AM, Balakrishnan R, Rajakumar MK, et al: Rupture of patellar ligament after steroid infiltration. J Bone Joint Surg 51B:503–505, 1969.
34. Keene JS, Lange RH: Diagnostic dilemmas in foot and ankle injuries. JAMA 256:247–251, 1986.
35. Lancourt JE, Cristini JA: Patella alta and patella infera. J Bone Joint Surg 57A:1112–1115, 1975.
36. Lennington KB, Yanchuleff TT: The use of isokinetics in the treatment of chondromalacia patellae: A case report. J Orthop Sports Phys Ther 4:176–178, 1983.
37. Letts M, Smallman T, Afanasiev R, Gouw G: Fracture of the pars interarticularis in adolescent athletes: A clinical-biomechanical analysis. J Pediatr Orthop 6:40–46, 1986.
38. Li G, Zhang S, Chen G, Wang A: Radiographic and histologic analyses of stress fracture in rabbit tibias. Am J Sports Med 13:285–294, 1985.
39. Matheson GO, Clement DB, Mickenzie DC, et al: Stress fracture in athletes: A study of 320 cases. Am J Sports Med 15:46–58, 1987.
40. McCarroll JR, Miller JM, Ritter MA: Lumbar spondylolysis and spondylolisthesis in college football players. Am J Sports Med 44:404–406, 1986.
41. McDermott AGP, Marble AE, Yabsley RH, et al: Monitoring dynamic anterior compartment pressures during exercise. Am J Sports Med 10:83–89, 1982.
42. Messier S, Pittala KA: Etiologic factors associated with selected running injuries. Med Sci Sports Exerc 20:501–505, 1988.
43. Michael RH, Holder LE: The soleus syndrome: A cause of medial tibial stress (shin splints). Am J Sports Med 13:87–94, 1985.
44. Micheli LJ: Overuse injuries in children's sports: The growth factor. Orthop Clin North Am 14:337–360, 1963.
45. Micheli LJ: Low back pain in the adolescent: Differential diagnosis. Am J Sports Med 7:362–364, 1979.
46. Micheli LJ: Back injuries in dancers. Clin Sports Med 2:473–484, 1983.
47. Mital MA, Matza RA, Cohen J: The so-called unresolved Osgood-Schlatter lesion. J Bone Joint Surg 62A:732–739, 1980.
48. Mubarak SJ, Gould RN, Lee YF, et al: The medial tibial stress syndrome: A cause of shin splints. Am J Sports Med 10:201–205, 1982.
49. Obremskey WT, Seaber AV, Ribbeck BM, Garrett WE: Biomechanical and histological assessment of a controlled muscle strain injury treated with piroxicam. Transactions of the 34th Annual Meeting, Orthopaedic Research Society, Vol. 13, February 1–4, 1988, p 338.
50. Osgood RB: Lesions of the tibia tubercle occurring during adolescence. Boston Med Surg J 148:114–117, 1903.
51. Orava S, Puranen J: Exertion injuries in adolescent athletes. Br J Sports Med 12:4–10, 1978.
52. Orava S, Puranen J, Ala-Ketola L: Stress fractures caused by physical exercise. Acta Orthop Scand 49:19–27, 1978.
53. Oxlund H: The influence of a local injection of cortisol on the mechanical properties of tendons and ligaments and the indirect effect on skin. Acta Orthop Scand 51:231–238, 1980.

54. Palumbo PM: Dynamic patellar brace: A new orthosis in the management of patellofemoral disorders: A preliminary report. Am J Sports Med 9:45–49, 1981.

55. Pappas AM: Elbow problems associated with baseball during childhood and adolescence. Clin Orthop Rel Res 164:30–41, 1982.

56. Pedowitz RA, Hargens AR, Mubarak SJ: Modified criteria for the objective diagnosis of chronic compartment syndrome of the leg. Am J Sports Med 18:35–40, 1990.

57. Porter RW, Hibbert CS: Symptoms associated with lysis of the pars interarticularis. Spine 8:755–758, 1984.

58. Pratt W, Aronow L: The effect of glucocorticoids on protein and nucleic acid synthesis in mouse fibroblasts growing in vitro. J Biochem 241:5244–5250, 1966.

59. Resnick D: Disorders due to medications and other chemical agents. In Resnick D, Niwayama G (eds): Diagnosis of Bone and Joint Disorders, Vol. 3. Philadelphia, W.B. Saunders, 1981, pp 2363–2384.

60. Rorabeck CH, Bourne RB, Foweler PJ, et al: The role of tissue pressure measurement in diagnosing chronic anterior compartment syndrome. Am J Sports Med 16:143–146, 1988.

61. Schlatter C: Verletzungen des schnabelformigen fortsatzes der oberen tibiaepiphyse. Beitr Klin Chir 38:874–887, 1903.

62. Sherman FC, Wilkinson RH, Hall JE: Reactive sclerosis of a pedicle and spondylolysis in the lumbar spine. J Bone Joint Surg 59:49–56, 1977.

63. Sinding-Larsen C: A hitherto unknown affliction of the patella in children. Acta Radiol 1:171, 1921.

64. Slocum DB: The shin splint syndrome: Medical aspects and differential diagnosis. Am J Surg 114:874–881, 1967.

65. Soren A, Waugh TR: Spondylolisthesis and related disorders. Clin Orthop Rel Res 193:171–177, 1985.

66. Stanitski CA: On the nature of stress fractures. Am J Sports Med 6:391–396, 1978.

67. Stanitski CA: Repetitive stress and connective tissue. In Sullivan JA, Grana WA (eds): The Pediatric Athlete. Park Ridge, IL, American Academy of Orthopaedic Surgeons, 1990, pp 203–209.

68. Steiner ME, Micheli LJ: Treatment of symptomatic spondylolysis and spondylolisthesis with the modified Boston brace. Spine 10:937–943, 1985.

69. Viitasalo JT, Kvist M: Some biomechanical aspects of the foot and ankle in athletes with and without shin splints. Am J Sports Med 11:125–130, 1983.

70. Wiltse LL, Newman PH, MacNab I: Classification of spondylolysis and spondylolisthesis. Clin Orthop Rel Res 117:23–29, 1976.

71. Woo S, Maynard J, Butler D, et al: Ligament, tendon, and joint capsule insertions to bone. In Woo S L-Y, Buckwalter JA (eds): Injury and Repair of the Musculoskeletal Soft Tissues. Park Ridge, IL, American Academy of Orthopaedic Surgeons, 1988, pp 133–166.

Index

Entries in **boldface** type indicate complete chapters.